SHADES

writers on depression,

OF

suicide, and feeling blue

BLUE

EDITED BY AMY FERRIS

SEAL PRESS

SHADES OF BLUE

Seal Press
A Member of the Perseus Books Group
1700 Fourth Street
Berkeley, California   94710
sealpress.com

"Unraveling" by Hollye Dexter was excerpted from *Fire Season: My Journey from Ruin to Redemption* (She Writes Press, April 2015)

Library of Congress Cataloging-in-Publication Data

Shades of blue : writers on depression, suicide, and feeling blue / edited by Amy Ferris.
pages cm

ISBN 978-1-58005-595-6 (paperback)
1. Depression, Mental. 2. Mental health. I. Ferris, Amy Schor.
RC537.S4818 2015
616.85'27--dc23
2015019705

ISBN: 978-1-58005-595-6

10 9 8 7 6 5 4 3 2 1

Cover and interior design by Domini Dragoone
Printed in the United States of America
Distributed by Publishers Group West

TO KRISTA, MERRIK, AND KEN:

Two gorgeous goddesses and one sexy mensch who lifted me, held me, edited me, supported me, and gave me every bit of goodness and generosity to bring this book to life. This collection would not have been conceived or born without you.

Contents

Introduction:
The Balls-out Truth About Depression............................ 1
Amy Ferris

Riding With the Top Down 5
Beverly Donofrio

Suicide, a Love Story... 10
Mark S. King

Three Girls, Laughing 17
Beth Bornstein Dunnington

Medication Makes Me Whole 24
Angela M. Giles Patel

Bye-bye, Crayola 28
Caroline Leavitt

Death, Depression, and Other Capital D Words.................35
Marika Rosenthal Delan

Colors at the Piano 41
Linda Joy Myers

The Deal Breaker 47
Lira Maywood

A Slip of the Noose.. 53
Jimmy Camp

A Body of Grief... 61
Zoe FitzGerald Carter

If I Love You, You'll Leave 70
Debra LoGuerico DeAngelo

Hello, Catastrophe 79
Elizabeth Rosner

Unraveling 87
Hollye Dexter

Letters I Will Never Send 94
Alexa Rosalsky

Nothing Helps, Except Love 97
C.O. Moed

Search for the Silver Cup 106
Betsy Graziani Fasbinder

The Merry-Go-Round 113
Mark Morgan

Thorazine 116
Karen Lynch

Learning to Sit Still 124
Chloe Caldwell

Depression is a Patient Stalker 130
Ruth Pennebaker

Allies in the Sky 136
David Lacy

Off With the Fairies 145
Christine Kehl O'Hagan

Learning To Love My Depression 153
Sherry Amatenstein

Skirting the Abyss.. 160
Barbara Abercrombie

God's Perfect Child 167
Patti Linsky

Irish Wake-up Call 176
Kitty Sheehan

The Dialectics of Suicide 183
Samantha White

Forty-four Steps.. 191
Kathryn Rountree

Upon Being Told to Be True to Myself 197
Jenna Stone

Viral Goodbyes 202
Matt Ebert

Someday This Pain May Be Useful 207
Jennifer Pastiloff

Riding Shotgun 213
judywhite

Surviving the Spiral 220
Regina Anavy

A Kind of Quiet Most People Have Forgotten 227
Pam L. Houston

INTRODUCTION:

The Balls-out Truth
About Depression

AMY FERRIS

This is what I know this morning.

Post-coffee.

Pre-wine.

Yesterday my friend asked me, Did you ever try it? Yes, I said, yes, I tried suicide. Obviously, this was all around the news of Robin Williams and his death. Yes, I said . . . I was young, much younger, and so sad. I was miserable and unhappy and felt all alone in the world. I felt like nobody knew what it was like, this damp darkness. Everything was pitch black. There was no color anywhere. It was dark and lonely, and the best way I can describe how I felt at that time in my life was like being in the middle of a forest, and it's eerily dark, and you don't know which way to turn so you take baby steps. Teeny steps because you don't know where you are, and you can't see anything, and you don't know how to find your way out, and you reach out for something to touch, but it's not there. You fall down, and you don't know how to get up, so you start by getting up on your knees, and then slowly, very slowly, you straighten up . . . and start to walk through the darkness, and you're not sure you're gonna make it out, but you silently hope and wish and pray that you do. And I said to her—my friend—you know that saying, there's a light at the end of the tunnel? Well, the truth is, there is no tunnel. No tunnel in the pitch blackness. Forget about finding the light at the end . . . you can't even find the tunnel.

So, yes . . . I tried suicide. The pills, the stomach pumped. And all that follows. But I was lucky. Fortunate. Blessed, whatever you wanna call it, because at nineteen someone wanted to save me, help me, hold me. And then I became a Buddhist, and then I battled my demons and unhappiness and self-hatred every single day. Well, not every day. Some days they got the best of me and I could barely move. But I fought fiercely. And some days I won, and some days they won. And some days it was a match. And some days I wanted to die, and some days I wanted to not only live, but live with passion and find beauty in my life and find love. And then what I found out, I found out that you gotta save your own life. Because the person holding your hand, they can get really tired. They hold on so long and so tight that their arm aches. And that's when I had my epiphany, my breakfast at epiphany moment: if you really wanna save yourself, you gotta be willing to throw someone else a line, grab onto someone else and save them, help them, hold them. You gotta be willing to see another person's suffering and pain and look them in the eye and say, I know how you feel.

I. Know. How. You. Feel.

I have your back.

I'm gonna hold you, and I'm gonna hold you tight.

And the truth is, the balls-out truth is this: those of us who suffer from bouts of depression, who don't believe we're good enough, who can barely make it out of bed some days, who struggle with self-esteem and the whole concept of self-love . . . when we use our own pain and suffering so that we can understand another person's heart . . . it doesn't eliminate our pain, or make it vanish, or go pouffff—but it does make it bigger than ourselves; it makes it worth the struggle. I look at the folks I know—some very personally, some on the periphery—who have gone through hell and back a million times, and they use their life every day to inspire, encourage, and awaken the good and greatness in others because they know what it was like to be flat-out broken, broken into little pieces.

So, yes, I tried it.

And I'm awfully glad that I didn't succeed at it.

I'm glad, so very glad, that I was a failure at that attempt.

Because I get to rise up every single day and work through my life stuff, face my own demons—like all the other beautiful, imperfect, breathtaking survivors you'll read in these pages—and then strut my stuff and tell each of you that you are awesome. You are magic and glitter and all that's extraordinary in the world. Because the truth is, even in our darkest moments, even in our saddest moments, even in our most broken moments, we have magic in us; we have glitter and sparkles; we are goddesses and gods, Buddha's, kings, and queens.

When I decided to take on this topic—depression, suicide, mental health issues—I thought I knew what courage was, what it looked like. I was wrong. I say that without any hesitation. I have often thought of suicide as a way out. A way out of my pain, my heartbreak, my sorrow, my mood swings, my abusive (past) relationships, my fears and crippling self-doubt. For me, truthfully, it was a second thought, impulse. The first thought being, How do I get out of here? I understand why folks take their life. I do. I understand that moment, that fierce mighty blinding moment. But I also understand why we're told to count to twenty, breathe in and breathe out, put the gun down, place the pills back in the bottle, remove the scarf. Sit. Breathe. Make a call. Ask for help. Reach out. Reach out again and again. And again. Life is precious, it is precious even in the worst of times. Because even in the worst of times there is always something—a memory, albeit, a small teeny memory—that can reel us in. Back. Home. It takes massive courage to say, "I'm not happy." To say and declare out loud, "Please, help me, hold me." It takes huge courage to share our lives—the messy, dirty, crappy, and complicated pieces of our lives. It also takes enormous courage to keep that pain a secret. After all, we live in a world where the round yellow happy face was the single biggest seller for years and years. People love happy. A frown would have never sold. It takes massive huge courage to wear a frown. It takes guts to wear it, and own it, and say, "Here's my story, maybe it can help you . . ."

So this book is for you, all of you. The men and women, girls and boys, who always—always—wear their scars like stardust.

You are amazing beyond belief.

You are.

Yes.

So go on, strut your gorgeous stuff today knowing—absolutely knowing—that you are not alone.

This I know for sure.

This I'd bet my life on.

Riding With the Top Down

BEVERLY DONOFRIO

It's 1971. I'm twenty-one, and I'm beginning to believe everything will turn out all right. I can drink in bars legally, and I'm not trapped in the house without a car anymore because my son is old enough to stick his thumb out and hitchhike with me. Jason is three, fun to be around now, and can do most things on his own, which is good because I am too young to be a mother and can barely take care of myself. We sing to Beatles songs and dance all over the house. Whenever he wakes up before me, he pours his own cereal and milk, and then watches cartoons. He doesn't bug me to get up until nine or ten.

Sometimes, I borrow my mother's car and take Jason to the frog pond, where we sit all afternoon, frog eyes sticking out of the water, turtles climbing onto logs. He turns thoughtful, and says, "You're my mother, but you're like a sister too. Right, Mom?"

I had to hug him for that one because this is my new child-rearing philosophy: If I'm happy, my kid will be happy, so I'm having fun. He sleeps at my parents' house a few times a week. I bring our laundry for my mother to wash on those days, watch the Soaps with my sisters, stay for dinner, and then head off with my best friend to the Italian Club bar.

All those cute, strutting guys at the Italian Club bar.

Dancing to the jukebox.

Riding in the backs of pickups with the lights turned off in the moonlight . . . running through sprinklers on the golf course.

Once when I was tripping, I saw in the bark of an oak tree all the roads of the world, so many choices to make, so many directions to take. I felt hope like bells ringing. I would leave this town and return one day driving a red sports car, the top down, my long hair flowing, and show everyone how wrong they were about the pitiful girl who got pregnant in high school.

Turns out, that happy time never got the chance to pick up speed. While a friend borrowed my house to sell his garbage-bag full of pot, I was off with a guy in the woods singing to his guitar. It wasn't my pot, just my house. But the old judge at the trial wheezes, "A mother on welfare selling drugs for profit? I'm not inclined to go easy on you, young lady. But there is the child to consider." My name is plastered on the front page of the newspaper. Now I'm not only a single ex-teen mother on welfare with a kid, I'm the leader of a drug ring and will spend the rest of my life a convicted felon.

Now when people give me a look in the grocery line, it isn't only because of the food stamps, but also probably because they know who I am and wouldn't touch me with a ten-foot pole. I don't blame them. If they get too close, I might contaminate them with lousy luck.

The guy I'm in love with doesn't want to touch me with a ten-foot pole either, but the sex is too good, so he comes by on Friday nights after the bars close and parks his car on another block. He's a school-teacher and says if people found out about us he'd get fired.

Every week in the town hall, my probation officer harasses me with questions I refuse to answer: "Been to any orgies lately? You shoot some heroin? Isn't that what you hippies are into?"

I feel like I did when I was a kid and lost my mother in the department store, like I'll never see her again, and there will be no rescue. I'm so lonely, I eat half a loaf of Wonder Bread toast slathered with butter and jelly every night just to comfort myself.

I grow so fat I jiggle.

Nothing fits me anymore, so for Jason's first day of kindergarten, my mother buys me a new pair of jeans. Jase and I walk down the corridor holding hands, and instead of thinking about how much I'm going to miss my son, I'm worried the other mothers will stare because I'm too young to have a child, and I radiate *White Trash*.

When we reach the classroom, Jase doesn't want to let go of my hand. I pull a chair out for him and he sits up straight, his hands folded on the table, and stares ahead, being brave. He looks so grown up with his hair parted on the side; he's wearing a pinstriped shirt with a button-down collar and looks so frightened I think my heart will break.

After school, he hands me a crayon drawing of the two of us without arms and teaches me a new song he learned. The next day, I wave him off on the school bus, go back to bed, and don't get up till he comes home.

Jason has a life and I don't have a clue how to get one.

I apply for a job as a file clerk at the steel mill, and another one at the hospital to train to give EKGs. Both of the men interviewing me ask who will take care of my child the half day he isn't in school; what will I do when he's sick? I say my mother will take care of him, which is a bold-faced lie because she has her own job. And the real truth is I have no idea how I'd get to and from work every day. I don't have a car, and there's no public transportation. It doesn't matter anyway because I never hear back from them.

I'm like the frogs Jason catches and traps in coffee cans, hitting their heads on the plastic lid. When Jason tries to hug me, I feel like he's dragging me under. A day doesn't go by when I don't yell at him for something. My life is already ruined, and now I'm ruining his, too. My parents would love to have him. And he'd love to live there. If he doesn't like what's served for dinner, my mother makes him something special. There's dessert every night, ice cream in the fridge, boxes of cookies, a dog, a cat, a man in the house, and my two younger sisters.

Jason would be better off. Life was never fair, and now it's cruel, unsafe, ugly. Whenever something good happens, something worse happens in reaction. Good people who try to change things—Gandhi, President Kennedy, Martin Luther King—are assassinated. Friends of mine are killed in the Vietnam War, which nobody with half a brain believes is about keeping America free. A friend home from 'Nam tells me his job was to pick up body parts, put them in bags, ship them home. Picturing this, I can't sleep for nights on end. A Buddhist monk sets himself ablaze on TV. People riot, cities burn, police are brutal.

I am so filled with sorrow for the world, I can't bear it.

And I can't bear myself either.

I'm a fat, ugly sad sack who anyone in their right mind would run from. Even worse, I am not a good person. I have a terrible temper, and I'm ungrateful, selfish, argumentative, and don't know when to keep my mouth shut. I also wouldn't give up saying "fuck" in every other sentence, even if I could. I'm sure I've deserved all the bad luck and punishment I've received in life, and I don't know how to change myself so I won't keep deserving it. I'm in terror that life will clobber me the most when I least expect it, so I must be vigilant, which exhausts me. Dragging myself out of bed in the morning, my legs feel like concrete, my eyes do not want to see, my ears do not want to hear; I want to disappear and be nobody.

Suicide would release me.

Suicide would be a relief.

Suicide is the only way out I can think of.

My death will be a gift to my son. He's only five and will hardly remember me, if he remembers me at all.

Jason is staying overnight at my parents' house. At 8:00 PM, I climb into bed and dump a hundred aspirins onto a dishtowel that I've laid out in front of me. It's an amount, I'm told, that will eat a hole through the wall of my stomach and make me bleed to death. Since I sleep sixteen hours a day, I'm counting on sleeping through it. I begin taking the pills two at a time and notice how the walls are dotted with my dried blood from the mosquitos I swatted when I was pregnant and didn't have screens. It had never occurred to me to wash the walls. There's something wrong with me. I thought I'd be an author, live in New York City, have outlandish and interesting friends, travel the world, have plenty of money. But I'm facing the truth: I've been damaged goods from the day I was born. Whipping myself with my mind like this, I swallow maybe twenty pills.

And then a message comes to me like a feather floating into an open hand: *It's always darkest before the dawn*, and then another, *When winter comes can spring be far behind?*

It's as though a dam breaks. I burst into tears and cry until dawn. And then I do something I never thought of before: I call the psychiatric clinic at the hospital.

Many years of therapies, six different therapists, meditating, prac-ticing yoga, praying the rosary, and more than a few bouts of depression later, I return to my home town to ride in the Memorial Day parade. My high school friend is bringing up the rear in a red Corvette, and I'm sitting in the passenger's seat, waving.

Suicide, a Love Story

MARK S. KING

This is the story that haunts my waking hours. It is a story with many ghosts.

It started when AIDS began its murderous march through my community, when gay men learned the intimacies of death, when so many perished we couldn't properly grieve for them all. And when our hearts were crushed from the weight of mortal questions that such very young men were never meant to answer.

Those answers, all these decades later, still elude me. This is what remains.

The hoarse sound of my brother Richard's voice nearly thirty years ago, phoning me after a period of frustrating silence during the declining health of his lover, Emil. Richard, my role model and a dozen years older than me and also gay, was saying that Emil wanted to see me.

"Tonight," Richard said. Within an hour, my boyfriend, Charlie, and I walked through their front door.

Richard led us to a sofa in the den, piled high with a mountain of blankets. Emil's head—which looked small, ancient, and childlike at once, despite being less than fifty years old—peered out through heavy folds. A curved reading lamp reached over Emil's body, casting a dramatic yellow glow across his face.

It was as harsh as the fluorescent lights I had often seen above the hospital bed of so many dying friends, shining straight down, showcasing the sickness beneath.

"Hey there, Emil," Charlie said, with a jarring friendliness. "How's it going?" I had learned not to lead with a question like that. Even in my early twenties I knew the social protocol for the dying.

"Hello, Charlie," Emil said weakly. His voice was a strained breath that worked without the cooperation of vocal chords. He looked shrunken.

The blankets moved slightly, and Emil produced a tiny, aged hand. It trembled slightly as he motioned to Richard, who acknowledged the signal and left the room. Charlie and I groped for words and finally surrendered to the silence.

Richard returned with an envelope and placed it in my hands. I smiled toward Charlie and noticed that Richard and Emil were without expression, lost in their silent, exhausted daze. I opened the envelope and pulled out a $100 department store gift certificate. I said how thankful I was, but the words came out as a strange pleasantry, as if the gift was a birthday present from a coworker. I was confused and it showed.

"For all your help the last few months . . ." Emil breathed.

Richard managed an almost perfectly horizontal smile, and I knew at once that he had bought it. I thought of him driving across town for the item, on strict orders from Emil to purchase the certificate and from what store, and Richard wondering if his lover would be alive when he got back.

Emil cast sleepy eyes on Richard, and I knew it was time to leave. I leaned forward toward Emil and barely brushed my hand across the blanket as a farewell. Richard led us out and stood on the porch as we drove away. I watched him close the front door. The porch light blinked out.

Only three nights later, Charlie and I would be summoned once again. We were bleary-eyed from the chaos that had begun with Richard's phone announcement an hour before, delivered with stunned, impassive clarity that Emil had passed away.

Richard pointedly directed us to the den, where Emil was nowhere to be found. He had spent his last days by his lover's side in the master bedroom. His body was still in their bed, away from view. I could hear a vehicle approach. Charlie turned to the windows behind us and pulled the blinds away.

"No," I said. "Don't. We better not look." He released the blinds and the car—or hearse, or coroner's truck—drew nearer and was now chugging just outside the window and beside the front steps.

We stared at each other, dissecting every sound as they took Emil away. We heard wheels, barely squeaking across tile floors, rolling out of the master bedroom and across the house. The front door creaked. There were muffled voices of instruction. A heavy car door screeched its objection to being slowly opened and then closed again. I wanted to pull the blinds wide open and see for myself, but I didn't dare.

The vehicle changed gears and began the retreat down the driveway. We held our breath as it drove down the hill and faded away.

Richard walked into the den and we sat up straight. I couldn't speak, couldn't spoil the reverence of the moment with pitying words.

Richard asked me to stay the night, and Charlie gave Richard a silent hug and left. Richard and I didn't stay up, didn't talk much at all. He withdrew to his bedroom and I fell asleep on the sofa to the sound of my brother's distant wailing.

I was awakened in the morning by Richard's voice. He was on the phone across the room, speaking to someone culled from the worn pages of an address book he held cradled in his lap. I quietly rolled over and watched him. He was beyond the grasp of any healing embrace.

Every call began the same, with his weary hello and then softly announcing he had some very bad news. And then he would say it out loud, something he had been terrified of ever saying, but that now would be repeated a dozen times on the morning of his lover's death:

"Emil has died." In those moments, I learned the meaning of utter dread at last.

Richard usually made it through the first few moments, but then would be barraged with condolences and have to say "thank you," and "yes, he certainly was," and "I know he is no longer in pain" a few times during each call. And it was that part that would break him, and he would convulse again into sobs, so that his goodbye would be hard to understand.

He would catch his breath, finding the next name in the address book through teary eyes, and then pick up the phone again. And again.

It is one of the most powerful images of my brother that I have. I sometimes dream of it.

These are the memories, so very dark but never distant, that confound my joy in having lived with HIV for thirty years. My prayers to survive the deadliest days, even above the lives of others, were answered with the loss of nearly everyone close to me. My great triumph of inexplicable good health is so tragically arbitrary it can be hard to bear. I am often lost at the junction of guilt and gratitude.

The sorrow visits me without warning. It is the filter through which I see the graveyard, the photos found in a drawer of dear young friends who will not age, the borrowed clothes in my closet that need never be returned. The reminders are hidden bombs, sad remembrances waiting to detonate.

Only a few years after my brother lost his partner to the epidemic, Richard would personally deliver another woeful explosive to me. It was a story of grief within grief. The rolling stone of pain can gather plenty.

"Did I ever tell you about the night that Emil died?" my brother Richard asked me.

I cocked my head. "Well, I was there, Richard, so I mean—"

"You were there *after*," he said, and downed his drink. "Don't you wonder what it was like just *before?*" He asked the question nervously, a perfect match for the cigarette he held in one hand—a long-broken habit, suddenly resumed—and the cocktail in the other, which he'd requested shortly upon arriving to my apartment.

"It's not like I was trying to keep it from you, Mark," he said, and he offered the glass for replacement. It was an odd thing for him to say.

I walked to the kitchen and unscrewed the vodka bottle, beginning to feel an aged and familiar misery. Richard talked as I cracked an ice tray.

"Emil had one of those tubes that went way inside him, in his chest . . ." He was beginning a story I wasn't sure I wanted to hear.

"A Hickman catheter," I said.

"Yeah," he answered, and he reached for the drink while the ice was still twirling. "But something was wrong with it the night before. It was swelling. So we took it out."

I took a seat as Richard paced.

"The next morning the nurse came and Emil was being stubborn. He didn't want the new Hickman." He gulped his drink and took a breath. "I got an inkling what he was up to when the nurse said 'Emil, starving yourself is not a pretty way to go.' But Emil kept saying, 'no, no, I won't do this!' and I remember he looked so weary, Mark. Just exhausted."

This wasn't the visit I had planned. I wanted Richard to help me think of a birthday gift for a close friend who laid dying in an AIDS hospice. Something for the man who had nothing. Something I would retrieve for myself after he was gone. But my sad choice couldn't compete with the story that was now rumbling out of my brother.

"I walked the nurse out and went back to Emil. He reached up for my hand, and he said, 'you knew that today would be the day, didn't you?'"

Richard looked at me but didn't acknowledge what must have been a growing expression of shock on my face.

"I knew Emil wanted me to say yes, so I did. But inside I was screaming *NO! NO!*"

Richard stopped, and I found the silence torturous.

"Well," I said, "it sounds like he was . . . in charge of himself."

"Oh, he was in control all right," he responded. "He told me to go get the book. The one about how to kill yourself."

Richard's next few remarks would be lost on me. I couldn't get past The Book.

"So I'm reading him the chapter we had picked out," Richard was saying, "and it suggests washing down the pills with alcohol. We had some Seconal and I found some Scotch."

I knew about assisted suicide but had never heard of the mechanics of it firsthand, or considered the logistics a caring lover would undertake, or witnessed the haunted result like the one that now sat chainsmoking across my living room.

"I made some toast for him just like the book said," he continued, "and while we waited for him to digest the toast, I opened the capsules and put the stuff into a glass."

I imagined my brother sprinkling powder into a glass while Emil looked on. I wondered what kind of small talk that activity encouraged.

"I poured the scotch, a couple of good-sized shots, and he wanted it right away." His voice trailed to a whisper. "I wanted him to wait, to wait, to wait . . . I wanted to hold him. I wanted to do it right, you know? But he kept reaching for the glass, and I would say, 'no, Emil, wait, *please wait*, I want to say I love you again . . .'"

Tears were filling Richard's eyes. His whole body began to shake, knocking his glass loudly on the coffee table as he set it down and brought his hands to his face.

And even so, he went on.

"Emil downed the glass in one gulp and made a face, and then he just laid back on the pillow." Richard looked up at me and managed a sad grimace. "Emil always said that when you go, you go alone. I hated that for him. I wanted him to feel me there, you know? So I held his hand real tight . . ."

I stared at my brother. Tears streamed from his face. His eyes searched around the room, trying to focus on something, anything, that would bring comfort or clarity.

I couldn't tell what I was feeling about this. Was it pity? Was it shock? How many kinds of pain can we distinguish within our soul?

"The book said to wait twenty minutes after his heart stopped, you know, before calling the doctor," he said. "I kept leaning over him and trying . . . trying to hear his heart. But I couldn't because my own blood was pounding in my ears! And those next twenty minutes . . ."

His voice constricted and gave out. Neither of us moved.

"What were you doing" I finally asked, startled by the sound of my own voice, "during those twenty minutes?"

"Screaming," he said simply.

Silence engulfed my apartment, surrounding the word.

I put my arm around him and he continued to weep. *Please be all right*, I thought. *Please be happy again, Richard. My brother. My brother.*

He received my embrace but his heart had taken distant refuge. It had long been numbed by the effects of the spent cocktail glass, sitting impassively on the coffee table, occasionally clinking with the sound of shifting, melting ice.

Three Girls, Laughing

BETH BORNSTEIN DUNNINGTON

We were three girls together, laughing—Iva, Rena, and I.

Five years after Rena died, I named my newborn daughter for her: the Hebrew name Rena, and in English, Marena. Something my daughter has had to explain her entire life. "Marena with an 'e,' not an 'i,' not the traditional spelling." No, not traditional, as there was nothing traditional about her namesake, Rena Shapiro: brilliant, funny, irreverent, sunflower-seed-eating, legs crossed on a chair at Yale. A mensch. "I love your Betsey Johnson shirt," I said to her once, early on. "Hang on," she replied, and before I knew what hit me, the shirt was off, revealing a massive bra holding in her size double-D breasts. "Take it, it's yours," she said. "It'll look fabulous on you! Better than it looks on me."

Rena holding court, regaling us with tales, laughing her hearty, deep, authentic laugh. She called me "The Mother of Us All" because I played Susan B. Anthony in Virgil Thomson's opera of the same name. Rena loved telling the story of when eighty-five-year-old Thomson, who wrote *The Mother of Us All* with Gertrude Stein (Stein's last work before her death), came to see our Emerson College production in Boston. On opening night, a large set piece fell down as soon as the orchestra started playing, and from the audience, Virgil Thomson—already old, already famous, already almost dead, certainly almost deaf—screamed out, "Somebody get a nail!" After that, Rena would occasionally imitate Thomson, turning something even marginally funny into something hysterical, because it was Rena's take, her interpretation imposed on anything that lifted it up, elevated its status.

"More than a fruit bowl, it's a work of art!" she would say about something she loved that rarely, if ever, had anything to do with fruit. "I love you more than life, but less than art." Rena-isms. I think she actually coined the phrase, "They're dead to me." Grand, larger-than-life Rena. College was her happiest time, and she was a force of nature back then.

Rena in a mental hospital years later, after Dick left her—ripped black fishnets and a short skirt, her platinum blond hair cropped like Edie Sedgwick, but still fiercely unique; Rena made it her own. Her 1981 college yearbook photo shows Rena in fake fur and a tiara with the caption, "What becomes a legend most?" The yearbook editor gave her an entire page, three pictures of her in different poses, a brochure advertising her goddess status, even at twenty-one.

Now, again, years later, Rena in the last mental hospital, the one she would soon talk her way out of, the one where she would say to the doctors who weren't as smart as she was, "I promise I won't kill myself if you let me out." And they did.

Rena in a paper Burger King crown: gold, torn on the side, just slightly, but showing that she had worn it before. Rena, the King of McLean's, who at twenty-eight would kill herself, as she told us she would. "Cut it out!" we all would say. "Stop it." Because we didn't want it to be true, didn't believe it was even a possibility. What did we know in our twenties about that level of despair? Rena, who couldn't even pee by herself. "I have to pee," she would say at a party, a Newport Menthol Light dangling from the corner of her mouth. "Come with. Come with." And of course we would, six of us crowding into a bathroom with her because Rena demanded and attention was paid. Rena, who called me The Mother of Us All, was in fact the real mother of us all.

Rena finding her way by herself to a hotel room where she would take all the pills she had apparently been stockpiling in the Burger King Hospital, the hospital where she must have read *Eloise, Pippi Longstocking,* and *Harriet the Spy,* her favorite children's books, to the other patients, because through it all books and words were everything. Something she and Dick shared, their love of books. They spilled out of too-full bookcases in their Boston and New Haven apartments; you would trip over them walking in the door. Rena and Dick: the whirling dervish and her wildly talented playwright husband. Everything swirled around them, once.

But before that, and long before hand-written notes were sealed with her beloved cat stickers and a decayed body was discovered in a hotel room, it was three girls together, laughing—Rena, Iva, and I.

"I met someone today," I told my freshman college roommate, Iva Newton. We lived in a dorm room at 100 Beacon Street in Back Bay. It was a small room, too small for us: me, a tall, loud, musical theater redhead from Winthrop, Massachusetts, who needed to sing all the time and who wore green, high-waisted polyester pants, the style in 1977; and Iva, the hippie chick from Southern Pines, North Carolina, who arrived in Boston with ripped jeans, waist-length blond hair, and skis strapped to her back. Iva—introspective, southern, softer against my louder, redder self. We found our way toward each other after an all-night talk just a week or two into school, discovered that the outsides were different, the pictures were antithetical to each other, but the words, the dreams and desires (which would shape our whole lives, although we didn't know it at the time), they were exactly the same. So much so, we could see the same vision, look into a kaleidoscope and decipher the same patterns, the same configurations. We even finished each other's sentences. And so there really wasn't room for a third girl. Until Rena.

It was later, a month or so down the road, when it was clear that no third girl was going to make her way into our world. "I met someone today. Rena Shapiro. She's Israeli and she's going to translate 'Exodus' into Hebrew for me so I can sing it at the Ethical Society event this weekend. She's on her way over."

Rena, sashaying into the certainly-too-small-for-her-larger-than-life-presence dorm room, wearing a Joan Crawford-style black and white polka dot dress with a crinoline, like a movie star, like a goddess. All red lips and blond hair. "I'm going bald," she would announce to everyone, from dying her hair so much over the years: purple, pink, black, white. Rena, deciding on the spot that Iva and I were her people and that she would adopt us, let us bask in her light, her star status. And we did, gratefully and willingly. Rena, looking into the kaleidoscope and seeing the same colors as Iva and me, the miracle of three girls sharing the same vision, no jealousy, no two against one—that girl thing, especially in teenage years. No, we were a triumvirate, a perfect threesome. Beth, Iva, and Rena.

Iva flew in from London in 1988 for Rena's memorial, her youngest child clinging to her leg at the New York City service, where she tried to talk about Rena but had lost her voice. And me, singing Gershwin's, "They Can't Take That Away From Me," the song I was asked to sing in her letter to me, not told, as would have typically been Rena's way, but instead she asked, because above everything Rena was kind, and she knew it would be hard for me to sing the same song I had sung six years earlier at her wedding to Dick. I sang it because I never said no to Rena, to anything she asked of me. "I have to pee, come with." Okay. "I'm firing an actress from a play I'm directing at Yale. Get on a train to New Haven tonight. You're going on tomorrow. It's the lead." What? Okay. "Walk with me through the streets of Queens in the middle of the night. I need to find a place for Dick to live to get him away from Kitty." Really? Okay.

I recently posted a video of us on Facebook; I seem to post this video every year. It's my twenty-second birthday party and we had just graduated from college. We're all there, at my parents' house in Winthrop: Rena, Dick, Iva, Nancy, Ricky, Allison, Mario, a dozen or so others. My Nana Anna is there, my brother Michael, still in high school, and my parents—they're young and beautiful and so thrilled for us. My aunt Harriet is holding up a big cake and someone starts singing "New York, New York," and we all join in; we DO want to be a part of it, New York, New York, and after the song is sung the camera pans around the room, landing on Rena, and she says, "We love Beth. We love her the most of all. She's the greatest, in the words of Michael Kenney. She's going to New York to be a star and will take us with her. She's The Mother of Us All!" I don't remember who Michael Kenney was, I think he went to college with us, but Rena loved throwing out random names like that, and what I take out of that video, out of that day, is that Rena held me up, told me I was it, that I would take the world by storm. Once she was gone, there was no one saying those exact words. No cheerleader saying, "Take it, it's yours." There was a quiet space where there had once been so much sound.

This year was the twenty-sixth anniversary of Rena's death. Twenty-six years ago, sitting in my New York City apartment, I got the call from her mother in Boston. "Our girl is gone."

No. Oh God, no.

Life as I knew it was over.

"Our girl is gone."

And the weight of those four words, of having to tell everyone else, holding the phone away from my ear as one by one our friends screamed, cried, called out for her, insisted, as I did, that it wasn't true. But it *was* true. Rena was gone. Our girl, who couldn't even pee by herself, found her way to a lonely hotel room on Cape Cod. She didn't tell anyone. She needed it to work. She couldn't live with going from what she had been, a larger-than-life twenty-something icon, to an anonymous girl in a line at recess at a series of New England psychiatric hospitals. My husband, Steve, and I would drive up and she would break out of the line and run to us, not looking behind her, letting

Steve pick her up and hold her in his strong arms. Then she was asked to return to the other patients. Once it came to that it was over. Once it came to that there was no turning back, even though she promised the doctors that she wouldn't kill herself. The doctors who weren't as smart as she was.

I picked her up at that last hospital in Boston, and we walked down Boylston Street together as if it was any other day, any other day before mental hospitals. "I need to go into Barnes and Noble," she said, ushering me into the bookstore. "I need to find a book on euthanasia." "Cut it out!" I said. "Stop it." What we all said to statements like that when we thought Rena was just being a drama queen, just being herself. I didn't see it. My mind refused to even entertain a world without Rena Shapiro. It simply wasn't possible. It didn't matter what she said. It didn't matter that she told us.

I think the video I posted of our college friends at that long-ago birthday party is the only footage of Rena when she was well, before illness, before my wedding nine months before the end of her life, when she was clearly not herself, not holding court. All the other bridesmaids were in the hotel bathroom—Iva, Nancy, Susan, Allison—they were putting on makeup and playing with their hair, paying attention to themselves, not to me. Probably what all twenty-something bridesmaids do. Rena never looked in the mirror once. By now she was thin, not robust, not voluptuous, as she had been. She sat next to me on the hotel room bed in her black bridesmaid dress, and me in my wedding gown and veil, asking me what I needed. Asking how I wanted her to hold her bouquet as she walked down the aisle. She actually practiced while the other girls were laughing in the bathroom. In the photos, she's the only one holding that bouquet high enough, and you can see that it took effort, that she had to think about it. This was the last thing she would do for me and she wanted it to be perfect. I didn't think about the fact that she didn't look in the mirror at my wedding. I wish I had. I wish I had known that this was a sign. But I didn't. And I spent years blaming myself for her death.

"I am a tourist in my own life," she wrote in her suicide note. We made copies for everyone and handed them out at the memorial in the packed, standing-room-only New York City event space where everyone who loved her came to celebrate her life. But it wasn't a celebration; we were in despair. A room full of theater people who had no words, except what we wrote about her, and read, or sang. There was only grief that day . . . the loss was too great.

"Please don't be too sad," she wrote to us. "I would not have done this if I didn't absolutely have to. I know I would have been a wonderful teacher and mother. It just wasn't meant to be."

But early on, in 1977, Rena, all red lips and white-blond hair, all sashay and savvy; and Iva, my beloved friend still, and a survivor of that time with me, a survivor of all we have lived through since: cancer, the end of her marriage, other disappointments, but also triumph, such great triumph—our film, our theater company, our thirty-seven-year friendship, our careers, our five collective children—and me, nicknamed "The Mother of Us All" but knowing that there was once a girl named Rena Shapiro who was really the mother of us all . . . I prefer to remember the early days of three girls walking arm in arm in arm down a Boston street, when life was good and the world was open and ahead and filled with promise and possibility. The possibility of three girls, laughing.

Medication Makes Me Whole

ANGELA M. GILES PATEL

The most dangerous times for me are the moments after I remember that I forgot to take my medication. This is the time when I convince myself that I am on the path to weaning myself from the required daily dose, that I am already hours into a medication-free life and can keep going, that there is no time like the present, that I will be okay.

I have been on antidepressants since I was fifteen and first prescribed a tricyclic. I am now forty-four. There must have been something I said that jolted my mother, though I cannot recall it among the string of arguments we had. I was unhappy and articulate, which meant that I could tell her with venomous precision just how much sadness I was experiencing. And I did so on a regular basis, telling her how I wanted to live anywhere else, how I hated school, how I wanted to disappear. I was the problem child, the oldest child. My two sisters were far better adjusted than I was, and I lived life as the moody black sheep in the family, perpetually aware of my inability to be normal.

If I felt like I wasn't being heard, I would stick handwritten lyrics to the refrigerator door. Little sad notes next to reminders that we needed to buy more milk. The Cure, The Smiths, Depeche Mode, Joy Division—they were the soundtrack to my high school years. When it became clear that I was well beyond the realm of teenage angst, or more likely, when it became clear that my mother couldn't navigate my waters in the midst of my father's vodka-tinged storms, she sent me to a psychiatrist. Finding someone else to help me was one of the best parenting decisions she made.

I went willingly.

I was diagnosed with major depressive disorder.

My therapist was a good fit for me. He took me seriously, listened to what I said, answered questions I had. He also prescribed an antidepressant. He fed my love of reading, recommending books that would give me a broader perspective than the one I had living in a small town in Southern Utah. *Soul on Ice, Zen and the Art of Motorcycle Maintenance.* The books were edgy and expansive. I wrote about how I felt, he read it, and we talked about it. There was never any real discussion of me not making it through my teenage years; it was always a question of how. We set a goal: I would make it through high school and move out to attend college.

I considered my need to use an antidepressant nothing more than a by-product of living in a dysfunctional home. I never balked at taking it, nor at the weekly sessions I had with my therapist. The small white pill made the edges less sharp and life felt easier. I thought the medication was temporary, that once I no longer lived at home, I would no longer need it.

In college, I let the prescription lapse and found myself sliding back into a space I thought was hundreds of miles away. What I was feeling was so familiar that it scared me, and I again began a regimen of therapy and medication. Rather than discussing how to endure my environment, the therapy focused on how I could best be me. Among the many things that make me who I am is the fact that I am a person with a clinical disorder.

I've been on five different antidepressants since I was a teen-ager, moving from one to another as I changed doctors or as newer medication became available. But the biggest change to the type of medication I was taking came in my thirties. One of my sisters died suddenly from a previously undiagnosed condition, and my world buckled in profound ways. A gap in my collective consciousness was created when what had always been the three of us suddenly was reduced to two. The hole in me that was created by her death changed me physiologically. It took exactly one month to learn that the run-of-the-mill antidepressant wasn't working. My body chem-istry had upped its game and thrown anxiety into the mix. Com-binations of medication were tried until I felt balanced. Although I stopped therapy years ago, I continue to see a doctor who helps monitor my medication.

And here I am.

Holding on.

Thriving even.

So nothing pisses me off more than to see someone talk about how they *used* to take medication for depression or anxiety, but *now* they don't have to anymore because they discovered yoga or running or god. The idea that somehow they have managed a victory that is important enough to broadcast, that what they have accomplished can be outlined and followed, is misleading at best. And although they won't say it explicitly, the implied judgment is clear: if you are not enlightened enough to be able to survive without medication, some-thing is wrong with you.

No shit.

Something *is* wrong with me.

What is wrong with me is not a bump in the road, or a case of the blues, and it is not something that can be addressed by the right herbal tea. It is not a pothole, it is a fucking canyon—one I can only navigate with help. This is why I have to take two burgundy-colored capsules every morning. If I don't, my mind turns against me. It's not that I failed to become enlightened, it's simply who I am. The kicker is that I am enlightened enough to know that who I am is someone whose mind can fail to be her friend.

I hate taking the medication. The idea that I cannot fully function without it breaks my heart on a regular basis, but I can't stop taking it. I've tried. It isn't pretty. I hate my *dis*-order and my *dis*-ease enough that I occasionally allow myself to become tricked by depression. I am not sure who said it first, but they are right—depression lies. One of the biggest lies it tells is the one that starts with the idea that medication is unnecessary. Maybe it is optional for someone who just needed a little boost to get through a rocky period, but for those of us who are clinically diagnosed with depression, proper medication is critical. To suggest otherwise is a failure to understand the true nature of the problem.

There have been a handful of times where I have stopped taking my prescription on my own, always after missing a dose. The immediate onset of withdrawal symptoms, coupled with a careening mood, were enough to snap me back to my senses within a few days. I have stopped my medication under supervision twice. Making it past the painful withdrawal period and becoming fully engaged with my depression felt perilous, and I was quickly placed back on medication after expressing my concerns. Even so, if I could trade the fact that my pharmacist knows my name before I open my mouth to ask for the prescriptions my doctor has called in, I would. I don't need that kind of recognition.

What I do need is space to be me. I need quiet and time to reflect. I need room to be still and recollect. Truth be told, I occasionally do a bit of yoga and I regularly run my heart out, but neither of those is a panacea. I also need my friends. They accept that my disposition is a part of me, nothing more and nothing less, just another feature I have, like my messy red hair. Above all else, they understand what it is to be gloriously unique. And I need a reliable pharmacist, preferably one who genuinely smiles when she sees me walk through the door.

Bye-bye, Crayola

CAROLINE LEAVITT

The first thing you have to know is that because of my own crummy childhood, I never wanted kids, and I told everyone that fact from the time I was ten. "Don't let anyone ever hear you say that, because they'll think there's something wrong with you," my mother warns me. I laugh. I want a life of travel and adventure and lovers. I don't want to be tied down by a child, to have to give up any of my life for his or hers. And then I fall in love and marry later in life and suddenly a baby is all I can think about, and I'm terrified it now might be too late. I'm in my early forties. I have fibroid tumors the size of grapefruits. My chances of having a healthy baby are slim as a swizzle stick. And I get pregnant immediately.

Being pregnant is bliss. My hair thickens. My skin shines. I love all of it! The morning sickness! The swelling of my ankles as well as my stomach! My obstetrician laughs at me. "Everyone else complains," he tells me.

Jeff and I have names picked out. I can't resist shopping for the baby, but then, nearly four months into the pregnancy, during an exam, the doctor stops smiling. "I'm so sorry," he says.

I can't quite hear what he's saying, only snippets, each one like a thorn. The fetus was always struggling, he tells me. It's nature's way of making sure the fittest survive. Dead. He says the word. Dead. "You'll have to have the fetus removed," he tells me.

The good thing about hospitals is that no one pays attention if you are walking down the corridor sobbing. No one bothers to avert eyes or to stare. I go to the alcove where the pay phones are and call Jeff. As soon as he hears me sobbing, he says, "I'll be right there." It takes him half an hour with traffic, and I can't get off the phone. I call everyone I know, as if someone will tell me, "This isn't happening." I keep one hand over my belly as if my yearning might keep the fetus alive.

When we get home, I take to bed, Jeff lying beside me. I am supposed to be at jury duty, but I can't go. I am supposed to be at work and I call my boss, a memo-pusher in a bow tie, to tell him I'm taking a week off, and then I beg him not to tell anyone the reason why, because I need to be able to come back to work and not be reminded of what I've lost. I won't be able to bear it. "Of course I won't tell," he says, deeply sympathetic, and I believe him.

An hour later, a friend calls. "They're joking about you," she tells me. "Bow-tie man is saying you are an old hen who shouldn't have chicks."

I shut my eyes. I hang up the phone. I pull the covers over my head and I can't get up. I feel the baby, dead, inside of me, moving. Pain sweeps through me, a tsunami, and I am drowning.

They put me under the next day to remove the fetus. Groggy, I wake up and go home and go back to bed. I can't move. I don't eat. At night, I stare at the ceiling and mourn my baby. Friends call and come by and in well-meaning gestures bring me books about grief that are so stupid, I wait until my friends are gone and then hurl them across the room. My friend Jo tells me, "I know you will always think of that baby as your first," and I love her for it. Others stumble and tell me it's for the best, or maybe I'm too old to have a child. I'm upset until my friend Peter makes me a booklet of snappy answers to the stupid questions.

"We'll try again," Jeff tells me, and we do, and six months later, I'm pregnant.

We tell no one, though people at work tell me, "I know you're pregnant. Why can't you just tell us?" But I can't risk making it real, so I keep silent.

My pregnancy this time is blissful. Delivery is easy, and there is only one frightening moment when they lift the baby up so I can see him, his starfish hands, his eyes as big as dinner plates, and Jeff begins to cry.

"What's wrong with the baby?" I panic, but he holds my hand.

"Nothing. He's perfect."

Later, a friend of mine, a professional psychic, will tell me that every day I was pregnant she would think of me and see a huge sheet of black wall. She thought this baby would die, too, and sick with sorrow, she wouldn't tell me. She wanted me to have the joy of pregnancy for as long as I could. "I was wrong," she tells me. "That black wall was for you."

Post Partum Factor VIII Inhibitor. A glitch in the immune system that makes your body generate a protein which stops all your blood from clotting. So rare, there are only one in six million cases. So rare, the hospital has no idea what is wrong with me, why my body is swelling up. There are five emergency operations, and one nurse later tells me, "The OR was like the elevator scene from *The Shining*. No one had ever seen so much blood from a patient." They put me in a medical coma for two weeks. They glue some of my veins shut. They put me on memory blockers so I won't remember anything, and there is even a morphine drip for the pain, which gives all the doctors and nurses jaunty animal heads. I float, thinking I am in a TV comedy, imagining I am in a sex clinic, and I cry to the doctors, "I can't have sex now! I'm sick!" There is always a ring of doctors around my bed peering at me, talking as if I can't hear.

They call in my family because no one in the hospital thinks I am going to survive. And then a German hematologist who is about to retire says, "I know what this is and how to treat it." And she does. Two hundred transfusions. Factor VIII Blocking Agents. Keeping still because to move could cause a fatal hemorrhage.

But the thing is, they won't let me see Max. Jeff has put up a big poster of Max on the wall, with the words "I miss you, Mommy. Please get better!" He's brought in a video of Max's first few weeks, and the nurses—the kind, wonderful nurses—give up their break room so I can watch it, weeping.

I'm in my second month in the hospital when I tell the doctors that I am going insane. "You have to let me see my baby!" I shout. "I'll jump out the window if you don't." They argue with me, but I get hysterical, and then there is a discussion, and finally they tell me I can see my baby, but just for an hour, and just for once.

I'm so nervous, I beg my friends Nancy and Lindy to go and buy me mascara and brown eyeshadow, a lipstick that is soft rose. I have Jeff buy me a new hairbrush. I stumble to the bedroom, dragging my IV, and put on makeup. By the time I get back to bed, my heart is hammering. A nurse walks in and studies me critically. "You look good," she says.

"It's Maybelline," I say.

When I see my baby, my Max, he looks like a stranger. He's bigger, and when he's set in my lap, he blinks at me. The hospital is worried about me tiring myself out, so they make everyone leave after an hour. *Wait!* I want to call. *Wait. Wait. It's not enough time.* When I get back to my hospital bed, I remember how Max smelled, how he had a dimple, how his eyes were so blue. I fall asleep for fifteen hours. Two weeks later, I'm allowed to go home.

I have to stay in bed for six months. I can't lift Max, I can't feed him, so he's brought into the bedroom so I can see him. He shies away from me. When he's set down beside me, he cries. I cry, too. "We're supposed to be bonding!" I weep. Friends tell me about their baby who was in intensive care for three months and now is fine. Babies don't remember,

I'm told. But I do. And from the way Max looks at me, I can't help but think that he remembers, too. That surely, he must feel betrayed.

I think of all I could have done for him. I was going to breast feed. I was going to have him sleep in the bed with us. I had planned to puree all his food, to take him to the park, and spend hours on the floor playing with him, and I can't move out of bed.

He doesn't know who I am, and now, every time I try to parent him, he screams.

"Give yourself time," Jeff assures me. "Give Max time." He gives us lots of time alone, but it never turns out well. One time, I am tickling Max and he looks up at me, alarmed. I'm losing my hair from the meds I have to take, and a hank slides down onto him, making him scream. Jeff rushes up and gets him. I take to our bed, clutching the hank of hair in my hand. I can hear my husband and son downstairs. The baby is laughing.

Of course, it happens. Slowly, gradually. Max tolerates me more and more, and I'm calmer with him. But it isn't until I can get out of bed and walk around and take him places—a year after I get sick—that we fall in love with each other, and then it's so dazzling, I am astonished. When he begins to walk, he walks toward me! When he starts talking, he calls, "Mommy! Mommy!"

No one understands why I don't want to leave him to go anywhere, why we take him everywhere with us. I breathe in his hair. I kiss him constantly. I can't imagine love could expand this big. That it could take over our lives like this, and we want it too. Jeff and I know it's because we've lost so much already.

And then of course, the years begin speeding by. He turns five and then twelve and then fifteen, and then suddenly he's behind a closed door in his room. He's secretive, or always on the phone. But at least he's here, and sometimes, when we go out together, he talks to me. Then my baby is eighteen. He is an actor, a boy of a thousand voices and roles, though he shines in the funny ones, the quirky roles, the soulful moments. He auditions and gets into Pace Performing Arts/ The Actors Studio/The Honors College, one of fifteen boys admitted.

He's ten minutes away in the heart of Manhattan, and I am stunned at how much I miss him the moment he's accepted. I know this is what he wants. I know this is what we want, but part of me, that hidden part, thinks, *Something else is about to be lost.* Something I can't grab on to.

This fear, the fear of the unknown. And always the refrain: I didn't know you long enough.

To comfort myself, I say, *I will still know you, but in a very different way.*

At the end of August, it is the day I've been dreading. We drive him to his college. We help him set up his dorm room, and then outside, we say goodbye. I kiss his face. I deep breathe so I won't dare cry and ruin his absolute wonder and joy at being here. I know that all the things I want for him, a successful career as an actor, a wife, children, will chip me away from him even more, moving me further from his center, and that is as it should be. I reach for my husband's hand, and we watch our son, his whole body humming with joy and wonder, vanish into his new life. As soon as we are back in the car, I start to cry.

I know people joke about the Empty Nest. I join a forum on Facebook, but some of the women are weeping all day and can't get out of bed, which makes me want to weep all day and not get out of bed, either, so I quickly get off. The grief is a dull ache. One friend of mine tells me that after her daughter left for college, she began wearing the same dress over and over until she realized it was the dress she wore for funerals. But it gets better. Max texts. We have reason to see him every other week. There's a Broadway show he wants to see and would we like to see it with him? His computer is acting up, can we go to the Apple Store with him and then to dinner? And when we see him, we really see him. He's not on his phone. He's not glued to some game on his X-box. He's with us.

And then he's gone again.

The sorrow rides under the joy, like a burr stuck to us, or a rudder propelling us forward. Life without Max. I miss him in all his stages. I miss him when he was baby. I miss him as a toddler. I miss him at twelve, when he wanted to go on American Idol and sing. I miss the last five minutes I had with him, when we had an animated discussion about Insomnia cookies. I miss it all because I know I will never have those moments again.

Quantum physics says that there is no time, that it's man-made, and that everything is happening all at once. I love hearing that. It means in a parallel universe, I can cradle my baby boy, I can kiss my toddler, and hug my grown-up college student. I can bring back those shining moments, and just for a little while, stay in them again.

Death, Depression, and Other Capital D Words

MARIKA ROSENTHAL DELAN

Who wants to die? I wonder if everyone feels like this? It must be normal, right?

I tell myself that like George Bailey in *It's a Wonderful Life*, all of us have been hopeless enough to consider jumping off a bridge. I convince myself it must be a given part of life to contemplate being out of one's misery. I ruminate on all these things but don't know if they're really true. Haven't we all wondered if life is worth all the trouble? *Don't we all start asking such questions when we reach the ripe old age of ten?*

I ask myself these things in my depressed and prepubescent state, not prepared to know the answers. My ten-year-old logic is this: If *I'm alone* in my sadness, it only deepens my feelings of loneliness. If *I am not alone*, it means there are a whole lot of terribly sad people walking around the planet. Either way, I don't want to think about it.

I will not speak of my secret. I don't tell Mrs. Fisher, the guidance counselor at school with the crazy red hair. She asks me why I miss school a lot. I tell her it's because my stomach hurts.

I pretend not to notice that every time I think of not being alive, I die a little inside. It's my own suicide of the mind, a plan of my own subconscious creation. I use the Garfield diary I get for Christmas to document my sentiments so as to never let myself forget. Under lock and key, in blue and bouncy fifth-grade hand, I write:

"I wish I was dead."

We planted a tree in honor of Lisa Rose that year in the front school-yard of McMillan Elementary. I was asked to speak at the memorial service, but I only recall one sentence of what I said. *Why hadn't I written it all down in my diary instead?*

The thing I remember saying that day about Lisa Dawn Rose: that despite the fact that she was always so sick, somehow she never had a care in the world.

I read words I had prepared in honor of my dead friend, written on standard-issue, blue-lined notebook paper. I opened my carefully folded page at an ugly veneer podium in white shoes and wet morning grass. I read the words I had memorized, too afraid I might forget one.

I heard them like an echo when I said them aloud, as if they had already been spoken. I wish I could remember every word, but instead remember the metal mesh of microphone, pressed against sticky Bonne Bell-covered lips.

I skipped my first school lunch on a Thursday one day after that morning in spring. I know it was Thursday because it was Turkey Turnover Day. When I showed up at the table without a tray, my friends seemed irritated at me. *Why hadn't I given it to one of them, they asked?* Every single person I knew loved turkey turnovers. I hated them. They made me want to puke. If my friends couldn't understand how disgusting turkey turnovers were or how much fatter I might get if I were to eat one, *how would they ever understand that sometimes I really wanted to die?*

It pains me that these are the things I remember: pink, partitioned lunch trays and shredded-turkey-stuffed pastries covered in gelatinous yellow gravy, a scoop of powdered potatoes by it's side; a development of an aversion to microphones.

How was I supposed to remember things that I really needed to know?

How would I ever remember how *she knew how to live even though she knew she was dying?*

I didn't write it down.

Why hadn't I written it down?

Instead I decide to pen my confessions of suicidal ideation on pages guarded by a comic book cat and a lock you can pick with a hairpin. I scribble over and over it later, in panicked circles, until it's no longer clear what was written there.

But the scribbles are there to remind me, so one day I rip out the scribbles.

It leaves the binding loose, being as it was the very first page.

Ten years and 10,000 more prayers to let me die later, a clinician scribbles some words in a chart on her desk where I can't see. I can't tell her I think a lot about dying, more days than not since the year I turned ten, but I tell her what she needs to know. I don't want something written that cannot be erased. I made that mistake once already and ruined a perfectly good diary. As she turns to get a prescription pad and boxes of samples from a grey-metal file cabinet, I strain to read what she has written. I can only read a little, but I fight the urge to grab the chart and scribble in circles over the words. I want to rip out the page with the words that I read before she turns back around in her chair:

Major Depression, recurrent, 296.32

Dispense Prozac 20 mg.

The sadness never left me after that diary entry in the winter of 1985, nor after that office visit ending in a diagnostic code and a bag full of little boxes of pills.

I didn't know at the time, but I was feeding my sadness all the food I tried but failed to deprive myself of. I grew bigger while my spirit withered away. For so long I thought this was what growing up was.

And thirty years later, how I pray that I never grow up. I feel sometimes as if time has moved backward in those respects, and I'm okay with that. I keep trying to learn in reverse to see the world again through the eyes of a child. Jesus said we must become as little children to enter the kingdom of heaven. Maybe that's the key to living the way Lisa Rose always did. Maybe that's why she knew exactly what to do.

In *Their Eyes Were Watching God,* Zora Neale Hurston wrote "There are years that ask questions and years that answer."

So many questions.

All this time.

And even after all of it, I still don't have answers to all of them. There are those questions the years have answered loudly and some that grow exponentially larger with time. Looking back, it's clear it was all of the usual suspects that had started the landslide of *things that made me want to Die,* things like Disordered eating and Diets that promised my fat would Disappear; things like Divorce.

Things like Death.

These things happen and the world keeps spinning like it doesn't even notice it fell apart. It goes on and so do we, mustering the best we possibly can amidst the D words and the mud that we slide in. *Mud.* Just another word for soaking-wet *Dirt.*

Sometimes I cry a lot and then pull myself back together, wipe my eyes, and take a deep breath. Just like I did when I was ten.

But I no longer pray to die in my sleep. Thoughts of escape by death are no longer things I pray or wish for. Now I wake in the middle of the night wondering if I have taught my kids the things they really need to know.

I wake in a panic full of questions, full of last requests.

God, please don't take me before I have lived enough,

before I have loved enough.

Before I have learned how it is that we become as little children.

I keep thinking about the fact that my son is only three years away from the age I was when I wrote those ominous words in my journal. Watching holiday movies lately must have us both thinking a lot about life and death. He asked me last week after watching *A Christmas Carol*, "Mama, what does it mean to be alive?"

I asked him where he completed his training to be a Zen master.

The questions children ask are often the hardest ones to answer. They seem simple enough at first, but they cause you to examine your own questions and those still waiting for answers. The ones you skipped over, leaving the little oval empty, your pencil hovering until you waste so much time on it you decide—*I better come back to that one later.*

It awoke me that night in sweat-soaked clothes—his question and my inability to answer it, even though I must know some of the answers.

Perhaps my fear isn't that I don't know the answers. It's that I know some of the answers are the ones that change you forever. Like the ones that you learn around the time you turn ten.

Pushing nearly forty, my memory grows dim with each passing year. *I still can't remember what kind of tree we planted that day for Lisa Rose, but I pray that it flowers every spring.*

I'm writing the important things down now so that I'll never forget. For that day when my son asks his question again, through the lens of someone no longer a stranger to loss. And when that day comes, I will have prepared these words to be saved now as a digital file—never to be lost or taped up in a cardboard box somewhere where diaries with locks go to become old relics.

My beautiful Child,

Sometimes you will find yourself in the back and forth between know-ing the largeness of your life and being so hurt by the smallness, you think you can't bear either one.

There will be times that you will be filled with boundless joy, and times life will steal your very breath and leave you praying that you don't panic and take it back.

Sometimes you will fall and shear the skin from your knees, but you have witnessed the miracle of your body heal the wounds. Like the scab that forms where the skin has been broken, it will fall away in time to reveal that while it was aching so badly, your very cells were knitting themselves back together.

You must keep living, even though sometimes it means dying a little, and when it feels like all is lost, never forget—even death can't make love die.

Love,
Mom

Colors at the Piano

LINDA JOY MYERS

Back then, when my body was small and pale, everything had sharp sounds, and the colors would scratch or caress my skin, and flashes of knowledge would go off behind my eyes. I lived with my grandmother in the middle of the empty howling plains, sandwiched between amber-colored wheat and the great azure sky; or in other weather, between grey, wind-blown weeds and thunderheads that reached to the heavens, purple, green, or indigo blue. When it was grey and purple outside, the wind whipped up and pressed you into the earth, pushed you and pulled you until you couldn't stand up, you couldn't catch your breath. Then, you knew that everything was bigger than you, and you couldn't do a thing about it.

Inside the small house on Park Street in a town in Oklahoma, storms brewed. Gram, who'd rescued me from the mean lady who hit me for no reason, where my parents had sent me for reasons no one could ever figure out, was the "good fairy" for the first couple of years, plying me with smiles and Cream of Wheat with brown sugar, offering piano lessons, which opened up a world. The piano would lay itself before me, a puzzle of black and white keys, its language locked behind hieroglyphs of black and white notes on a staff, mysterious to decode.

The sprinklers were hissing on the lawns on a hot July night, the other kids playing catch, their laughter lifting into the air, when the mysteries of the musical staff opened themselves to me: E, E flat, F, F sharp, A, A flat. Middle C. Stunned to read this new language, I played the notes and watched as each bloomed into its own color before me. The wine red of B flat, the dark purple of E flat. D flat was dangerous and jagged. The sharps were bright—F sharp was a warm orange, D sharp a warm beige. C was white, neutral.

As time went on, my fingers grasped at chords and melodies, and layers of color emerged into the smoke-filled house with its maroon ceiling, my grandmother hunkered down in the couch emitting something that was not quite a color, not quite a sound, though she talked or shouted or screamed, depending on the thing that would come over her. It didn't have a name. It made me shiver and shrink; it was cold and soon enough I watched it take over my world.

My mother ambled toward me and Gram while the Texas Chief's silver engine shivered in the station like a pony who'd scrambled across the big plains, catching its breath. Her beauty, ivory skin—red lipstick always perfect—her throaty voice greeting me, her fingers along my cheek; the sound she emitted was wispy when she arrived, delicate as the tissue paper in her perfumed suitcases, but too soon she and her mother were shouting accusations. Mother was wrong, according to Gram; Gram was wrong, according to Mother. One thin line of words would lead to torrents of words and tears, and even screams. I learned to hide in the bedroom, hoping they would stop. Then the shattering of dishes, the sound of the world ending as they careened toward the cliff of no return, each facing the other like tattered warriors in makeup, wearing nice dresses, their pretty faces twisted. One time I ran between them and begged them to stop. Another time I bent down to pick up the pieces, but Mother stopped me.

On her yearly visits, mother would play Franz Liszt's *Liebestraum* for me. "It means Song of Love," she told me, her eyelids fluttering as her graceful pale hands swooped up and down the keyboard. The colors that had shattered the night before began to settle into place as I huddled near her warm body, wanting to soak up all this beauty before it disappeared again. The music was blue and red and swirling, passionate and promising, and then it was over. An ache began in my chest then, a feeling like an umbilical chord knotted and connected between us, and I knew in my body how wrong it was that she had left me, that she kept leaving, year after year. You try to keep the goddesses on their pedestal when you are young, because if they fall down into pieces, you shatter too. The world is too fragile for anyone. She left over and over again, climbing on that silver train, its whistle the color of smoke and the blue of a lonely night.

Back then, I didn't know that my grandmother had left my mother when she was only six years old, the same age I was when she rescued me, seeding a generational pattern that mother would repeat. No one spoke of these things, and I would not know how perfectly the pattern had played out until after they died. No one would talk about the ghosts of the past that hovered around us. What I knew then was this shattering brokenness between them.

By the time I was twelve, my grandmother faded from her welcoming smiles and my best and only friend into a harpie with snaggled teeth, a wicked backhand with the walnut yardstick, a woman who spewed hate, forcing me to mirror her moods or be beaten, demanding my absolute allegiance. Yardstick on her lap, she had me write in my own hand hate letters she dictated to my father, signing my name. In high school, as I eyed the door for escape—I had nowhere to go—I tunneled my psyche into music. It beckoned me with its colors and its sounds, and put its arms around me where she couldn't reach me, though she was only a few feet away. Once in awhile she'd break through the barriers of notes to swing the yardstick, but most of the time it was my moat where I was safe from her.

When I was twenty, my mother made it clear that I was not welcome as her daughter in Chicago where she lived. "No one knows I was married, so I can't have a daughter, right?" I gazed at her in disbelief, blood draining from me as I tried to make sense of this denial. There were no colors or soft edges that could protect me, so I took it in the stomach where it would live for a long time. Yet, I didn't take this rejection at face value. For the next thirty years, I tried to convince my mother that I was a worthy daughter, sharing my three children with her—she chose to see each one twice in her life—my degrees in music and art, my value as a therapist who could help heal others and make a difference. Through those years, I searched to understand why we were all painted with such dark colors, why such a broken and shattered family. The darkness that haunted my grandmother and mother came to rest on my shoulders and in my body, a heavy weight of muddy colors. Year by year in therapy, I would return to the grey and smoky house in the lonely plains, trying to understand why the women I loved turned from light to dark, changed like magic creatures from one thing into another, why they turned their faces away from each other, and me.

I was fifty and she was eighty. My mother, whom I had not seen for four years for the sake of self-preservation, was small on the bed, white sheets all around her, her hair resting on the pillow around a face that could still make my heart stop. She would get a lung biopsy and then be diagnosed with brain cancer. I always saw her beauty in these quiet moments, and sorrow filled my heart that as a little girl she was alone, like I was, and in some ways we had the same history. But then the edgy angry part in her arose, and she found something to criticize, and the whole crazy play started up again, but I was determined to draw upon my thirty years of therapy and make our last act different.

Again, in front of nurses and doctors, she denied I was her daughter, but I bore the stab wound quietly as I saw glances of pity fall upon me. I found out that she harassed the nurses with such nastiness the doctor ordered a psych evaluation. Finally. It had been clear for years that something was wrong with my mother.

The psychiatrist's eyes were full of compassion as I told him about the shattered dishes and lost girls and my grandmother's craziness. It had a name: manic-depression. "Yes, this runs in families," he said gently. At that moment, my mother was running up and down the halls, trying to find us, to silence him, to control us as if that would stop the raging forces in her mind and body. That week my mother was admitted to the geriatric psychiatric ward. On the way, she denied I was her daughter again, but this time I understand it as her illness speaking. This thing of pain had a name. It was a disease. It was not really her. I smiled, though my heart was racing. It was official: I came from certifiably crazy people. What did that make me?

My grandmother on her deathbed asked me to forgive her for hating my father. Her dark eyes were bright and the muddy grey air that always surrounded her was gone. She seemed surrounded in light, and the room was golden. A priest had given her the last rites, forgiving her for her sins. She became the grandmother I knew when I was little again, who gazed at me with love. Two weeks later she died.

I returned to Chicago the last few days of my mother's life because she could no longer shout at me, her powers of speech stolen by the cancer. She had denied me until then, but finally nodded when a nurse asked if I should come. I approached the room and saw someone unrecognizable in the bed, a bald woman, emaciated, her arms flying up and down randomly, eyes rolling. I backed out of the room to look at the number. It had to be the wrong room. This was no one I recognized, but I looked again. Just then she saw me, and a wild keening sound arose in her, tears burst from her eyes, and she waved her arms toward me. The grief for all we had lost, for Gram, for the wasted and painful years burst in me, and we sobbed together for a long time, our tears mingling on our bodies. I had a vision then of the unfolding of time, how it wafted back through the generations, that she and I were made of these moments that had passed between us as well as all the moments we had lost. Our lives and psyches were woven of this wispy stuff of soul and now we were together. It was like those days at the piano where the notes and their colors filled my world, and now the dark B flat and the scary D flat changed into welcoming colors of amber and gold, white light and forgiveness.

It was the beginning of the rest of my life.

The Deal Breaker

LIRA MAYWOOD

An empty hook hangs on my living room wall. Until recently, it held a medium-sized picture frame in shades of brown and gold. In it was a photograph of a couple, eyes half closed, his arm around her shoulders, her right hand tenderly cradling his cheek as he leans down, so close that their foreheads almost touch. Her smile is open, joyful. His is tender, a private smile for the woman he loves. The inscription: *Once in a while in an ordinary life, love gives us a fairy tale.*

We used this photo for our wedding invitation, and it was a storybook wedding. I felt like a fairy princess in my gown, forehead encircled by a crown of tiny white flowers. He sang to me as I walked toward him down the aisle: "You're everything I hoped for; you're everything I need . . . You are so beautiful to me." It was 2009, and we had been together for five years. In his toast, the best man held up our invitation photo and said that in all the years he'd known Mike, he'd never seen him smile like that.

Less than a year later, I was a widow.

On our second date, we stood outside a bar on Sunset Strip necking
like horny teenagers, oblivious to Saturday night traffic and the occasional whistle or catcall. "I feel like I'm sixteen," I murmured into his
ear. In reality, at sixteen I couldn't have imagined that a tall, long-
haired rocker boy would ever want to kiss me. I didn't date until my
twenties, and it had taken us thirty-five years to find each other.

Our third date began with lunch at Venice Beach and ended with
me nestled in his arms on my couch, listening to his heartbeat and
saying a silent prayer: *Thank you for this man.*

We talked about everything from politics to lucid dreaming. I
told him the plot of my novel-in-progress and he gave me insightful
feedback. We walked arm in arm down the boardwalk, stopping to
listen to street performers or browse the market stalls, and when the
wind picked up he removed his leather jacket and draped it over my
shoulders. We danced barefoot on the sand at the drum circle while
the sun went down, then stole away to a more private spot where we
stood kissing until I had a crick in my neck and the night wind chilled
our bodies wherever they weren't touching. That whole perfect day felt
like something out of one of my stories, the kind of romance I'd imagined on the page but never lived.

Before we made love the first time, we put our potential deal
breakers on the table. I confessed my fears about sex, the result of adolescent trauma. He shared that he had struggled with depression since
the collapse of his marriage three years prior and was taking antidepressants. Somewhere in the back of my mind a distant warning bell
was ringing, but I ignored it. I told Mike it didn't matter. Having never
experienced a fulfilling sexual relationship, I dismissed the potential
side effect of sexual dysfunction. If he would be patient with me, I
would be patient with him.

Our first time together was wonderful. I had no idea sex could
feel that good. And it just kept getting better.

Nine months into our relationship, Mike decided he no longer
needed antidepressants. It was October and he was in the throes of
artistic creation, working night and day on an elaborate Halloween

costume. He was amped, couldn't sit still or focus on anything but his project. He would mutter under his breath while he worked, often a string of obscenities—not in anger but as if he were repeating a mantra. He became jittery at night, with restless legs that he couldn't stop from shaking, and slept little.

The inevitable crash came in early November. He stopped wanting to go out or do anything. He'd come to my apartment and sit slumped on the couch for hours, staring blankly at the TV with listless, dull eyes. His sex drive went from supercharged to nonexistent. Sometimes he would hold me at night; other times he didn't even want to be touched.

I'd never seen Mike have more than one drink at a time, but now he was going through half a bottle of tequila in a night. Alcohol put some fire back into him, woke him out of his dead-eyed lethargy, and I didn't mind until he started passing out on my bathroom floor. Sometimes he was a maudlin, tearful drunk but rarely angry that I recall, except once.

We were drinking quietly at my apartment, jazz on the stereo, and without warning or provocation he hurled his glass at my dining room wall, taking out a chunk of plaster as shards of cobalt blue glass littered the floor. I retreated to my room, unnerved by the violent gesture, and sat on the bed sobbing. I'd lived with an angry drunk once, and swore I would never do it again.

When he came in to apologize, I told him tearfully that I didn't want to lose him. What I really meant was: I don't want to leave you. Don't make me leave you.

Around Thanksgiving, he agreed to go back on the antidepressants. "I'm not right," he admitted. I counted the days, praying that the medication would be titrated up to effectiveness before our first Christmas together and the January anniversary of our first date. I wanted the old Mike back, the one with the mischievous sparkle in his eyes who made me laugh and argued as passionately as he fucked. His depression was like a thick fog that seeped into every corner of the room and sucked the energy out of both of us.

I kept telling us both that it would get better, that he'd get back to normal with the medication, but it wasn't that simple. For five years, he rode the medication rollercoaster as his doctor adjusted dosages, adding and subtracting different meds. We'd have a few good months, and for a while he'd almost be the man I fell in love with again, then one day I'd come home and find that he hadn't gotten out of bed and his eyes had that flat, lifeless look that spoke of a dark, dark place.

Twice it got so bad that I feared for his safety. The first time was just thirteen months into our relationship. When I called to ask if we were still going out that night, he said he wasn't sure he could get off the couch. He'd been lying in the dark for hours and didn't know if it was day or night. "I don't know where to go from here," he added, his voice sounding small and lost. "Come over," I told him. When he walked in the door, with several days' growth of whiskers and lank, greasy hair, I wrapped my arms around him. His skin and clothes had a sour tang. He curled up in the fetal position on my couch, and I sat beside him, alternately holding his hand or rubbing his shoulders.

In a flat, blank voice he told me, "I can't do this life anymore."

Two years later, on the verge of being fired from his second job in a row, he would say it again. After several days of the can't-get-out-of-bed depression, he disappeared one afternoon while I was running errands, calling me from the airport just before he boarded a flight to the Florida Keys. It was, he told me once, the only place where his life had ever made sense. I didn't know if he had gone to the Keys to get perspective on his life or to end it. When he said those words again—I can't do this anymore—I was distraught.

"Just come home," I begged him. "We'll get through this together. Just come home."

Both times, he came back to me. Both times, we made it through the darkness together and came into the light again. After Florida, we started our own business and he threw himself into it with the same manic intensity he gave his art. We got engaged. We formally promised to stand by each other in good times and bad, to love each other forever. I thought that would be enough. I knew the pit of depression was always waiting there to swallow him, but I believed our love could keep pulling him out of it.

The call came at 5:25 PM on Wednesday, March 3, 2010. The caller identified herself as a sheriff's deputy and asked, "Has anyone told you what's going on?" I hadn't given the office phone number to anyone but Mike, so I assumed it was related to the agency where I was temping. "I don't know what you're talking about," I answered, impatient. I was five minutes from clocking out, eager to run down to the car where my husband was waiting for me. Then the deputy said Mike's name, and I had a terrible feeling.

I asked a coworker for a ride to the hospital. It wasn't far, just a few miles away, but the drive seemed to take forever. I pulled out my phone and saw six missed calls, four from my mother-in-law. I called her back. "He used a gun," she told me, her voice quavering. My fleeting hope that it hadn't been a serious attempt died with those words. I began to panic that I wouldn't get there in time. Every red light made my chest constrict, my heart beat faster.

The hospital chaplain, a spindly woman with gray hair and a large crucifix, met me at the ER entrance. She led me into her office and told me in a soft, calm voice that Mike's condition was very critical and he wasn't expected to live more than a few hours. Numb with shock, I followed her to a curtained cubicle in the ER.

When I stepped through the curtain, the nightmare was real. I saw him lying there, absolutely still, a sheet pulled up to his neck, most of his head covered with a white cloth. Slowly I approached the gurney. His right eye was full of blood, and when I saw that, I knew that what the chaplain had told me was true. There was no way he would recover from this. The respirator, breathing for him, made a shushing sound. The line on the EKG machine wasn't flat—it showed that his heart was beating, but surely it lied. He was already gone, lost to me. The chaplain told me I mustn't touch him, especially his hands, because the police still had to test for gunshot residue. I gripped the metal sides of the gurney, white-knuckled. My chest felt so tight, I couldn't draw more than a shallow breath. The lump in my throat threatened to choke me, but no tears came.

When the blessed numbness of shock began to wear off, the pain was unbearable. For the first time, I had an inkling of how bad Mike's pain must have been; for the first time, I understood how ending it all might seem like a reasonable response to such pain. I couldn't stand to contemplate the rest of my life without him in it.

"I don't know how to do this" became my mantra, the words I repeated over and over when I wanted to howl like a wounded animal or just lie down and give up. Implicit in those words was the hope that living without him was something I could learn to do. "I can't do this" was not an option I would allow myself. Mike had the right to take his own life, but he wasn't going to take mine.

I talked to him sometimes, addressing the pewter urn on the bureau or our picture on the wall—that moment of joy captured as proof that we *were* happy together, in spite of depression and lost jobs and financial struggles. We loved each other so much. I would ask his picture, "Why did you leave me, baby?"

It took over a year, but one day I knew. I finally understood the gift he thought he was giving me.

He left me so that I wouldn't have to leave him.

A Slip of the Noose

JIMMY CAMP

Sick Boy. Angel. Bobby Two-Tone. Baby Crazy. Johnny Tri-Hawk. Cutter. Not their real names. Most everyone had a nickname. No last names.

I was just Jimmy.

Still am.

Most everyone had someone looking for them. Good or bad. Parents. Pimps. Cops. Brothers. Dealers they fucked. No one wanted to be found. Most everyone wanted to be anonymous. Invisible. Lifeless. Disposable. Most of us lived in *Hell* at some point: 7021 Hollywood Boulevard.

People were looking for me too. I didn't care. Good luck. Try to find me here. Wouldn't matter anyway. Just turned eighteen. My older brother came looking for me once. Just after Thanksgiving. In his topsiders and Lacoste shirt. I'm sure. He ran into Charles somewhere on the boulevard. Charles went to high school with us. He was adopted. His mom was crazy. She took in strays for money. Foster kids. Retards. Cripples.

Charles was eighteen.

No one was looking for him.

Charles took my brother down to Oki Dog. Told him I might be there. Oki Dog was on Santa Monica Boulevard. We went to Santa Monica Boulevard to roll fags. I was at Oki Dog a lot. I'm sure he got my brother to buy him a forty, or a pastrami burrito. I wasn't there. A few days later I saw Charles on the front steps of the El Nido, a hotel on Wilcox. Off Santa Monica Boulevard. Down from the police station. He lived there with a skinny, blonde tweaker chick named Polly. He told me he took my brother to Oki Dog looking for me. We thought that was funny. Usually there were bums drinking Thunderbird on the steps at the El Nido. There weren't any that day.

I called the house on Christmas Eve. Outside the dollar movie theatre. I wanted to go home. My brother answered the phone. My parents were at church. My dad was the pastor. I wondered why my brother wasn't with them. He told me I was ruining their lives. I probably was. He hung up. I didn't call back. I went and saw two movies for a buck with Maria. She was a German. Seventeen. A whore. No one was looking for her. The cops were all over Hell that night. Couldn't go there. Children of the Night had a big Christmas party for runaways with runaway advocates. The cops came and popped them all. A lot of them were staying in Hell. They narc'd out a bunch of other kids that were crashing there. The cops were looking for them. Most of them came from the Valley or the OC. People in the Valley and the OC want their kids home at Christmas.

We crashed in an underground parking garage that night. The Garden Court Apartments, an apartment complex on Sycamore, under the stairs by a bunch of hot-water heaters. That became our place. Maria and I sort of lived together. Not anywhere. Together.

It was warm.

For Christmas Eve.

Tom Mix, John Barrymore, Stan Laurel, Oliver Hardy, Marilyn Monroe, Louis B. Mayer. Not their real names either. But they all *wanted* to be found. Visible. Full of life. Dead now. They all lived at

The Garden Court Apartments at some point, 7021 Hollywood Boulevard. It was next to the Chinese theatre. If you hung around the bus benches in front of the Chinese theatre, Japanese people would scurry off their buses and give you a dollar to take your picture with them. Especially if you had a Mohawk in 1983. I did.

The Garden Court Apartments had gargoyles and a big fountain out front. It was the place back in the day. Grand pianos in all the rooms. The cat's pajamas. The bee's knees. Tinsel Town. Before Hollywood became a shit-hole. Before they boarded it up.

We called it Hotel Hell.

Hell for short.

I started doing drugs by accident. I was twelve. I got an electric guitar for Christmas that year. I got some brown corduroy overalls and cowboy boots that year too. I got a small amplifier. A chord. Strap. Finger Ease.

Finger Ease was a spray you sprayed on your guitar strings. Like string lube. I would lie in bed at night playing my guitar under the covers. I would spray the Finger Ease on the strings. I would hear helicopters. I figured out that if I sprayed the finger ease on part of my pillowcase and inhaled it I could hear more helicopters. I figured out if I covered the spray tip with a sheet and inhaled it directly I would hear cooler helicopters. I figured out it worked with any aerosol can. I didn't learn it from anyone. Didn't see it on an ABC after-school special.

Hairspray tasted really bad. It was sticky. Pam cooking spray was greasy. My mom used to spray stuff on her fingernails to make them dry quicker. It didn't taste that bad. Don't remember what it was called. Pink can. Wasn't sticky. Wasn't greasy. It became my spray of choice.

Inhaling fingernail-polish dryer was fun when you're twelve. At first you would lay back and hear the helicopters. After a while you would start hallucinating. If you did enough, you would pass out. There were no real side effects. Except for the brain damage. Or the seizures. Or Death. I never experienced seizures or death.

Nor did I care.

Not at twelve.

I did it mostly after school in my room. Often at night in my bed. I would go in the bathroom. Lock the door. Pretend I was going to the bathroom. One time I was sitting on the toilet seat, tripping, and these ratty-looking Charles Dickens orphan-type characters were sitting on my shoulders. Three of them. Smoking cigarettes. Laughing. Dropping ashes on my head. I was worried my mom was going to smell the smoke. I walked out. Left the fan on. Shut the door. The stairs were right by the bathroom door. I looked down the stairs. Mrs. Tagan, the principal of my school, was standing at the bottom. It was like a hologram, like Princess Leia. She put her finger on her chin and shook her head at me. The Charles Dickens guys ran to my room. Laughing.

I had to steal money from my parents so I could replace the fingernail-polish-drying spray. I was kind of a stealer early on. Not sure why. The cans weren't that big. I would go through two or three a week. I started to just steal them directly from the drugstore. Save a step. I was kind of smart.

One day I was getting lit in the bathroom. My mom yelled at me to come downstairs. I was in trouble. For something. Don't remember. I stumbled down the stairs. She saw my eyes. She smelled the fingernail spray. She went up to the bathroom. Found the washcloth and the can. She flipped out. She called Pastor Tannenberg. He came right over. He sat on my bed. Took off his shoes. Put his feet up. Tried to talk to me. It was a little weird. The Pastor with his shoes off, on my bed.

Real drugs are expensive. Heroin. Speed. Coke. Hard to get. Homeless runaway street kids don't have money for real drugs. In order for street rats to get enough money for real drugs, they had to do things. Rob People. Steal stuff. Turn tricks. Bad things. Bad kids.

A noose around the neck.

Gun in the mouth.

Fake drugs are cheap. Easy to get. Spray cans. Liquid paper. Airplane glue. Robitussin. Kids could panhandle enough money in about an hour to get fake drugs. Hopeless. Fucked-up kids. They would mostly get liquid paper. Empty it in to a paper sack. Inhale. Hear the helicopters. You would see them walking around Hollywood Boulevard with dried liquid paper all over their faces. I didn't do that shit anymore. Hardly. It was for twelve-year-olds. The last thing I wanted was to be in an abandoned apartment building in the middle of the night full of runaways, junkies, whores, rapists, thieves, trash, hearing helicopters and seeing crazy shit that wasn't really there. It was bad enough seeing what *was* really there.

Sometimes I would play guitar on the Boulevard.

Enough money to buy a forty.

Some food.

Food was easy to get. You could listen to a greasy-haired, Ike Turner-look-a-like mother fucker dressed like a priest yell at you for forty-five minutes and get a free English muffin topped with chili and cheese. You could go to McDonalds just after it closed and wait by the dumpster. They would come out and throw away the fish filets and Big Macs they didn't sell. Sometimes the guy would just give them to you. Sometimes they would set them on top of the dumpster. Sometimes they would make an effort to mix them in to the trash just to fuck with you. Depended on who was working.

I don't remember the first time I did heroin. I was in Hotel Hell. There were three or four of us. I can't remember if speed or heroin was first. It was the first time I shot up. There wasn't any water in Hell. We needed water to shoot up. We didn't want to risk leaving Hell in the daylight and coming back in. Risk. You could get busted if the cops saw you. If one person got busted, it would get real tight and nobody could get in and out at night. People would get pissed if you brought the heat on them. We found an old half-filled bottle of Canada Dry club soda lying around. Made sure it was flat. Made sure no one pissed in it. We used it to cook our drugs. Three or four of us on the same spike.

This was when AIDS was still gay cancer.

We weren't gay.

No worries.

A slip of the noose.

You had to do bad things to get real drugs. I had a conscience. I only did bad things to bad people. Bad people don't call the cops. Justified it. Didn't want to go back to jail. Or hell, the real hell, when it all crashed down. And you always knew it would.

Laura was sixteen. Darrell was her boyfriend. Skinhead. We had all come to Hollywood together. She was from the OC. We scoped out an apartment building. Light up front, dark out back. Jump two fences and *bam-bam*. Fuller Street. Runyon Canyon. Used to be a big mansion there. Pool. Tennis court. Errol Flynn lived there. Once it decayed along with the rest of Hollywood, it became home to the Manson family. Hobos and bums. Street scum.

We knew it well.

It's a park now.

Laura stood on Sunset, between La Brea and Highland. With the whores. We waited in the dark lot. Laura pulled up in a car. Middle Eastern dude. Wedding Ring. Baby seat. Married. A baby. Picking up a sixteen-year-old girl. To fuck. Bad guy. Fair game. We jumped him. Gold chain around his neck. Yanked it off. Like a movie. Held a knife in his face. Wouldn't give it up. Wallet was in the trunk. Dropped the keys. Kicked them under the car. Punched him in the face. He started screaming. "Help me! Help me!" Went through his pockets. Hundred bucks. Two fences. Chucked the keys. Storm drain. I wonder what he told his wife. We separated. Headed for Runyon Canyon. Met up at the old tennis court. Laid low. I went for a walk. Picked up some provisions. Stayed up all night. The next morning we scored a room in a shitty Chinese hotel. Took some friends along. Showered. Crashed out. Partied some more. Chinese lady came in screaming to get out or she'd call the police. There were six of us. Back to Hell. Had twelve bucks left. Laura and Darrell split the next day. I stayed. Misfire.

Santa Monica Boulevard was a gold mine.

Lots of bad people.

Lots of money for big-kid drugs.

Old queers in nice cars looking to fuck teenage boys.

If they asked, I said I was fifteen. They liked that. Made them worse. Easier to hit. My first time but not my last. Older guy. Bald. Glasses. Volvo. Nice place. Went to his bedroom. Said I needed the bathroom. He was naked on the bed. Under a sheet. I could see his boner. Sat down on the bed. I felt him gently put his hand on my back. I reached down. Pretended to untie my oxblood Doc Martin boots. Pulled a butterfly knife. Tucked him in real tight. I could see him breathe. Couldn't see any movement. His hard on went away. Looked like a mummy. I wondered if he had a gun. Hidden. Somewhere. Turned the TV on. Taxi. Alex, Louie, Nardo. Not too loud. Loud enough. Took his money. MasterCard. Leather pants. Nice leather jacket. Gold jewelry. Car keys. Cut the phone cords. Bedroom. Kitchen. Left real quiet. Like a movie. The needle not quite full.

Our lives meant nothing.

To me.

I used to be a little boy. A baby. At first, I was the good one. My mom would come in to my room in the morning, and I would be lying there in my crib wide awake and happy as could be. Didn't cry much. I had curly brown hair and deep chocolate eyes. I was born on my mother's birthday. Her favorite. Sweet. Until I wasn't. No reason. They started taking me to a child psychiatrist when I was eleven. No one really explained why. Someone for me to "talk to." She was nice. "How was your week?" "How was school?" "How did that make you feel?" "I don't know." Eventually they stopped taking me. No conclusion. Didn't really talk about it. No deep repressed memories of abuse or neglect. No fucked-up childhood. No hopelessness.

Then.

It just was.

I put the noose around my neck.

The gun in my mouth.

The needle in my vein.

The blade on my wrist.

I tried.

Gave it every opportunity.

The reckless lack of the value of life.

My life.

Missy—*Ribs*—she hated it when we called her that. Her pink hair. The ink up and down her back. Exposed and not. The optimism of adventure. Every day. The slap of my face. The kiss. Holding hands. On the railroad tracks.

I wasn't holding Missy's soft and kind hand as she jumped from the Colorado Street Bridge.

The full pursed lips. The deception. The institution. The wind in her hair. The sun in her face. I wasn't there to kiss Michele's neck one more time before she slammed the needle full of heroin into her jugular.

I wasn't sitting there with Peter in his truck eating organic pistachios discussing prehistoric glacial activity in Yosemite when he closed the garage as the engine ran. His magical eyes bulging and his face turning blue.

Lives full of beauty. Hope. Life. Apparently.

The rope always seemed to break.

The gun misfired.

The needle just shy of *enough*.

The blade dull.

I stood on the bridge.

Put the needle to my neck.

Had the keys in the ignition.

Yet, here I am.

A Body of Grief

ZOE FITZGERALD CARTER

When my mother killed herself, I thought, *Finally! I can relax.*
No more worrying, anticipating, or trying to talk her out of it. No more tense discussions about sleeping pills or helium or morphine. No more wrapping my mind around a "death date" only to have her abruptly change it when she realized she wasn't quite ready to go. No more flights back and forth across the country with my two small children or—even worse—without them.

For months, my primary job had been to help my mother plot her escape from advanced Parkinson's. So when she finally got down to it and stopped eating and drinking on the first hot day of July 2001, and died ten days later, it seemed like I had traversed the apocalypse and survived it. The most planned, discussed, delayed, and fought over death in the history of mankind had finally transpired. I was sad, of course, but mainly I was exhausted and spent.

I was also frantic to pick up the missing pieces of my "real life," much of which I could barely recall. After a hastily assembled memorial service, a final good-bye to the termite-riddled childhood home in D.C., I returned to Northern California, determined to get down to it. Make up for lost time.

I threw myself into volunteering at my younger daughter's preschool. I picked up the threads of a novel I'd been writing a year earlier. I bicycled like a lunatic up the steep, winding roads into the Berkeley hills. I tried to remember who my husband was and why I had married him.

For a week or so, I was a whirlwind of released energies. Churning out words, flying down hills, staying up late, driving the carpool, having sex, throwing parties, and playing music. No more waiting for the phone to ring with my mother's pinched voice on the other end proposing yet another day—another way—to die. No more lying on the couch all morning because to commit to any one activity was to invite interruption: a call from a doctor or a caretaker; another conversation about death. ·

Everything was back on track, I thought, cooking up hearty dinners for my daughters and husband, playing my long-neglected guitar. Strapping on my bike cleats and grabbing my helmet for yet another ride, I reveled in my newly awakened muscles, the growing wingspan of my lungs.

And then the whole construct came to a skidding, tire-rolling, helmet-flying halt. But it wasn't my bike that crashed. It was my body.

First there was a freaky eyesight thing that made me think I was going blind. A vague, difficult-to-define disturbance in my vision that started a month or two after my mother's death. It danced like a vibrating cloud across my eyes. A thin, shimmering curtain between me and the world that made me feel permanently stoned—or half asleep.

I tried to ignore it. Will it away. Mind over eyeballs, or tumor, or whatever it was that had moved into my frontal lobes like an unruly guest. But walking with my children along the Berkeley waterfront one day, our blond terrier mutt running ahead of us, I noticed that it had gotten worse. There was now a contrail effect. I turned my head to search for the dog, and for a second, the image of the trail bled into the image of her running along the beach, creating an arty double exposure effect.

Terrified, I forced myself to keep chatting with my eight-year-old, who skipped happily beside me; to hold tightly to my four-year-old's hand, slowing my pace to match hers as we moved down the path, squinting to protect my brain from the glittery, painful sunlight reflecting off the bay.

I just wanted to be normal; to be a nice, normal woman enjoying her life with her husband and children. Homework, soccer practice, dinner with friends, writing, cooking, walking the dog.

But I was not normal, I was going blind. Waking up in the middle of the night in a fearful, acrid sweat, I would lie there wondering: If I was a character in a novel, would this strange eye malady be a metaphor? A cosmic joke? Or just bad luck?

Maybe if I could figure that out, it would leave me alone.

Then came the tics. They would start in my left eyebrow, move down my arm, and pop up, especially at night, in my calves. Then a random, searing pain radiating across the left side of my upper back like an evil sprouting wing. And just to keep things lively, there were dizzy spells, stomachaches, night sweats, and insomnia.

Having been exceptionally healthy my whole life, I felt like I had entered the twilight zone. My formerly peaceful nights were now dogged by wakefulness and primal fears. I feverishly wondered if my mother's death had infected me; if her sickness and despair had leached itself into my flesh while I slept beside her. I told myself I was an idiot. That none of my symptoms, with the exception of a possible brain tumor, were even serious. They were just annoying, transitory spasms. This too would pass.

These stern self-lectures were invariably followed by images of my children growing up without a mother, my husband finding a new wife, and the bed would turn into a thrashing sea of twisted sheets and anxiety.

Mornings were better. I stayed off the computer for a few days and my eyes got a little better. The contrail vanished and the veil retreated to the periphery like in a hazy-edged antique photograph. But then, in the midst of a steep climb on my bike, I grew dizzy and breathless. My heart began to erratically bump and thrash in my chest. Steady one moment, pounding like a motherfucker the next.

Arrhythmia, my young male cardiologist, Dr. Wu, told me. Lone incident unless it becomes chronic. Could be hereditary. Could be hormones. Drink less coffee. Drink less alcohol. Control stress. See you in six months.

WHAT? Control my stress when my heart—*my heart*, the thing solely responsible for keeping me alive—has an uncontrolled glitch? How does one stay calm when one's pulse sounds like a wacked-out metronome (*boom-BOOM-budubudu-BOOM*), Dr. Wu? *Really?*

I did not go back to see Dr. Wu. Nor did I stop drinking. I was frankly too stressed to do either of those things. Which could explain why I had a headache more days than not. The pain was never terrible, more of a low-grade grumble than a full-on roar, but I found myself hoarding Advil, irrationally afraid that I would find myself in a remote location without a Rite Aid or CVS. I stashed bottles of it in my purse, in my bathroom, in the glove compartment of my car—even in the little pouch on the back of my bike. As long as I had those milky brown pellets nearby I was okay.

But I was *not* okay. And the idea that my body might be falling apart for a reason had started to dawn on me. Maybe this lurid array of symptoms really *were* a metaphor or a message or a secret code that I was just too stupid or stressed out to crack. I even suspected that my physical breakdown was connected to my mother and the traumatic way she had departed this earth. But I was too busy going to doctors' appointments to think very deeply about it.

There was the ophthalmologist who told me I probably had a bad case of eyestrain—either that or a neurological disease. The neurologist who told me that I did *not* have a neurological disease but couldn't explain my vision issues. The crisp, overworked primary care doc who sent me off for a CT scan to see if my headaches were caused by sinusitis. They were not.

None of these doctors had anything helpful to say. Apparently, I was as much a mystery to them as to myself. My days were now spent tracking symptoms, going to doctors, surfing the web, and diagnosing myself with everything from ALS to cancer. I grew fractured, distracted, and miserable. I stopped calling my friends or playing my guitar. When my husband reached for me in bed, I pulled away, curling tightly into myself, wanting to be alone with my fears, my inch-by-inch body scans.

The final straw was when I walked my dog in a wooded park at the top of the Berkeley Hills and brushed my shins against a branch of poison oak. Instead of the usual constellation of itchy blisters that quickly faded, both shins turned into a pulpy, oozing mass from the knees down. My legs were literally weeping. And the blisters, rather than receding, crept upward. One day I itched my left arm and the spot blistered and turned red. Another patch popped up on my stomach. Afraid to scratch myself, I was plagued with itching. My left ear! The back of my right knee! My skin teased and tortured me, revolting in every sense of the word.

And so, on a fine spring afternoon, I lay sobbing on the bathroom floor, trying and failing to tape thick sheets of white gauze over my weeping shins. My body was coming apart at the seams. From eyes to ankles. From the outer layer to the inner cavities. From my tweaked back to my unsteady heart.

I was furious at my own powerlessness, just as I had been when my mother would not stop talking about killing herself. I was furious at *her* for not being there. Not only in that moment, but for all the moments to come. I needed her to listen to me, goddamnit—to care about *my* problems for a change.

With something akin to horror, I realized how perfectly I had recreated my own trauma: the helplessness, the fear, even the endless doctors' appointments. After that brief interlude of joyous reconnection, I had slipped right back into a familiar universe of *dis*-ease: isolated and ashamed of the dismal place I inhabited. (Enumerating physical symptoms was no more attractive than discussing my soon-to-be-dead mother.)

Only this time I had only myself to blame because there is really no blaming a dead woman.

In my memory, that was the day Dr. H's receptionist called and the universe, which had been fucking with me for weeks—smirking nastily from the sidelines while I flailed and spluttered and took on water—unexpectedly threw me a lifeline.

I had heard about Dr. H from my friend Mary, a Buddhist therapist who shared my bristling distrust of mainstream medicine. According to Mary, Doctor H was scary smart and totally unorthodox. She would "run your pulses," do muscle testing, and give you Chinese herbs. Best of all, she could diagnose conditions that other doctors missed or were stymied by.

Excited—and desperate—I had called her office only to find that she wasn't taking patients. Listlessly, I had left my name on her wait-list, not expecting to hear back. But then, months later, while I lay crying on the bathroom floor, my legs oozing in sympathy, her receptionist called to see if I was still interested. I was.

From the moment I arrived, it was clear Dr. H did things a little differently. The small, messy waiting room was covered with scarves and potholders to raise money for Charlotte Maxwell, a breast cancer clinic in Oakland that offers alternative treatments to underprivileged women. Dr. H herself came out to collect me, a tiny, grey-haired woman in a colorful Guatemalan shirt. She had bright blue eyes and a distinct, but not unattractive, beard on her round cheeks.

Without preamble, she took me into her cramped, equally messy office. Plopping herself behind a small wooden desk, she poured herself a glass of water and asked me what was going on. As I began to talk, I felt myself relax. There was none of the usual shuffling of papers, the barely hidden impatience, the sense that my issues were too diffuse or unrelated or just bizarre to consider. There was only curiosity, questions, and more questions. About my symptoms, but also my life: Who did I live with, what did I eat, what events may have precipitated my health crises?

At some point, she had me get on to her patient's table where she took my blood pressure, looked at my tongue, and had me repeatedly raise my arm while she pressed down on it, simultaneously touching various parts of my body. "Energy testing," she said, unapologetically. "It works."

Back at her desk, she gave me the verdict: "Your liver is sluggish, your nervous system is overloaded, and your ability to deal with stress of any kind is severely compromised. The tics, the muscle spasms, the headaches, the arrhythmia—even the poison oak—it's all part of the same thing."

Looking across her desk at me, her expression was sympathetic but not in a pitying "poor you" way. More in a "things happen and you deal with them" way. Kindly, but matter of fact. I found it immensely comforting.

"You need to grieve for your mother," she said, scribbling things on a sheet of paper as she spoke. "Write. Meditate. Walk. Bike—*keep biking!* The arrhythmias aren't going to kill you. Think of them as information. Your body is talking to you, letting you know it's stressed. You need to listen to it. You're going to be fine. You're young and healthy. We just need to get you back into balance."

She wrote out several pages of instructions. Everything from cutting out wheat and dairy ("Just for now, while we build up your threshold") to taking a Chinese supplement called Freeing the Moon to deep breathing and meditation. Then she referred me to a local homeopath and an acupuncturist, both of them women, both of them close colleagues of hers, and told me to come back in six weeks.

Sitting outside in my car, I cried and then I laughed and then I stared at a neon-lit nail salon trying to figure out what the hell had just happened. For the first time in weeks, I felt a deep sense of hope and relief. I was not dying or having a nervous breakdown. I was not crazy or stupid.

I would follow the instructions Dr H gave me, both that day and at many appointments to come, and I would eventually get better. I would also read books with titles like *When The Body Says No* and *Why People Don't Heal* and realize that there is a whole science behind the physical expression of trauma, stress, and unexpressed grief. And then I would get angry all over again at the way most doctors see us as a single symptom or, at best, a compilation of symptoms, not as holistic organisms.

But one thing I knew for sure that day: I had received far more than good medical advice; I had received the gift of being fully seen. Not just for the malfunctioning parts of my body but also for the sad, neglected parts of my being. The unacknowledged emotion that had been willfully tossing up symptoms like a tantruming child.

For the first time in years, I felt mothered.

I laughed with the obviousness of it. And then I cried again. My mother had stopped mothering me years before she died and that was perhaps the greater grief, even greater than her death. The huge, layered rock that I had been dragging around with me, cumbersome but manageable. Until, suddenly, it wasn't.

But thanks to Dr. H, I could begin to break it apart. To chip away at the pieces, let them crumble and roll away.

I wondered, briefly, if Dr. H would consider adopting me.

There were, of course, no miracle cures. But within a few weeks of that first appointment, many of my symptoms began to disappear. First my eye issues resolved, then my headaches receded. I came to realize that the arrhythmias were at least partially connected to the wine I was drinking and I gave it up.

Most importantly, I learned to grieve for my mother. To toast her at my family table, to visit her grave, and even to write a book about her. To forgive her for the ways she had not mothered me and remember the ways she had.

Thirteen years later, none of those particular symptoms have reappeared. There *are* still times when my body talks, but these days I know enough to listen. Although Dr. H retired a few years ago, I have found other wise and loving women to help me decipher that language; the way it often expresses our deepest needs.

When I think of those days, I can still perfectly recall the fear and frustration of dealing with my imploding body. But what I remember most clearly are the blissful moments when I lay on various tables—Dr. H's, the acupuncturist, the homeopath, all of them women, all of them older than me—and answered their gentle questions, felt their sympathetic hands on my forehead or on my aching back: their soft mother hands on my skin. And my spirit began to heal.

If I Love You, You'll Leave

DEBRA LoGUERICO DeANGELO

Before you go all "Oh no! All mothers love their babies!" on me, just hear me out. It's not about pity. It's about finally looking at the truth. Just looking. Without judgment. And this is the truth: My mother didn't love me.

But don't blame her. I was part of that equation. I wasn't the gurgly, giggly baby every mother dreams of. Quite the opposite. I was serious and sullen. I didn't make eye contact. Eye contact is a key factor in mother-child bonding. When Mom—or anyone else—would look at me, I'd just look away at cars going by or tree branches waving in the breeze. It would be three more years before my parents discovered that I was legally blind. Everything beyond about five inches from my face was a blurry kaleidoscope of color and motion. Make eye contact? I couldn't see faces, let alone eyes.

No eye contact, and no smiles either. Returning smiles is another crucial step in parent-child bonding. I was a year old before I smiled. Developmentally, that's about eight months late. I couldn't return what I couldn't see.

But wait, you say, that can't be the whole story! Blind babies smile at the sound of their caregivers' voices!

"Caregivers." Plural.

Boom, there it is.

My mother became a physician in the 1950s, when women were supposed to become secretaries or teachers—if they became anything at all other than housewives. Maybe they could be nurses. But not doctors. My mother was a feminist decades before the first bra burned, and she didn't even know it. But she did know she wasn't going be a secretary. She worked her way through medical school as a waitress, one of only two women in her graduating class. That MD behind her name was hard-fought, and she wasn't about to toss it all away on motherhood. She went back to work when I was two weeks old. And so began my lifetime of longing for "someone." I was too young to know who.

As for my dad (also a physician), long hours meant that he wasn't around much either, save for the weekends. In my early years, he was affectionate and loving, but I continued craving "something else." Unfortunately, alcoholism and World War II PTSD eventually eroded his mind, but even in the thick of that, he was at least aware of me, even if marginally—which is more than I can say for my mother.

In 1959, there were no daycares. My parents relied on a rotating wheel of grandmothers and aunts to care for me. Each would stay for a couple weeks, then pass the baby baton to the next shift worker and go home. My needs were met by serial "mothers" who showered me in love and affection.

And then left.

Forever.

You see, "object permanence"—the realization that things still exist after they disappear—doesn't develop for about twelve months. Prior to that, when something, or someone, goes away, they're gone and never coming back.

Dead.

With death comes grief. I don't remember people or incidents from my first year. But I vividly remember weeping myself into exhaustion, stuffy-nosed and gulping salty tears and mucous, an aching hollowness in my chest; the smell of a tear-soaked pillow. Each time one of my caretakers "died," I grieved. Grieving people—even tiny ones—don't smile much.

When "object permanence" developed, I realized my "mothers" didn't die after all. They'd arrive, cuddle me, kiss me . . . and leave. I started to recognize the pattern. Some kids develop separation anxiety when they realize a caregiver is about to leave. I protected my tiny heart preemptively: I stopped attaching myself to anyone. Attachment brings abandonment. Abandonment hurts. The way to not hurt is to not attach in the first place.

Don't trust anyone!

Because . . .

They.

Will.

LEAVE YOU.

I was Little Baby Poker Face. I offered nothing emotionally and gave nothing back. I didn't exactly melt Mom's heart. I looked at her like I would any stranger: I don't know you. Surely, this made it easy for Mom to leave me and focus on her career. I'm sure she figured it was no big deal—clearly I didn't even like her.

She was so wrong about that. Yearning for her love is a thread stringing through my entire life, but I kept that precious secret locked inside. I didn't let it show. I didn't cry when she left. But I knew she was gone. She told me that whenever she came home from work, no matter how late, I'd be standing up in my crib, silently grasping the rails, waiting to see her. And just stare.

Mom eventually exhausted her relatives and turned to a parade of babysitters, none of whom I cared about. After losing so many "mothers," I'd learned the "don't attach" lesson well. I was attached to myself, though. I was my own best company. All I needed were some books or my little red record player, or the swings in our big backyard or neighborhood cats to call through the fence. I started protecting my inner child while I still *was* that child.

By my twenties, I'd weathered several bad relationships and a disastrous marriage. I went for counseling to talk about my emotionally abusive husband. I ended up talking about my mother. In one session, I spread out photos of me from birth until present. The therapist studied my photographic timeline and made an observation: "You've always been sad."

Sad?

What does that even mean? This is how I've always felt. I can't comprehend any other way to feel. If you're colorblind, you don't imagine colors you can't see. It's impossible. You just accept that this is how the world looks, and that's that. What the hell are "red," "green," or "happy"? My therapist labeled my lifelong sadness "infantile depression." At least it gave my chronic, low-grade longing a context. Every "mother" I ever had, including my actual parent, abandoned me. No wonder I was so wary of getting attached to anyone. I was *still* protecting myself.

Flash forward to now. I've discovered that infantile depression is actually a symptom of something larger: Reactive Attachment Disorder (RAD), which results from having multiple caretakers and no stable attachments during infancy. The infant never learns to bond. Usually, you must be raised in a Romanian orphanage or bounced from foster home to foster home to develop RAD. But I developed it while being passed from the loving arms of one grandmother to the next, and aunts and babysitters, and on and on and on.

An infant with RAD is withdrawn, sad, and listless: irritable for no obvious reason. She neither seeks comfort, nor responds to it. She doesn't smile. She watches others closely but doesn't engage with them. She doesn't reach out to be picked up and is disinterested in playing peek-a-boo or other interactive games.

That's *Baby Me.*

Add to this my gazing past faces I couldn't see, and nowadays I'd be whisked off for early autism intervention. Back then, my parents just called me "serious" and handed me to whichever caretaker was on duty. I was The Serious One. My bubbly, bouncy sister, born four years later, was The Smiley One. But she also had serial caretakers. What was different?

She had me.

I was a constant presence in Susie's life from day one. Caretakers came, caretakers went, but Susie smiled and made eye contact anyway. Mom finally had her dream baby. There's a photo of us that says it all. Mom is holding Susie in her lap, joyfully beaming down at her. They're gazing at each other in mutual adoration. I'm scooted right next to Mom, but her free arm isn't around me. It's tucked under her leg, and her shoulder is slightly turned, creating a protective barrier: against me.

Once Susie was born, I ceased to exist. Was I crazy jealous? Did I hate Susie with ever fiber of my being? No. Susie was my constant presence too. She was the first person who didn't leave me. Besides, she was amusing—a big doll that moved, drooled, and babbled. And when she smiled at me, I finally smiled back.

That said, I wasn't spontaneously cured. I didn't become an animated, cheerful child like Susie. I remained serious and solitary, more comfortable with books and animals than other kids by the time I started school, which is when my parents planted some glittery, cat-eye, coke-bottle glasses on my face. I could see! But I was teased mercilessly for wearing them. I was the weird little goggle-eyed fatty they avoided at recess.

And then came puberty.

Fatty stretched into curvy.

Contact lenses replaced glasses.

I started making friends, and eventually boyfriends.

Lots of them.

In high school, I became one of the "popular" girls.

Go fucking figure, right?

I discovered two things in high school. One, that alcohol, lots of friends, and partying like a rock star dull your aching, longing hollowness—for awhile anyway. Two, that after you have sex with boys, they hold you and kiss you. In exchange for spreading my legs and putting up with a boy pumping away at me for a couple minutes, I'd feel loved, even if just for a little while. In my mind, that was a totally fair trade.

They say girls become promiscuous because of troubled relationships with their fathers. *They* aren't always right. Sometimes it's the other parent that's the issue. Promiscuous girls may not be burning with desire for male attention. They may be burning with desire for love—mother love—and they'll do anything to get it.

Ironically, in my desperation to find the unconditional mother love I craved, I married precisely the person who couldn't give it to me. I longed endlessly for love and got nothing but emotional abuse and scorn in return. Broken people tend to marry other broken people. We recognize the cracks.

You know what else broken people do when they marry each other? Have babies.

Thank God for parenting books, because I was winging it every step of the way (I owe you big time, Penelope Leach). Not only was I lacking any mothering template to follow, my mother didn't have the chance to redeem herself when she had her first grandchild. She died of a brain aneurysm when my firstborn was 2. That was the only time she said "I love you" to me in my whole life—when she was in the hospital, just before she died. She was on morphine. I suspect it was the drugs talking.

To be fair, that was the only time I said "I love you" to her too. I didn't have any drugs to blame.

Ironically, although my relationship with my mother was strained, her death was a torpedo through my soul. I grieved myself into a stupor. Not only did I lose her, for real this time, I also lost my lifelong dream of a relationship with her. My father was severely disabled from a stroke nine years earlier, so he was essentially gone too. I felt orphaned. There wasn't much left but my dysfunctional marriage.

So, now what?

How about have another kid? That always helps everything, right?

My daughter was born two years later. By then, my marriage had become exponentially worse, but our children were—are—bright and beautiful, charming and charismatic, despite growing up in a minefield. Any random little thing could explode in your face at any moment. Did I mention my raging husband was an alcoholic? No? Oh, that's always a fun embellishment.

I had to get out, but I didn't know how.

Yes. Therapy again—and an abundance of support from friends—and over the next decade, I managed to patch up my self-esteem enough to extract myself from that marriage and go it alone. Baby Me had taught me well: being alone is better than being hurt. When I emerged from that train wreck of a marriage, I was astounded, and rather pleased, to discover that I was relatively intact. I managed to get my life, relationships, and career back on track, but I still had ISSUES. I was anxious about everything, imagining perils and horrors other people wouldn't even dream of. I hovered over my kids like a lunatic dirigible. Chronic anxiety is one facet of untreated RAD. Others include depression and negative thoughts, and post-traumatic stress disorder (PTSD), which in turn can cause emotional detachment, hyper-vigilance (compulsively scanning one's surroundings for danger—real or imagined), anxiety, and insomnia.

Bingo.

And, there's a peak inside the head of someone who raised two children without benefit of a role model. No clue at all about mothering. I was winging it the whole time, but I had to. My "don't attach" strategy failed me. When I held my newborns for the first time, I fell wildly, completely, crazy in love. My warm feelings careened out of control down an unfamiliar path. Love? That's like that red and green that I can't see! But there it was, gushing through my heart.

It scared the living shit out of me.

Because they might leave me too.

The "what ifs" started galloping in my mind: *What if they get sick? What if they're injured? What if they're kidnapped? What if? Whatifwhatifwhatifwhatifwhatifwhatifwhatif!*

Instead of enjoying my children as they grew, I was obsessed with protecting them. I compulsively hovered over them, guarding them from any and every potential harm. I filled them with unnecessary fear. But the terror of losing them was utterly overwhelming, and still can be. If my negative thinking gets loose, I'll be right back on the hamster wheel of anxiety, running like mad. The thought of losing one of them catapults me into full-blown panic, so I try not to "go there." Consciously, anyway.

Anxiety is the constant white noise in my head.

Over time, I've learned to ignore it, but any random negative thought can catch me by surprise and crank up the volume. I'll have to talk myself down from the window ledge of terror: "Right now, we are all just fine; Right now, we are all safe . . . "

Rinse and repeat, rinse and repeat . . . until I can exhale.

Although parenting was a learned skill for me, and a C- one at that, I'm satisfied with one thing: My children know I love them. I may have fumbled things in myriad ways, but if you peer closely at my motivation, it was always love. I made a point of saying "I love you" to my kids because I know how it feels when your mother never says it.

We're all adults now, and little by little my kids seem to be forgiving me for my shortcomings and neuroses. We're all slowly healing. I can still topple into the chasm of obsessive worry and drive them nuts with my highly creative fears. I still ache whenever they leave and can't relax until I get that text that they're home safe, but I don't dissolve into a pool of despair anymore. I've finally convinced myself that they'll continue to exist, even if I can't see them.

So, I've learned to let go of them, sort of.

But not their stuff. Crayon scribbles, swim team ribbons, nasty, ratty teddy bears—I still have them. Even now, I don't like washing their empty coffee cups after they leave because letting go of anything that reminds me of them is letting go of *them*.

I still have all my son's baby clothes.

My son is thirty-one.

I have every ribbon from every gift my daughter ever gave me. I can't throw those away—that would be like throwing *her* away!

I'm not a hoarder, dammit! I'm over-attached!

Irony, you little monkey.

My reluctance to let go of anything that reminds me of my kids doesn't end there. When I started dating a man on the opposite side of the country, one who periodically came for visits and then left, my "collecting" rose to the next level. Every card he ever sent me, every dried rose, sure. But also store receipts, napkins, wine corks, beer caps.

Hair.

HAIR, people.

If I found a hair on his pillow, I'd keep it in a little box. A quite full little box.

Once he splashed a drop of tomato sauce on the counter while cooking dinner. I cleaned around it for months. I was lovingly showing "Joe's spot" to my sister one day, and she said, "You mean *this* one?" and wiped it away.

I was crushed! She wiped Joe himself away! Had she not, it would probably still be there, even though Joe and I are now married. I don't really need that spot anymore. But I still kinda wish it was there.

Just in case.

Hello, Catastrophe

ELIZABETH ROSNER

My darkest blues started this way, fourteen years ago. I was on a plane heading east, from California to New York, toward what would turn out to be my mother's death. I didn't know that at the time, only that she had been rushed into surgery with such urgency that I had to drop everything and fly. I prayed the entire journey, at least for the grace of time to say goodbye. During the seemingly interminable wait for my connecting flight in Chicago, I tried to reach the hospital for some hopeful update about her condition. "She's not answering the phone in her room" was the only information I could get from the operator. "I can't tell you anything else." My father, sister, and brother weren't answering either. I flew through clouds and weather, landscape invisible below, tears streaming down my face. The last time I had seen her, just three weeks earlier, she was lying in a hospital bed while receiving a transfusion. Her oncologist assured me she had at least three months to live—"worst-case scenario," he said— but my mother whispered to me when I kissed her cheek: "I'll never see you again." I kept telling myself she was the kind of person who said those things.

When I finally landed at the Albany Airport, my father and siblings were all there. For a delirious moment I allowed myself to believe that everything was all right, that this was why they had all come to meet me. But the second I looked at my father's face, I knew she was gone. My legs gave way and I fell onto the grimy airport carpet, where I stayed, sobbing. Passengers steered around me and I didn't care for a second what they thought or imagined. Grief was in charge now. It wasn't going to let go for a long, long time.

Until that moment, the year had promised to be one of the best of my life. I'd signed a publishing contract for my first novel with a major New York house, along with an advance to write my second novel. Just as I was celebrating the most exquisite reward for years of hard work and perseverance, my mother's breast cancer recurred with a vengeance. She died so quickly that even her doctors were surprised.

Her funeral passed in a freezing blur; we sat *shivah* according to the Orthodox customs; I watched my hair turn gray at the temples, seemingly overnight; I flew back to my life in California. The tears came so often and so relentlessly that I developed eye infections. Sitting in a paper gown for my annual physical, my doctor asked if I might consider trying Prozac. "My mother died," I wept. "I'm very sad. Aren't I supposed to be sad?" Her inquiry both angered and disappointed me, implying that a finite amount of sorrow was "appropriate" for mourning one's only mother. Although I came from a long line of depressives—my mother included—it felt bizarre and wrong to abbreviate my grief, especially by way of a pill. And I'd never been particularly impressed by the way medications treated my mother's mental state. She had eventually been diagnosed with bipolar disorder, but for years her mood swings seemed just as unmanageable when she was on meds as when she was off.

Within a year of her death, my first novel was published to a few days of great fanfare. A week later, on what was to be the first day of my multi-city book tour, terrorists flew two jetliners into the World

Trade Center. *More falling, much more falling down.* It was only in a delayed reaction many months later that I realized I had felt forced to disregard my own tremendous sadness in order to defer to the larger, much larger, tragedy of 9-11. As a daughter of two Holocaust survivors, this kind of deference to other tragedies was second nature to me.

Eighteen months later, I managed to resume my optimistic journey in publishing. My first novel came out in paperback with a new cover, promising a new life. Also as promised, time had eased some of the grief over my mother's passing. And I fell in love.

Here is where the story starts to sound happy, right? I met the man of my dreams—handsome, brilliant, talented, passionate, fun. *If only my mother could have met him!* I often thought. She would have been ecstatic. She would have said things like, *"You two would make such gorgeous babies!"* and *"He reminds me of someone I was in love with when I was young!"*

But we did not have babies.

That *perfectly amazing love of my life* was actually a man who had told me on day one that his lifelong approach to relationships was, "I cheat and I leave." He spoke those shocking words out loud. I heard them. It was quite possibly the one and only time he told the truth. Some part of me could have chosen to cut and run in the opposite direction; certainly a woman paying a different kind of attention would have done that. Unfortunately, I wasn't that woman.

I was the woman who believed her heart to be infinitely vast and infinitely powerful. I was the woman who deserved to be *chosen* as the one he would never be able to leave, the one who would finally and irrevocably prove to him that he didn't *need* to cheat and leave. He didn't need to look anywhere else for anything. I had enough of everything for both of us: a beautiful home, a sizeable bank account, and a career with travel for two! I would fly him to Europe for the first time in his life. I would introduce him to my French editor and treat him to champagne in a Paris hotel room. I would sit across from him on the TGV to Bordeaux, adoring and generously supportive, planning the rest of our fabulous shared happily-ever-after life.

My novel won prizes. We drank a lot of wine. We laughed and made love and acted like superstars. We wrote parallel journal entries about our trip and after returning home, we threw a party for all of our friends. We called it "The French Commotion," inviting a houseful of guests to bring their favorite French snacks so that we could regale them with our tales, and then judge them all in a hilarious scarf-tying competition. We were the King and Queen of our dance community: beautiful and successful and brilliant and magnanimous. We ruled.

That is, we ruled, but not quite in a shared monarchy. In an almost-but-not-quite-secret recess of my mind lived the haunted awareness that I was living in "the best of times and the worst of times." The stealthy infidelity he had perfected with his previous wives, girlfriends, lovers was (of course) happening to me too—I just couldn't name it clearly yet.

Desperately ignoring my inner terrors, I completed and published a second novel. We took more trips: to Italy, to Kenya, to New York City, Chicago, and Los Angeles. I paid for everything and in far more ways than monetarily. There were signs everywhere, you see. Comments from my dearest girlfriends about ways he seemed to hug them a little too long; hints that he'd been seen at a restaurant with "some blonde," and always, relentlessly, the dancing, oh yes the dancing. Outrageously flirtatious, overtly sexual; writhingly, blatantly seductive. This was the stuff that happened right in front of me. Who knew what went on in the rooms I didn't enter, didn't know about? He knew. And he wasn't admitting any of it. He was, you could say, simply practicing what he preached. Lying and cheating. Only this time he didn't leave.

We argued about boundaries and rules and agreements and compromises. It was a form of torture: daily, hourly, minute by minute. I threw him out for a while after he explained to me that the reason he wasn't paying much money for sharing my home was that he was contributing to our life by way of "being monogamous against his will." I said, "You mean I'm paying you not to fuck other women?" I kicked him out, righteous and furious, but tragically I continued seeing him. Can I blame any of this foolishness on persistent grief over my mother's death? Hard to say. More likely I was holding on to images of her own tragic mismatched dance with love. I maintained a fatalistic conviction that this man and I were destined to be together, that life without him could never be better than life with him. About a year later he moved back into my house, and then I got cancer.

The diagnosis came on the morning of my forty-ninth birthday. The fact that breast cancer killed my mother and two of my dear friends was not lost on me, yet somehow I accepted the diagnosis with a surprising degree of equanimity. Only later would I recognize this state of relative calm as a variation on a perpetual awareness—something I had learned early and often from both of my parents—that terrible things were always happening and always about to happen. Moments of happiness merely existed in order to seduce you into dropping your guard. What you really needed to do was practice a state of hyper-vigilance at all times, bracing yourself for the next cataclysm, which was one small step around the corner, one breath from now.

The diagnosis was "invasive cancer" and required not only one but two surgeries, the second one less than three weeks after the first. It also ensured that I would have to go through chemotherapy and radiation treatments. *Hello, catastrophe,* a voice whispered with something like satisfaction. *I knew you were around here somewhere!*

Meanwhile, in the realm of the heart, I was dancing on the edge of a precipice. My nervous system was in a condition of constant alarm, but given my family addiction to drama, this seemed normal. In retrospect (that horror show of perfect accuracy), I have a sad certainty that my immune system was paying the price for my cumulative adrenal overload. I would have slugged anyone who suggested that we "give ourselves cancer," but I did and still do have an aching sense of sorrow about the means by which the "universe" chose to wake me up from my sleepwalking.

I shame myself by writing this. I shame myself by remembering my complicity in this destructive relationship. I shame myself and yet I long to cleanse myself of the shame by typing these words and sharing them. *I didn't know how to love. Now I do.*

Here is one thing I want to say: for a very long time, I could not find a way to forgive myself for loving an insecure, cowardly, broken person who was ruthless enough to cheat on his so-called partner while she was going through treatment for breast cancer. It wasn't him I couldn't forgive (though it's pretty obvious by now that I haven't quite forgiven him. It remains an item on my spiritual to-do list). It was *me* I couldn't forgive. The woman who had "given herself cancer."

Truth?

The day I heard my diagnosis, my first thought (unbidden) was, *Maybe now he'll stop sleeping with her.* I pretty much knew who she was, you see, no matter how many times he told me Gaslight-style that I was "going through menopause and acting paranoid." That I was "living in the past," a sadistic reference to the previous time he had been sleeping with "her" and lying about it. He was a disturbed wreck, but what did that make me?

What finally "cured" me and enabled me to throw him out for the second and final time? I got a letter in the mail from his girlfriend, the one I knew by name, the one exactly sick and twisted enough to participate in his sick and twisted game. She typed it and mailed it "anonymously." He was lying to her, she said, and sleeping with yet another woman. She signed it, "your sister in shame."

On the worst days, I could not eat or get out of bed. The mild nausea I had experienced during cancer treatment was nothing compared to the soul-shaking nausea I felt now. I could not stop crying, could not stop hating all the women (there were several it turns out) who had chosen to fuck someone else's boyfriend, including while she was at home in bed because she'd just finished a daylong infusion of chemo. I hated him for using me and treating me like garbage, and I hated myself more than anything. I hated that I believed I *loved* him. I hated that I couldn't understand why any of it had happened to me. I hated that I hadn't been smart enough or brave enough or strong enough to say *No thanks* all the way back on that first day when he told me the rare truth. "I cheat and I leave." I thought cancer was the worst thing that could have happened to me, but it turned out there was something even worse.

I hate revisiting the story as if it happened to someone else, as if I've moved so far beyond it that I don't feel those feelings any more, as if I can share with you my lessons and growth and recovery. That's all true to a degree: I have moved far beyond it. Not just in time but in *space*. I have experienced phenomenal amounts of growth and I have been recovering. "Ing." As in, a work in progress. A path I am walking. A process.

How the deep dark blues faded, eventually, though imperfectly: It began with a dog. A rescue. As in, *she rescued me.* Her ridiculous cuteness tugged at my frozen heart, brought back my smile, my giggle. There were glorious devoted friends who stood by me, no matter what, even when I talked the crazy talk of maybe taking *him* back. I attended Al-Anon meetings and committed myself to transformation (a work in progress). There were long-distance visits to family, and various careful conversations about how I had to be exceptionally gentle with myself because I was so much better a human being than I knew. I found my ability to travel alone to the kinds of gorgeous places I had once only romanticized about: beaches and vacations and visiting writer/teaching jobs. I found my way back to writing and, eventually, to completing and publishing my third novel.

I didn't take any antidepressive drugs; I never wanted to. Instead, I swam and meditated and walked with my dog. In case it doesn't go without saying, I stopped dancing. No way was I going to go anywhere near the places where he was still doing his pathetic dirty work. It also helped to hear that yet more women were lining up to take my place beside him so that they could learn the same lessons themselves. I wasn't the stupidest one after all.

There was even a wide-hearted, deep-souled man who showed me for a brief but oh-so-significant interlude that my heart wasn't dead, my body wasn't either, and I could maybe even trust someone again. I could feel excitement and joy and rapture. I could touch and be touched. I could let my body be seen with its scars, not to mention the messiest ones on the inside. The blues faded this way little by little. I discovered it was possible to fall back in love with the world. I could wake up grateful to be alive and not in pain, grateful for my annual all-clear MRI reports, grateful for the sweet black dog and the gorgeous oak trees and the fragrance of roses and the suggestion of rain. I still don't want you to read this, but I am writing it anyway. Today the color of my blue is paler and sweeter than before, much more beautiful than frightening. I call it the color of sea foam. It helps me stay afloat.

Unraveling

HOLLYE DEXTER

In 1994, my husband Troy and I woke one night to find our house in flames. To escape the fire, we jumped from second-story windows with our toddler son—and then watched our house and home-based businesses burn to the ground. We were released from the hospital homeless, possession-less, and jobless. Over the next two years, we were bankrupted, lost our cars and another home, and watched our friends pull away one by one. As the outer layers of my life were stripped away, I began to spiral downward into a deep depression, where I found myself on the brink of losing my marriage.

Driving with my family on Highway 101, I see a cemetery on a hillside, overlooking the Pacific Ocean, and ask Troy to stop. Dead Christmas trees with sparse, weathered ornaments lie toppled over on their sides. Multicolored pinwheels spin in the wind atop the smallest graves. I need to confront death to see what life means to me. I walk through and read the headstones. I sit on gravesites. I lay down upon them, trying to absorb the meaning of life. Troy waits by the car, arms folded tight against his chest. He reluctantly tolerates my strange behavior while I meander and ponder. Did I really want to die? Or do I really want to live? Is there a God? Was there a soul once connected to this body now decomposing in the ground, or are we all just a freak accident of nature? What's the point of building a life if God can stomp through like a cranky toddler knocking all your building blocks down?

I step carefully between headstones, taking photos. Cissy sits quietly in the car reading Nancy Drew, but Taylor's high-pitched plaintive voice calls through the crack in the car window, "Can I get out? Daddy, can I get out?" As Troy stalls for an answer, the wide-open grass and multicolored pinwheels are too tempting. Taylor bursts out of the car and tears across the graveyard giggling. "Look, I'm an airplane!" He runs, arms outstretched, leaping over the graves of other children. I am breathless as my joyful, alive, rosy-cheeked four-year-old boy runs toward me. Five months before, he lay listless in his bed as flames raged and Death hovered over him, the carbon monoxide seeping into his veins. My throat constricts, my ribs caving in on themselves. It's time to stop contemplating all this death bullshit.

"Let's go," I say. Troy is happy to oblige.

Troy and I have spun off into different galaxies. Without him, I am lost. I turn away, creeping inside my own silent spaces to grieve. I start smoking again. I drink a lot of cheap wine. I sit outside in the carport, hiding from my children with my glass of chardonnay and cigarettes. Maybe I thought the nicotine and alcohol would fill that emptiness, but it only makes it ring more hollow. I am so broken down, I can't even find the will to paint or create. I still pray, just in case, but I am empty inside. I pray not for money or things, but for healing, for a sense of peace, for a glimpse that God is there in my life. I feel nothing but a cold empty silence in return. I remember Troy's words: *Hell is the place where God can't hear you.* I begin to believe that God is just something I made up in my head during my fucked up childhood, like an imaginary friend. "Jesus loves me," I sang to myself. "Who's Jesus?" you might have asked. "Oh he's my invisible friend. He's always nice to me, always helps me, he wears a white robe and sandals and he lives on a cloud." It worked for me, then. As an adult, the more I think about it, the more ludicrous it seems. But then, there was that voice in my head the night of the fire. That voice that said *check the baby.* That voice that woke me three times. Maybe that was God. Or maybe it was maternal instinct. But where is the voice now, when everything is falling apart and I am more afraid than ever? I beg on my knees for just a glimpse, a simple feeling of calm, a sign, or even the ability to sleep through the night. My grief is pervasive, a long sad shadow I drag behind me.

Every crack in the foundation of our marriage has widened until we wake one morning to find the Grand Canyon running through our living room. I can't reach him anymore. We are driving. Troy is distant, and I am desperate to find the place where we once connected. I needle him for a reaction until he explodes. He is yelling at me, and it all feels so hopeless. I can't hear him. I feel fuzzy, numb, like I am leaving my body. I lift the door handle and then . . .

"Jesus Christ!" Troy slams on the brakes and grabs for me. My upper body collides with the dashboard, one leg hanging out the open car door. He yanks me up hard by an elbow, his eyes wild with fear. A clump of my long blond hair hangs from his tightly closed fist. "What is WRONG with you?" he screams.

I don't know how to answer that. I whimper like a child as he drives me home.

Deeply ashamed, I lie in bed and cry big, huge, ugly sobs until there is nothing left in me. I am unraveling.

This is not the first time I've tried to throw myself into traffic. There was another place (Arizona), at another time (1973). I was nine years old. My mother, my brother, Kyle, and I had just fled Walt, her insane, drug-addicted, gun-loving boyfriend. My mother's plan was to run across state borders to Kyle's father, Gene, hoping to win him back. Gene was the only one who had ever been good to us, until he ran away. We were homeless, and school was about to start. So we drove, twelve hours straight, and I had a hopeful, optimistic heart, because during those few years we lived with Gene, everything was okay. He didn't hit us. He wasn't a drug addict. He read me books and held me on his shoulders. If he and Mom would make things right now, I knew everything would be okay again. We'd have a place to live. I'd go back to school. Driving through the Arizona desert I'd said the Lord's Prayer at least fifty times while holding tight to the lucky rabbit's foot in my pocket.

When we got there, Gene rejected us. He said he was happy now, and he didn't want to come back. My young heart couldn't take any more. My dog Rusty had just died, my Grandma had just died, and everyone told me they had "gone home." Home sounded like a good place. So I set off toward the main boulevard and stood at the curb surveying the traffic, waiting for a car that was going just fast enough. And then, the screeching of brakes, the horns honking, my mother dragging me into the house.

"What is WRONG with you?"

My mother could barely handle her own problems, let alone a suicidal kid. The next thing I knew, I was sent to live with my Aunt Laura, and that's when I became the master at tap dancing. I decided I wouldn't disappoint anyone again. I would be perfect- a saint, in fact. And in private, sleeping in my aunt's sewing room, I would hyper-ventilate until I made myself faint. Those were my little moments of peace—my mini deaths.

Because I buried it and never dealt with that incident in my nine-year-old psyche, it was bound to play out again. Here she was today, that nine-year-old girl trapped inside a thirty-one year old life, pushing me out of a moving car.

I haul myself out of bed and stand at my bedroom window, watching the traffic go by. I feel like I've added 100 pounds to my 110-pound frame. My knees ache, my back aches, my head aches from the full weight of revelation: the woman who convinced everyone she had it together is falling apart. I am deeply ashamed for what I put Troy through, and that I risked harm or death to myself, which would have hurt my children. But it wasn't premeditated. I did it suddenly, without thought. I am losing my fucking mind. It's just one more thing to lose.

In my head, I struggle daily with suicidal thoughts. Although I don't act on it, and made a vow to myself that I never would, the thoughts persist. I don't know that "intrusive thoughts" are a common symptom of post-traumatic stress disorder. I just think I am defective. I push the ugly thoughts away and try to busy myself with creative projects, gardening, cooking. I try, I mean I really, really try, to shield my kids from this darkness in my soul. But children are intuitive. They are natural empaths who feel the energy in the house no matter if you are the Meryl Streep of feigning cheeriness. My daughter, Cissy, is older now, independent, so she gets some reprieve from my inner turmoil. But Taylor is with me night and day, my constant companion—my emotional Siamese twin. He absorbs everything, including my underground depression. It is in a small ordinary moment as I'm applying a rub-on tattoo to his arm, that I come face to face with this. I pat his arm and start to walk away, but he screams, "Nooooooo!"

I turn to find him crying. Taylor only cries when he's hurt physically.

"What's wrong?"

"*That's not how I wanted it!*" He's never screamed at me before. I am stunned.

"Well . . . why? What did you want?"

"I hate this. I hate this! Just go away and leave me alone!" His face is red, his arms thrashing wildly at the air. He is completely unhinged. My heart pounds, my mouth dry. This is not my calm little Buddha-boy, not my Taylor. What is happening?

I stand up straight, pretending to be in control, "I see you're wanting to have a tantrum," I say, my voice shaking, "but you may not scream at me. You can have your feelings by yourself, and talk to me when you're calm." I walk out and shut his bedroom door behind me, my heart thrumming through my chest. And then, my four-year-old child, who still wears pull-ups at night, screams this behind his closed door, "*I hate myself! I hate my life! I want to die!*"

My knees crumple beneath me as I clutch the doorjamb for support. I can't breathe. He is too young to know what these words mean. No, these aren't his words. My son is screaming what has been inside my head every day for months. He screams out everything I have been suppressing. I can no longer hide what is happening inside myself, inside the walls of this "Happy House," inside the confines of my marriage. The jig is up.

I hesitate at his door, compose myself, then push it open. He sits on the floor, his face red and sweaty, his eyes wild and confused. I pick him up and rock him.

"We never say ugly things like that about anyone, *especially* not ourselves. Okay?"

He nods.

"Your Mommy and Daddy love you so much. We prayed for you to come to our lives. You are an answered prayer—our precious gift," I say, "and the fact that we are all even here on this Earth is a miracle. Our lives are a gift." I hold him close against me, wiping his tears and my own with the sleeve of my shirt, unable to say any more. With every word, I am learning a hard lesson. Am I going to live my life as a hypocrite, expecting my children to believe in the value of their lives, when inside I believe mine is worthless? No. I cannot live this way any longer. I am not going to let another generation of children grow up as damaged as I am. Doing my best is no longer good enough. I have to do better than my best. I have to find a way to heal myself, for only in doing that can I heal my family.

Facing death has awakened me to the truth of my own life. I have to unravel completely to find out who I am, what I'm made of. Everything I once felt certain of is shaken loose like soil from the roots of an upturned tree, leaving me raw, exposed. I have to find a way of taking root within myself.

One day, as I'm sneaking a cigarette on the side of the house, I hear Taylor's voice, "Mommy? Mommy, where are you?"

I duck beneath the window, hiding from him. I down the rest of my wine and stomp out my cigarette. And then I become disgusted with myself. I have a Gandhi quote taped above my desk. "Happiness is when what you say, what you think, and what you do are in harmony." I am so far from harmony, I am dissonance. Here I am lurking around, ducking beneath windows so my kids won't see how broken I am, knowing a life without integrity is hardly worth living. I remember something my therapist said: *You don't have any control of what happens to you in life, but you can control how you choose to react to it.* So I have a choice. I can lurk in the shadows with my cigarettes and wine—which is not effective at all- or get up off my sad, sorry ass and take my power back. I have a marriage that means the world to me, and two children who need a strong, loving mom to guide them. I can't afford to wallow in my sadness another moment. If I don't clean up my act, my children absorb my bullshit.

So this is when I start reading positive, uplifting books about healing my spirit, even though I am cynical. I get videos on yoga and start to practice it every day, even though I suck at it. I write and write, even though I believe no one will ever want to read it. I go to therapy every Wednesday where I do nothing but cry, but still, at least I'm doing it there and not at home.

My faith has become anemic, at best. There is nothing in my outer world to make me believe. No signs or proof of God. But children cannot thrive in a hopeless world. If I am going to raise mine to have a better life, I must find my way out of faithlessness. I dig deep in my memory, remembering all that I survived in childhood. Surely there is a reason I was not struck down in traffic that bleak day in my nine-year-old life, and because of that, Cissy and Taylor were born. Because of that, I got to experience spinning in place with Cissy in my arms, falling in love with Troy, Taylor's peaceful birth, sitting under a Jamaican sky with my husband, watching electric storms dance over the ocean.

And I don't even know what treasures my future life may hold. Emily Dickinson said, "Hope is a thing with feathers that perches in the soul." It's up to me now to find that thing with feathers and to make sure my children inherit it.

Letters I Will Never Send

ALEXA ROSALSKY

On the surface, I seem like a normal American teenager.
I go to school, hang out with my friends, play some sports, and spend way too much time on the internet. But beneath that seeming normality, *everything is not okay.*

I have never attempted suicide, but I've considered it. I've even written out a list of pros and cons. Looking back, I'm amused by how rationally I approached it. In addition to my list, I began composing notes to all the people who were important to me, even after I'd scrapped the idea of killing myself. I was hedging my bets in case I found myself back in that place someday. It was not a happy place to be, and I didn't think anyone would understand unless I explained it in writing.

It started when I was fifteen. Year after year, the pile of letters grew along with my regrets, notes saying how sorry I was, how I wished there had been another way. No one ever saw them except for me. Some were tear-stained and some were written with such anger that my pen tore through the paper. All of my fears, regrets, and hopes were written down in letters that I would never send, addressed to people who would never read them.

One day, I realized how strange that was. I'd just finished writing another letter, put it in an envelope, and hid it.

That's not how letters work, I thought.

I was compiling a diary of depression under the guise of letters to friends and *it wasn't okay*. I knew it wasn't okay, but I had no idea what to do. I couldn't send the letters.

I'm not big on sharing, even the small things, so revealing everything I had kept hidden for so long all at once was terrifying.

I couldn't even consider it.

I still can't.

It would be too much.

But doing nothing, continuing on that path was just as bad. It took me another few months to realize that. And then things started to get really bad.

I've never been much of a troublemaker, I don't tend to act out or do anything that is considered rebellious, but I do have a temper. I was pretty bad at not getting angry. I would lash out at people for the smallest things, slamming a door so hard that the house would seem to shudder. The anger led to doing more things I regretted—to more little notes hidden away, to more anger, and a downward spiral.

I could have (probably, maybe) stopped anytime I wanted, but I didn't want to because the anger felt much better than the hopelessness. But I knew something needed to change. The pile of letters was just too deep.

I wanted to give up.

I didn't want to go on living anymore, everything was going wrong and it all seemed to be my fault. It was scary, like monsters in the closet scary, and being brave was getting so hard.

I didn't want to put on a happy face and pretend things were okay.

I wanted to be done.

So I went for a walk.

I found myself standing on the top of a cliff. It was a long way down, and I felt calm, happier than I had been in a while. Being up high, away from everyone, everyone I knew, alone where there was nothing to hold me back, nothing. All I wanted to do was jump, to let go of everything and have one moment of absolute freedom, to end the helplessness and hopelessness and pain.

It was the first time I'd felt at peace in a long time.

I didn't jump.

I wanted to, but I didn't.

I don't know why.

Even though at the time, it seemed to make perfect sense.

I'm glad I didn't jump.

And I decided that writing what were basically *suicide notes* whenever I was upset was probably not the healthiest means of coping. I stopped writing angry things. I tried not to bottle up all of the bad feelings inside. It was not fun. It was not easy. I did not always succeed. Sometimes while taking notes in English class, I'd realize that I was no longer writing about symbolism. Instead, I was writing things about myself, things that I did not like. Knowing that there was a problem, a major problem, made a huge difference. I began talking to people.

But it is still not easy.

Now and again, bad days seem to last for an eternity, and the doom-and-gloom feelings surge back and a little voice in the back of my head says *jump*, but now it's easier to ignore, defused. Like the constant hum of the refrigerator, it eventually becomes background noise. It is always there, persistent and annoying, but not crazy-making. I just don't listen that acutely to it anymore.

I still have all the notes I wrote, hidden where no one will find them. I can't quite bring myself to destroy them; they remind me that there have been worse times. Sometimes, I add to them. But they are not angry, and they're not addressed to anyone but myself.

Now, instead of a pile of suicide notes, I have a collection of letters to myself. They help me stay brave. They are a roadmap of my emotional life, reminding me where I've been and where I am going. And today, that is ever farther away from the cliff.

Nothing Helps, Except Love . . .

C.O. MOED

Planning my suicide was the only thing that kept me going.

For years.

From that first night, at age four or five or four, crushed and buried alive by feelings I didn't even know how to spell, watching the shadows of the trains on the Williamsburg Bridge, thinking over and over again that if I died if I died if I . . . could get really sick—until that night, at age thirty-nine, when something finally shattered and broke and I stood up, freed—I planned.

- Staring at a bottle of aspirins, the only drugs my parents allowed in the house besides cigarettes and booze, and the once-a-week bag of potato chips, thinking maybe taking all of those little white pills would become a portal out of the silent insanity I knew I was living in, no matter what anyone said.

- Wandering through 1970s East Village streets in the middle of a cold night because I just couldn't bear another moment of watching my sister's head get slammed against a wall.

- Walking away from a screaming relative, usually my sister or my mother or my father or my sister or my mother or my . . . there is no escape there is no escape there is no escape . . . except out. Out now. NOW NOW! Get one last drink at the bar and then . . .

- Drinking my weight in alcohol and then shoving tons of chemically produced baked goods and salty crunchy things down my throat, egging myself on, *Just Do It!* stopped only by my body throwing me into the bathroom for hours of puking.

- Promises made staring out the kitchen window of my own apartment during a happy Thanksgiving meal, a HAPPY one, thinking, *Okay, next year I don't have to be here I don't have to be here in this hell next year I will be dead*, and suddenly feeling so relieved I offer to make everyone coffee. Best Thanksgiving ever.

- Forcing myself to go to work because I wanted to die in my apartment, so I had to get paid so I could pay the rent because getting evicted would really fuck up my suicide plans, and as I turned the corner of 12th Street I suddenly felt like I had wings and I flew to work at the office of the biggest dickhead lawyers in New York City because I. Had. A Plan. Skipped around the office for weeks after that.

And on and on and on . . .

Back then, I couldn't tell you why I had such a fierce desire to kill myself. What I could tell you was that teetering on a high thin ledge, contemplating flight, was normal—like breathing or drinking or walking.

So how the fuck did I stay alive, one might ask?

Gene Kelly.

In the movies we went to long ago, I watched him sing and dance and smile and love. Every time we got on the F train I kept waiting for him to dance onto the platform, swoop me up, and take me the fuck away from my family.

I believed this. I looked for him every time the doors opened. Soon, that looking for him became something inside me saying over and over again, *Stay alive a little bit longer and I promise you I'll make your life like Gene Kelly's heart and soul. Just hang on. Maybe he's on the D train.*

So each time I made a Plan, this something inside would start tap dancing away like crazy. Why don't you try this *tippity-tap tippity-tap* why don't you try that *tippity-tap tippity-tap*, you got rhythm you got music just hold on, everybody is going to start dancing with you in a second *tippity-tap tippity-tap.*"

Dancing on that high thin ledge that beckoned escape and liberation was an exhausting war to fight day in, day out. For decades.

But somehow, *tippity-tapping* just wouldn't give up. If there was something it could *tippity-tap* to and keep me going a bit longer, it did:

- A teacher, after another exasperating reading of my great dramatic thesis about suicide, saying, "You know suicide is a double homicide. You're not just killing yourself. You're killing someone else." That not only ruined my plans, it pissed me off because it painted me as a vengeful loser instead of a tragic heroine. Also, it was too late to rewrite my thesis.

- The make-or-break moment with a really good therapist. It was summer and I hated summer, not just because it was the ONE season that epitomized a dateless Saturday night. Summer was when everyone's lives stepped outside. Watching happy families and loving relationships on the streets, in the shops, everywhere I turned, only proved how viciously incapable I was of being a human being. As it got hotter, I got worse and started saying

over and over again, "I don't want to live anymore I don't want
to live anymore I don't want to . . " Finally the therapist said,
"If you keep talking about killing yourself, I'm going to have
you committed." Gene Kelly started *tippity-tapping* like crazy
because only Jack Nicholson hung out in locked wards and he
was *not* my type. At least not then.

- Getting involved with a new-age spiritual community promising complete freedom from crippling scars. It kept me off the
streets and gave me amazing food, shelter, and life-long friends.
It also made sure that every cent I earned, from the time I was
fifteen until I was twenty-eight when I left, went to being there.
When you are giving all your money away, there's never quite
enough to buy expensive drugs to overdose on.

- Black ankle boots—so what if all six pairs look alike. I had fat
calves and couldn't fit into the knee-high black boots all the
pretty girls with boyfriends and real lives and happiness had.
So, no matter how horrifyingly inhuman I felt with my bovine
legs, nothing said "one more day" like black ankle boots. They
made me look like I belonged in the world too.

- The born-again church the cute coworker went to; the syn-
agogue my father, uncle, friends became bar mitzvah in; the
Buddhist retreat in the mountains I found online; the transformative workshops, the other transformative workshops.

- The peer-support groups that seemed to only meet in cold
basements.

- The late-night panicked phone calls to strangers I met in those
cold basements.

- The late-night panicked phone calls to friends who still tolerated me.

- The willingness to go out on a date with anyone no matter how uninterested or unwilling I was.

- The millions of words poured into tons of diaries.

- The sobbing through hundreds of movies, racked with knowing that I was watching my life. So what if I couldn't figure out how to find the door into it? It had to be there somewhere because someone made a movie about it.

- The debate in the *New York Times Magazine* about choosing your own death in the face of incurable disease. A hospice nurse said that her big question to sick patients wasn't "Do you want to live or do you want to die?" it was "Do you want to die or do you want the pain to stop?" Most just wanted the pain to stop.

During these decades of *tippity-tapping*, I heard about a book called *The Final Leap*, which of course I didn't read. Someone else read it and told me the most important part. It was about the people who jumped from the Golden Gate Bridge and then lived. Each and every one of them, as they moved from steel to air, suddenly wished they hadn't taken that one step of only a couple of inches.

Every single one of them.

It began to slowly dawn on me. It would have just been a matter of time. Regardless of my serious or not serious planning, one day in the near or far future, I'd plan an inch or two too much and find myself flying through irreversible air. Because you see, the thing about suicide plans is that they are like plaque on your teeth. You don't floss that shit off every day? All your teeth fall out. And in between, you reek of decay each time you open your mouth.

Here's another thing about *tippity-tapping*. Like flossing it changes things.

Each time I *tippity-tapped*, the proverbial ledge got wider. I began to have more room to *tippity-tap* back to life.

And each time I stepped back, there was space for other experiences. I didn't know I was having them until one day a woman said, "Every night, write three things you are grateful for."

Fuck you, I said, and then found an index card.

My three things: 1. paper, 2. pencil, 3. didn't kill myself today.

Every day, for weeks, that's all I wrote.

Then one day I wrote, "the wind on my face."

A couple of days later, "the sun felt good."

A week later, "coffee," and then after that . . .

Every extra line I wrote began building an even deeper wider ledge. I started noticing other things besides raging destruction.

But, you know, not committing suicide isn't the sunset in some stupid movie with big silent men and their horses. It's plaque and it's floss. Even as time went on and my ledge got bigger, I was still standing on it.

I saw this on *60 Minutes*. A North Korean guy escaped from an internment camp literally crawling over dead bodies. He said what made him want to attempt the impossible was the description someone told him about chicken and how delicious it tasted.

All he had eaten his entire life was gruel. But this story, told to him by another prisoner who loved him enough to share such dangerous secrets, was enough to inspire him to crawl over his friend's dead body to get to freedom and chicken.

As my ledge grew, I began to understand how I had stepped out onto it in the first place, and I began to learn words for all those feelings, that at age four or five or four I didn't know how to spell. I began to recognize the beginning of it all.

This is what I recognize—on the street, in the subway, on a bus, in a restaurant, on the ferry, in an airport. This is what I see everywhere: the shocked look in a little kid's baby-face watching someone they love beating the shit out of them with a word or a slap or gritted teeth dragging them by the arm. Before my eyes I watch that kid's heart get broken for the first time. I watch that heart literally get crushed and obliterated.

When my heart broke at four or five or four and then over and over again for the next thirty-five years, every slap, every punch, every raging word, every hateful glare—inside, outside, school, play, work, streets, whether I was a little girl receiving it or an adult giving it back—it all became a jackhammer obliterating me. The pain was so great, the rage so awful, that the only way I understood how to stop it was to stop being.

It was time to make some different plans. I decided to get back to that moment right before the jackhammering started. I decided to get back to that love.

At first I tried getting it back with a boyfriend and then a girlfriend and then a boyfriend and then losing twenty pounds and then several master's degrees and always lots of red lipstick. Nothing quite worked. I was still on that ledge.

Until one night when I was thirty-nine and something happened.

See, all that writing on an index card every night? I didn't know it at the time, but I was writing that love. Each and every word was Gene Kelly tapping furiously inside, saying, "You are your hope for joy. You are your chance for an amazing life."

"You are."

One day, while I was battling utter despair, that *tippity-tapping* decided I wanted flowers in my home.

Look, rich people get flowers for their home. Where I come from, it was plants that didn't need watering or plastic bouquets you got on Delancy Street. But my inner Gene Kelly wanted real, smelly flowers, and I found myself crossing streets to get them.

And there was a former classmate I may have said two words to. Ever.

Within thirty seconds he was telling me how he was practicing Buddhism, and within thirty-five seconds I was laughing in his face because it sounded so stupid, and within forty seconds I was giving him my number because if I was going to stand on a ledge for the rest of my life, I wanted it to be like his ledge because his ledge sounded way better.

I, who don't talk to people I see on the street, don't keep in touch with anyone, never call someone who says, "Call me!" Well, I called this guy repeatedly until one night I went and learned how he practiced Buddhism.

Of course, afterward I yelled at him on the street about how full of shit it all was blah blah blah . . .

Tippity-tap, tippity-tap, Gene Kelly said. Give it ninety days.

So I did. Two minutes a night.

Now, looking back, I can say, "Oh I was finally stepping through a door called my life." But then? It just felt weird.

And then one night, maybe a couple of nights after the first night, a feeling I had never questioned—just like I never questioned the air I breathed or how water tasted or even what made my legs move—a feeling that said, "Take another step out into air and you'll finally be free"—that feeling flew out into its own air.

And as it flew out into its own air, old pain finally lifted, and instead of being The Plan, it became just like the long scar on my tummy that I got when they ripped out my appendix in a hurry because I was about to die. A reminder.

This isn't some stupid sunset movie. Like my scar, that feeling is always nearby. When it acts up, it's just like when knees ache before it rains.

I know I don't want to die. I just want the pain to stop. Or I'm not saying out loud what I need, or I sit still for twenty minutes, or I really just want to punch someone in the face because they are treating me like I'm the reason their life isn't going well.

People ask me a lot what it was like growing up on the Lower East Side back then. Fucking normal you fucking moron, I usually answer. Okay, without the moron part.

But what do you mean what was it like? That would require something to compare it to. Like that kid in North Korea, what I felt every day—terror, rage, panic, helplessness, fury, self-pity, back to rage, and then panic again, and underneath it all, heartbroken—was normal. You have to be told about chicken.

During the years of writing down what I was grateful for, *tippity-tapping* away, flossing off all the plans of destruction, I met my nephew for the first time. Well, he had just been born, so it wasn't like it was a scheduling issue.

When I held him in my arms for the first time, I suddenly felt the Grand Canyon open up in my heart. I had never felt anything like that before and then suddenly I did.

One day, he must have been three or four or three, I scribbled something on a teeny tiny sliver of paper and then stuck it into the frame of a photo of me squeezing a billion hugs into him.

It said, "Nothing helps, except love and the experience of something different."

Search for the Silver Cup

BETSY GRAZIANI FASBINDER

We used to argue about it, my little brother and I. John always said it was his. I claimed it was mine. Deep in my heart, I knew the truth. I only told myself it was mine because as the fourth of five children in my family, so very few mementos of my little-girl life exist.

Ours was not a family that commemorated special events or took pictures of little faces aglow in the light of birthday candles. Particularly for those of us at the ragged end of the birth order. Perhaps this was because enduring life in our limping, lopsided, twisted family was hard enough without trying to fashion artificial faces for celebratory photos. No energy remained for bronzing baby shoes or saving science fair projects. Few childhood artifacts survived the baker's dozen of moves my family made around the country before I was out of elementary school.

Each "company transfer" triggered by one of my dad's alco-hol-fueled episodes had instigated yet another move to yet another factory, in yet another town, across yet another state line. I guess that's what they did in the 50s and 60s when you got hammered and pissed yourself on the dance floor at the company Christmas party. They didn't fire you or get you help. They just paid for a moving van to foist the problem off onto another plant manager and you moved with your bedraggled family in tow.

It didn't seem fair or right to my little-girl self that my younger brother had a little silver cup to commemorate his babyhood. It seemed to me such a substantial thing, made to last, fashioned not of construction paper that would wither and fade, nor cotton that would yellow, but silver that would survive the storms that would inevitably swirl around it. The cup survived the purging and the garage sales. It was spared the fate of the discard pile during each of our sudden cross-country moves.

It's a little thing, this cup. Two shot glasses would fill it with water or whiskey. Or blood.

Each time it was rediscovered among the boxes after a move, the slim-handled cup was grayer with tarnish and more dented from its haphazard care. Each time we unpacked the boxes in a new and unfamiliar house, I'd snag the cup and display it on the curio shelf on my side of our shared room. It sometimes took weeks or months for John to spy the cup among my things. Saying nothing, he'd make a grand display of snatching the cup from my shelf and placing it prominently among his Hot Wheels cars and the broken Batmobile on his shelf. I'd silently concede the point, knowing he'd forget about it again and I'd have it back in the next house. I have some wisp of a memory that a boss or secretary at the battery factory where my dad worked in Leavenworth, Kansas—the stopover where my younger brother happened to be born—gave it to my parents as a shower present. John's luck-of-the-draw in the geographical birth lottery.

While I'm searching through my brother's things all these years later, first for the answers to the overwhelming *why* of it all, a familiar part of me conducts a secondary search, hoping to find the little silver cup, just this one last time.

We enter the messy living room after cutting through the coroner's red tape and the sticker that seals his front door. We sneak under the tape before we're technically allowed to. And while we have been told to take nothing, I can't bear waiting another day. I must see.

The whole drive to Reno, I ran a movie in my mind of what would greet me and my husband, Tom, when we got to John's house. Would it be a scene from *Psycho*? *Helter Skelter*? I couldn't let myself admit it aloud, but I was sure I'd find a letter. A definitive answer. Explanation. Understanding.

After sneaking past the cluttered living room, I stand at his bedroom door, drawing breath into my belly and willing myself to enter. The light in the room is blue. Unearthly. I drop—or perhaps fall—to my knees beside his blood-soaked mattress with the manhole-sized crater and the headboard with the two broken slats, cracked by the impact of his body when the gun went off. My eyes take in the morbid detail that his blood, even in that quantity, could not hold its redness for four whole days exposed to the air. Instead of the crimson red I'd conjured in my mental horror movie, the massive stain was a putrid golden-brown hue. I stood in reverence to him, my spirit hovering somewhere other than inside my body.

I'd spoken to him just the day before he died. We'd planned Thanksgiving and Christmas ravioli making. He was making Harvest Beer as a special treat. He'd joked. We'd laughed. Plans had been made. What did the kids want for Christmas? Could he bring his dog to Thanksgiving? No, she didn't still have scabs all over and her fur had grown back. As many times—hundreds, thousands maybe—as I've replayed that last conversation in my mind, I still find no coded hint of what was to come later that night. Instead I find hints of a long future to come; a future that didn't happen. The phone call ended as all of mine did with my baby brother. He closed every call, every departure with, "Love you a bunch." His last words to me.

I pull the bedspread up without thinking. Perhaps it's to spare my baby brother the immodesty of others seeing what he's left behind. He was private and modest in life. I felt like an intruder. But I had to see it with my own eyes, smell the earthy fragrance of the last bit of my brother's human form. I had to look at the coroner's photographs to take in his last expression; just one more piece of the jigsaw puzzle that I was trying to assemble of who he was and how he'd left. I had to touch the bedcovers with my own fingers, feel the stiffness of dried blood, and the hardened tufts of amber-stained mattress cotton.

Not seeing is always worse for me. Hitchcock knew my kind; for me, what takes place off screen is far more horrifying than anything even the master of suspense could design to show on the screen. What I can conjure is almost always worse than what is.

And while the scene in my brother's bedroom isn't more horrifying than the one I'd conjured, neither is it less horrifying.

I've never been prone to depression. My hard-wiring is more tuned for anxiety and panic. That's why, I suppose, my mental movies are so often worse than reality and why I need to see things. John was different. He was wired for depression. He hid from sadness. And he hid his own sadness behind his wicked sense of humor, his extraordinary generosity, and his good-ol'-boy charm. And now his hiding and his sadness had proved fatal. Help was available. He was loved. But he made his choice behind a thick curtain. He made his choice alone.

The cup was not in the bedroom. After I'd etched the images of that room into my memory, I closed the door behind me.

I hunted under the cheap living room furniture and behind the two contraband slot machines my boys had always loved to play when they visited their Uncle John's house. His whole place looked like a bad garage sale, full of the broken junk everyone picks through looking for the good stuff. I moved to the kitchen and rummaged through the hodgepodge of battered gadgets and the mountains of pricey beer-making equipment that was his final, obsessive hobby. I plowed through the broken and rusty collection of tools and piles of meaningless paper that bore no secret messages or final wishes.

Or apologies.

Or words of love.

Or explanations.

All the while as I searched, that classic America song from the 1970s kept droning in my head. *This is for all the lonely people/ Thinking that life has passed them by/Don't give up until you drink from the silver cup/And ride that highway in the sky.* Had John felt life had passed him by?

I searched through papers and boxes, through closets and drawers. I hunted *mostly* for the answers to the *why*, a note or an email message yet unsent on his laptop. But I looked for the cup at the same time.

My husband sorts through bills and records, the paper flotsam and jetsam of a life not lived to its natural end. I search through the rubble, seeing evidence of tasks neglected and of more sadness than even I knew John carried.

As my hopes of finding answers dim, my craving for the cup becomes a full hunger of a hunt, mad and ravenous. The calm, decent, good man I'd married continues to sort through my brother's bills, assuming we'll be taking on the unfinished details of what he's left behind. I cannot confess to Tom the object of my ravenous search, for fear of it sounding silly and sentimental.

The whole time we're in the house, we know that we're trespassers, that authorities will soon lock the doors permanently. The stuff that remains of my brother's life will become the property of the county. The thought of that cup going to some probate auction, sold off as so much miscellaneous junk, seems such a small heartbreak, but it is unbearable.

The hours pass. Still no answers. No notes. No unsent emails. No reasons. No hints of an unrequited love that might have destroyed his heart. No crushing debt. No secret cancer diagnosis that would have doomed him to years of excruciating pain. None of these horrible, merciful, horrible explanations were to be located among the rubble.

Finally, my patient husband says, "I think I'm about done here. Are you just about ready to go?"

My heart turns to lead. My questions are unanswered and I don't know if I can leave the silver cup behind. I close my eyes and swallow past the dryness of my throat, clearing the way for some kind of acceptance. Some surrender. "Okay," I say, defeated. "I guess we've done all we can do here." I give one more glance around the room through the blur of new tears, my eyes raw and stinging. *How can there be any tears left in me?*

Then, I see it.

The little cup is sitting in the back of the glass-fronted shelves of my mother's secretary desk. She'd willed the desk to me, but I'd loaned it indefinitely to John because he really liked it. I'd teased him saying I wanted him to erect a plaque: *Generously loaned from the Betsy Collection.*

The cup was beyond gray, blackened with tarnish, shrouded with the dents and scars inflicted in all of the locations where it had been dragged and stuffed and jerked around, and treated with general carelessness. It sat on the shelf surrounded by nothing important: crumpled envelopes, a corkscrew with a horseshow on its end, a broken Rubik's Cube, and a Reno Rodeo commemorative belt buckle from 1997.

This cup is a little nothing, a small something, and an everything all at once. It is what I have left to remind me that my brother was a little boy with me when I was a little girl. Hard evidence that he *was.*

The little silver cup that I once falsely claimed is now as mine as any physical item can be anyone's. It's one of only two objects I'd grab on the way out of my burning house once I knew my people and dog were safe. That valueless, tarnished cup is one of very few material things I would profoundly grieve if it were lost to me.

They say, "Be careful what you wish for." But in my little-girl wishing, I never wished for or imagined that the cup might one day come to me in this way.

My mother's desk has been returned to me too. Though technically, we stole it from my brother's house before the probate vultures and courts and the official offices of the Washoe County Public Administrator could get their hands on it. This is what happens when someone exits stage-left without leaving a will. The mementos of their existence are confiscated, treated with no sentimental regard, and sold in unmarked boxes to junk dealers, who strip the boxes of anything with monetary value. Then the remnants are sold to other dealers that deal in junkier junk. The little silver cup and my mother's battered desk will not be among my brother's disregarded miscellany. I couldn't let it happen that way. I couldn't rescue him, but I could save one small enduring part of us.

Even as I write these words, the man I love is restoring my mother's desk to its former glory. The drawers will no longer stick and the drop-leaf front will be secure. There, on the glass-fronted shelf where I found it, the cup will find its home. I will keep it polished. I will protect it from further injury. I will treasure it and treat it as a precious thing should be treated—the way I wish my brother had treated himself.

The Merry-Go-Round

MARK MORGAN

A sudden and terrifying jolt through my body wakes me up, like stepping into a cold shower.

It always begins the same.

I should be accustomed to it by now given how often it occurs, but it never fails to surprise me—my eyes fly open, and the familiar dread hits fast and furious—pure fear and panic. In that moment I know, *not wonder*, but know, I am going to die.

My doctor has told me that I have some—*a little*—panic disorder, which sounds like being told you are *a little* pregnant. But I assume that it is his way of breaking the news to me. I can now add this to my other wonderful awards, which include generalized anxiety, obsession/compulsion, and depression.

A delightful combination.

As soon as I have finally managed to calm myself down after waking up in a sweat and believe I'm not actually dying, the anxiety rears its ugly head to remind me—once again—why I really should in fact be *scared shitless*. All of the past and future, along with the day's activities, run through my head: what I didn't get done, what I need to do. I turn and toss several times—vain attempts to fall back to sleep.

But the worries persist.

The damage done.

BOOM!

By a certain point I am completely aware of how long I have been worrying, and then that becomes *my greatest worry*: that I worry too much. Welcome OCD, I knew you were in here somewhere. And that worry *is the black-hole worst of all*. The calculus equation for which there is no solution. None.

By this time, the hamster wheel that is my brain has built up a good amount of momentum. Here's the drill:

The covers come off and on, off and on, half a dozen times. Maybe more. I know what's coming next and I don't want to feel it. I don't want to deal with it. I go to the bathroom and splash water on my face, I turn on the TV and go online. But it's unavoidable. The pit in my stomach and lump in my throat both show up, right on time, side by yes, fucking side. They are nothing if not dependable.

I cannot seem to lessen the sadness, the depression.

I wonder: *Am I addicted to thinking?*

I read about that somewhere.

If that's the case, it's quite unfortunate—hugely unfortunate—because my drug of choice is with me every moment of every day, and every night, day in and day out. It's me. What—*or better yet, who*—wakes me up at night is me. And it doesn't matter what problem, worry, or concern is going on in my life at that moment.

It's all interchangeable.

My brain will chew on it, stew on it, simmer, mull it over, roll it around, and pull it apart like taffy. It will have anticipated the outcome. And 99 times out of 100, it will have predicted the worst—it is programmed to scare itself shitless. Even when the outcome proves the inverse to be true in real life: that 99 percent of the things I worry about never actually occur, never come to fruition, never manifest—the program never learns from the exercise. Never. It never adjusts itself to the real-life end result, like a data-gathering, self-learning computer algorithm would do.

And funnily enough, I am obviously aware of all of this.

Of the deficiency.

Of the same exact virus in *my* operating system.

I'm writing about it right now.

Mark knows this.

I know this.

I.

Know.

This.

This is a fact, a truth. There is no disputing it. But my brain will not cooperate. It won't register the information properly, or won't accept it. Maybe it doesn't want to. Either way, it just doesn't stick. Compute. And just like a merry-go-round, I will know all of this when I go to sleep tonight.

Knowing that my mind is not me.

Knowing that my thoughts are not me.

That my fears are not me.

And then a sudden and terrifying jolt running through my body will wake me up.

And again, it begins.

Thorazine

KAREN LYNCH

When I was seven, my mother taught me how to kill myself. She said you must hold the gun firmly to your temple and squeeze the trigger without hesitation. Don't be a wimp about it. The bullet will pierce the soft flesh of your temple, travel through the occipital lobe, and take out the executive suite of your brain. Maybe she didn't say "executive suite," but her words made me picture a Wall Street financier doing the deed in his private office bathroom. Mom said those who failed to follow these simple instructions risked leaving themselves alive and hideously deformed. "Hideously," she emphasized.

Mom shared other useful insights she had acquired along the way, such as her certainty that she could perform a competent emergency tracheotomy using just a steak knife, should we be dining out and I ever begin choking. Though Mom had spent a great deal of time in psychiatric hospitals, I probably don't need to say here that Mom had no formal medical training. She was an autodidactic physician. I hate to sound like one of those "I blame my parents for everything" people, but her offer to perform surgery is the probable source of my neurotic phobia of steak knives, restaurants, and meat.

We never owned firearms during my childhood, which was a good thing given Mom's history; nonetheless, the vivid picture of my self-inflicted head shot made cameo appearances as I grew older. I had never touched a firearm until I became a police recruit, nor had I ever seen one in the hands of any of the hippie tribe who raised me, but Mom was so detailed in her instructions, at times it seemed she hoped I might somehow acquire a revolver and do myself in.

Mom's Thorazine came in a jumbo bottle, similar in size to a Costco bottle of Ibuprofen that might last an average family ten years. When she took the medication, our life was calm and relatively predictable. I would take the bus to school, then return home to find Mom where I'd left her, harmlessly perched in bed, reading historical novels and smoking cartons of Marlboro Lights. I loved the periods in our life when she took her meds, small lozenges of tranquility that kept the dreaded manic episodes at bay. But as inevitable as the changing of the seasons, Mom would stop taking her Thorazine, saying she hated the side effects of lethargy and weight gain. I pretended everything would miraculously be okay, convincing myself that she no longer needed the medication.

However, within a few weeks off Thorazine, Mom's mania would return, the upside to her being bipolar, and then all bets were off. Mom might then lock herself in the bathroom, hollering that she was slashing her wrists. There was never any actual slashing; no blood, or razors to be found. Her screaming was only a gesture designed to manipulate me into calling her ex-boyfriend to save her. Reliably, I would call him, playing my part in Mom's script, and Jim would arrive stage left—the Colt 45, Pall Mall-smoking white knight in a Chevy pickup. Mom had achieved her desired reaction, never intending to voluntarily remove herself from the planet. Like those who test positive for a disease, never showing any symptoms, Mom was a suicide carrier, not a victim.

When the time finally comes, I will disregard Mom's vivid instructions. Having no access to a firearm, and no desire to make myself hideously ugly in the event of failure, I will choose the most obvious and convenient of escape routes.

Maybe my future struggles with depression were inevitable from the beginning. If I were a standup comedienne, I'd open with, "I was committed to a mental hospital before I was born" . . . *badaboom*. But it's a fact. I was committed to Agnew's State Hospital for the Mentally Ill, along with Mom, several months before I was born.

By fifteen, I had endured many episodes of Mom's hospitalizations, followed by my abandonment or internment in a children's home. I was physically and mentally spent, overwhelmed at the prospect of dealing with yet another "nervous breakdown." With each of Mom's hospitalizations, my existence seemed more tenuous. I became dependent on the kindness of strangers and learned from past experience that some strangers were less than kind. The anxiety of what might become of me lurked in the dusty corners of my bedroom, taking on various shapes: the pimp, the rapist, the slave master.

One evening when Mom was still lucid, she took me to see the movie *The Exorcist*. Though the family in the movie, a single mother and her adolescent daughter, mirrored our family down to the similarity in family surname, Mc/MacNeil, I didn't foresee the impact the movie would have on her. Within days, Mom was convinced I was possessed by the devil. She choked me, exorcising me, screaming for Satan to leave my body. Though I managed to push her off me and escape, I stupidly returned to our apartment shortly after with the intention of gathering my clothes and leaving for good.

And this is how it happens.

I find Mom collapsed on the couch, smoking and watching television. She is exhausted from the exertion of the exorcism earlier in the day.

I cannot see what is ahead for us. I cannot see how close I am to freedom. I only know I cannot leave her like this. I am all she has, and as much as I hate to admit it, she is all I have. I cannot see it in this moment, as I measure Mom's mood from the doorway, but in seventy-two hours the police will arrest Mom at Aquatic Park for assaulting a woman picnicking on the grass. She will be sent to Napa State Psychiatric Hospital, and I will finally be free of her. I cannot see that Mom's boyfriend, Jim, ever the rescuer, will provide me a safe haven to finish school, or that I will receive scholarship money to attend UC Berkeley. I cannot see the husband who will one day love me, the career that will give me a sense of belonging and family, the birth of my sons, the adoption of my daughter.

I can only see another chaotic nightmare with Mom, and I decide this is the end of the road for me. This is where I get off the Mom rollercoaster.

It's June 2, 1974. I lock the door to the bathroom and pull the jumbo bottle of Thorazine from the medicine cabinet. I pour a handful of tablets, round and orange, into my hand. "Skf T79" is printed in black on each one. I am not thinking, *This is the end of my life.* I am thinking, *I am done with you, Mom.* I examine the print, wondering what Skf means, not really caring. I like these pills. They are bringers of peace, that much I know. When Mom takes them, life is tolerable for everyone around her. I think, *If she won't take them, I will.* I gobble the tablets without further examination, sucking water from the tap to wash them down. I repeat the process with another handful. I don't finish the bottle. Two handfuls should do the trick.

I unlock the bathroom door and sit down beside Mom.

In that moment, if I'd had the ability to see myself separate from her, I might have acknowledged it wasn't me I wanted dead, it was my mother. But at the age of fifteen, that thought was too shameful to admit. "Honor your mother and father." Though not religious, I knew that wishing your parent dead was a sin. I sit beside my victim and die by proxy. Or try to die.

A few minutes pass before panic takes over. Just hours earlier, I was fighting my mother for my life, and now I'm killing myself? I didn't want to die!

"Mom, I just took a lot of your Thorazine." Now I was putting my life in her hands, letting her choose for me. Maybe I wanted some validation that she hadn't really wanted me dead earlier, that she had not known who I was or what she was doing.

"Why the hell did you do that!?" Mom was instantly lucid, as if the last few days of manic behavior had never happened. She picked up the phone and called for an ambulance, then ran to the kitchen, grabbed a bottle of French's mustard and mixed it in a glass with hot water.

"Here, drink this," she ordered. I drank it. It tasted horrid, but not bad enough to make me vomit, the intended effect.

Within minutes, two cops arrived at the door.

"What seems to be the problem?" the younger one asked.

"I took a bunch of my Mom's Thorazine." The cops rolled their eyes at each other. Maybe I was the hundredth suicidal teenager they had met that day.

"We just needed an ambulance, not the police," I said.

"You're fine to go in a car, you don't need an ambulance," the cop replied.

"We don't have a car, and we can't drive," I said.

"You can take a cab," he said. He did call us a cab. I'll give him that.

When the taxi dropped us at the Emergency Room, the admitting nurse asked me questions about the number of pills I had taken and how much time had passed since ingestion. I had reported on myself early enough that stomach pumping would not be required. Instead, the doctor gave me Ipecac. I guzzled the bottle, then vomited into a paper bag during the whole taxi ride home.

It took two days for the Thorazine to get out of my system. The first day I was paralyzed, unable to move from my bed. I now viscerally understood the lethargy Mom had complained of. While I lay glued to the bed, I could hear Mom return to her manic state in the other room, screaming at demons, telling me I had better come help her or she would slash her wrists. I was supposed to come save her, but I couldn't move.

I survived that night, and I survived Mom. When I came home from school two afternoons later, Mom was gone, arrested at Aquatic Park. Jim came to my rescue again and acted as my guardian, saving me from the monsters that prey upon vulnerable girls.

Mostly, I thought I was fine once I escaped Mom. I made it my personal challenge to live a good life, to be happy in spite of my chaotic childhood. I believed I had overcome my past, and though I had a few garden-variety neuroses, after a few years of therapy, I assumed I was as happy as the next person.

I had been working as a cop for more than ten years and had found myself in countless intense situations. I was often required to make split-second decisions: shoot, don't shoot, use my baton, not my pepper spray. I had never frozen or freaked out. I had consistently made good choices. Then in the winter of my thirty-seventh year, the darkness caught up to me without warning. We were driving home from a snow trip; my husband, Greg, in the passenger's seat; our two sons—five and two—strapped in their car seats behind us. I had the wheel. As the snow began brushing the windshield and the visibility decreased, I panicked, suddenly acutely aware that I was steering two tons of metal down a freeway at 50 miles an hour with my husband and children in the car. I could not drive a moment longer, and I did not know what to do next. Here on this freeway, I was as paralyzed as I had been after the Thorazine ingestion. Greg coached me to the shoulder of the road and took the wheel.

My physician diagnosed me with anxiety disorder and prescribed Zoloft, which is also prescribed to treat depression. She warned me not to mention to my coworkers that I was taking the medication because of the stigma associated with it. My lifelong goal had been to live the opposite life of my mother's, and I had failed. I was now also a mental patient. The difference was, I agreed to take the medication.

Within a few weeks, my anxiety symptoms disappeared, and I noticed something else was missing. Though I hadn't been aware of it until the medication kicked in, for years I had been host to an internal voice on repeat play that would say, *Just kill yourself . . . just kill yourself.*

It was a chant that started after any argument with my husband, or anytime I felt badly about work, or really maybe it had been there most of the time. How had I not noticed it before? It had been mildly annoying background music, but now, with its absence, I felt infinitely lighter. Maybe it had been playing since Mom's first description of suicide. Yet I never would have described myself as depressed. I suppose, had I even noticed it, I would have assumed all people walked around with voices telling them to kill themselves.

The happy ending to this story would be that I went on Zoloft, it cured my anxiety and depression, and my life has been great ever since. That would be the happy story, but not an entirely true story. The fact is, depression is a lifelong challenge. Oh, let's face it—*life* is a life-long challenge. Zoloft worked for me for at least twelve years. Then, at fifty, I was hit with breast cancer and its subsequent trifecta treatment: surgery, chemo, and radiation. My cancer was early stage and I went through the treatment like a trooper, few complaints, happy to be alive, but when the circus of treatment was over, the daily rides into the city for radiation completed, the cards and attention from friends over, I was left in an abyss so dark and black that Zoloft was no longer enough.

And this is how it happens.

For the first time since the Thorazine episode, I seriously consider suicide. I feel that since death is inevitable, I might as well choose how and when to go on my own terms. I become obsessed with knowing if the cancer will return. I plan various ways of ending my life. My witty, if heartless, suicide note will read, "I couldn't stand the suspense."

The thought I keep coming back to is, how can we be expected to love life, be involved in it, engaged, and simultaneously accept the inevitability of our eventual death? I feel that God, if there is one, must be sadistic. I cannot climb off this thought cycle. I want to love life again. I know I am supposed to appreciate my life, but I cannot because it feels so pointless to love something that will eventually be taken away from me.

During this time, the impact on my family seems negligible. I cannot foresee my son graduating from college and getting his first job in New York City, or my younger son graduating high school, or my daughter winning gymnastics ribbons. I cannot see the beautiful places I will visit and people I will meet. I can see none of the dozens of joyful events that I am opting out of in this moment.

But this time, I recognize the black dog for what he is.

Unlike that day in 1974, I do not act on my thoughts. This time I ask a doctor for help and am prescribed a new medication. Within a few days of taking it, I magically feel the way I imagine happy people must feel. I even try to consciously return to my depressive state, just to see if I can make myself obsess over death and darkness, but I can no longer go there. The switch has been turned off and I cannot go back to that place as long as I take this combination of medication.

My current chemical stew may still need tweaking over the years. Nothing works forever. Like Huey Lewis, I feel like I'm always saying, "I want a new drug." But unlike my mother's Thorazine, there are medications available now that work without turning the patient into a zombie. I now accept, without doubt, that depression is purely a result of the chemicals swimming in our brains, and we can choose those chemicals.

Learning to Sit Still

CHLOE CALDWELL

On the plane from Albany, New York, to Portland, Oregon, I deleted my heroin dealer's phone number. It wasn't the first time I'd done that—more like the fifteenth—and each time I'd felt a strange resistance. I knew that I would miss my heroin dealer, who'd been only too happy to help me ruin myself. I loved people that enabled my irresponsibility. In hindsight, he was my doctor. And I was a happy patient.

I was stupidly optimistic and naive and cocky enough to think I'd be okay once I landed in Portland. All I'd have to do was sweat the toxins out in a few yoga classes like I'd done in the past. Then I'd be new. Like a baby. I was amazing, possibly even talented, because I could maintain a drug problem better than other people. *Watch me go! I can go to yoga and do heroin. None of you can even tell. It's because I'm more functional than you. More stable. I can maintain a drug problem better than you.* It would be like nothing had even happened. No track record. No consequences. No nothing.

Because I'd never really had a problem before. I slipped through life doing as I pleased with no major consequences, mental or physical, from my drug use. Unlike other people, I was able to *dabble*. Now I realize that there had been an issue with semantics; the word actually wasn't dabble, it was *replace*. I replaced weed with mushrooms. Mushrooms with acid. Acid with ecstasy. Ecstasy with Adderall. Adderall with Cocaine. Cocaine with speed. Speed with Oxycontin. Oxycontin with morphine. Morphine with heroin. And when drugs weren't available? Alcohol. Food. Sex. I was a grabber. I was addicted to everything and nothing. I reached for anything that would keep me away from being with myself. I realized something when a drug dealer asked me, "So what do you want?" I went in never knowing what it was I wanted.

"You're like William Burroughs," a friend told me when I was in my early twenties. "You can do all these drugs and not get addicted!"

But when I stepped off the plane in Portland, my reality was not matching up with my ego. Jake, the guy I'd been seeing long distance for six months, was there to pick me up. I'd swallowed one Klonopin that morning and taken three Adderall XR throughout the plane ride. And I learned an important lesson: never show up anywhere on Klonopin and Adderall. (I love the part in the movie *Silver Lining's Playbook* when Bradley Cooper snorts: "Klonopin! It's like, *what day is it?*") I was wearing a shirt from Banana Republic (wearing something from Banana Republic has always made me feel like maybe I'll get my shit together, unlike wearing something from, say, Rue 21). But clothes can only do so much; Jake later told me he knew it wouldn't work from the minute I got off the plane and noticed my eyes were red and glossed over. When I was on drugs, I didn't care how I looked. That was just a sliver of their charm, and drugs charmed the hell out of me. Plus, I was convinced they made *me* charming. After I swallowed or snorted, I was more fun, more interesting, more attractive. Less edgy. Less human. That night at Jake's apartment, I poured my multivitamin container out on the bed, chock-full of orange and green and white pills. He told me I took a Klonopin before having sex, but I don't recall it.

I'd told Jake on the phone one night before I arrived that I was coming to Portland to get sober. "You're coming to *Portland* to get *sober*?" he scoffed. Maybe it made no sense to him but it did to me. Portland may have had a bunch of junkies, but my drug dealer wasn't there. I was convinced that it was all about convenience for me. Really, I was going to Portland for a six-month yoga-teacher training, and because I had a community of writers and friends there. Getting sober was just a back-up plan, a distant and glamorized idea, something that wouldn't be difficult since *my* problem was more casual than a *true* drug addict's.

Shockingly, things with Jake did not work out. I was smack in the middle of a stupor, a spiritual crisis, a quarter-life crisis, an identity crisis, an anxiety disorder, and he wanted a grounded girlfriend that would watch football and reality cooking shows and drink beer with him. On my second night in town, Jake came home from work and asked me to open a bottle of wine while he showered. I sat on the deck drinking it and he joined me. He quietly told me that he wanted to invite me to his home with him for Thanksgiving but that he felt apprehensive because "I know you'll just bring a bunch of benzos." It was like a sucker punch. It was only then that I realized perhaps I *did* have nerves. I thought of how my senior year of high school, when I had to give a speech in class, my friend Anna said, "Chloe's lucky. She doesn't get nervous."

That's right. I don't get nervous. I don't have fear. All you freaks with your orange prescription bottles. I feel sorry for you.

So, if I didn't have anxiety, why then did I take two or five Klonopin the next day? Why did I constantly hit people up for pills? Why did I take any drug handed to me and put it in my mouth and check medicine cabinets? Why didn't my boyfriend feel comfortable taking me to meet his parents? Why did I need to go to my grandmother's on cocaine or a bridal shower on heroin? Why did I need to have pills in my pocket like worry stones? Why did I need to have that seventh drink? Why didn't I want to remember things? Why didn't I want to be present for my own *goddamn* life?

Fear. Anxiety. Fear. Anxiety. And so on—ad infinitum.

Whenever I popped a pill of any kind, I'd lose track of how much

I was drinking and popping. It always reminded me of a line in Jillian Lauren's memoir, *Some Girls*: "Now, I am the kind of person that never turns down pills. And if you are the kind of person that never turns down pills, then you must always, always turn down pills."

Drugs motivated me. They got me out the door. I thought this was adventurous of me. I thought, in short, that I was hot shit.

While I packed my suitcases for Portland, I listened to two Aimee Mann songs over and over: "Save Me" and "Long Shot." I liked singing the words "save me" and also the chorus in "Long Shot" that begs, "Please love me." "Save Me" opens with: *You look like a perfect fit for a girl in need of a tourniquet.*

In Portland, without my drug hook-ups, I was beginning to bug the shit out of myself. Was I a drug addict or a binge-eater or did I have borderline personality disorder? My anxiety was through the roof. I couldn't get through breakfast without crying. I remember once, while living in a house with roommates, opening the fridge and seeing syringes for their cat's medicine and also narcotics for the dog, and I stood there truly considering using these things. I shut the fridge door reluctantly. This was one of the hundreds of times I realized I needed to get help. Other times: falling asleep in the park with homeless people, having a cop drive behind me while I had a deck of heroin in my bra, hearing people tell me that I looked high in my Facebook photos. So I called a health coach and asked for help. I called The Grotto, a Catholic Shrine and botanical garden that offered free counseling. I called Cascadia, a drug and alcohol behavioral center. I started seeing a therapist and getting drug-tested. At one point, I went to see the movie *Smashed* with a friend and I sobbed, gasping for air. It was the scene where the main character smoked crack. I knew that moment too well. My life seemed to be made up of those moments. The moment where you say yes instead of no. It haunted me.

It turned out that yoga-teacher training is nothing like running into yoga class late and on heroin. Yoga-teacher training is a commitment, a physical and mental challenge, not a quick fix to make you feel better about your body. Turns out we actually have to *work*. During our first week, I was struggling in Parivritta Trikonasana. My legs were shaking and I kept falling over. My teacher tried every prop and modification with me before she finally shrugged and said, "Maybe you just need to get stronger." I held back tears. She meant it in a physical way, but I knew there was more to it. The body and the mind are connected, and I was embarrassingly, obviously, ungrounded.

When I was singing the words "save me" and "please love me" over and over, I thought I was talking to my friends. To the universe. To the man I would meet and fall in love with. To the city of Portland. But now I know that those words were for me. I see now that I can live anywhere if I can learn to build a safe home inside my own body and mind. No one else cares if I binge eat, get drunk alone, and secretly pop pills.

And in the same way that I've heard alcoholics say that their body starts rejecting alcohol, drugs have stopped working for me. The last time I took a Valium, I turned into an evil bitch, then slept for fifteen hours. Oh, and even worse—I got completely ripped off when trying to buy drugs from a stranger at a bar. I gave him $20 and he gave me some black dirt from outside wrapped in tinfoil. I found this out when I went to the bathroom to snort it. He'd already left the bar.

I have more time now that I'm not going the distance to get drugs. When I'm not looking for pills on Google, I have time for movies. For hours of coffee with friends. To get my hair colored. To sleep in.

What is working for me is Dialectical Behavioral Therapy. As I'm sure thousands of others have discovered before, DBT feels like it was written exactly for me. It will be an ongoing thing in my life. I'm embarrassed and yet relieved to find that the cause of my drug use is anxiety. All I wanted was simple and yet it was the hardest thing to find: A sense of well-being. And I was using shortcuts.

It's pull-your-hair-out frustrating to take the long way after using shortcuts. Last month, a yoga instructor and philosopher named Michael Stone visited our teacher training. He asked us, "What would it be like to have a feeling and just feel it?" And then, the thing that made me cry, that made me gasp for air, that made me understand myself more: "The cause for unhappiness is that one cannot sit still alone in a room." While in Michael's class, he had us doing formal seated meditation and then fast and slow walking meditation. While in the seated meditation, some of us would start to nod off. "Be *awake!*" he would yell. "Forgive yourself. When you're sitting, you're not going anywhere or planning anything. You are here, sitting in your *life.*"

Do you know anything more terrifying than sitting still in your own life? I don't.

Some days are better than others. On "good" days, I eat kale and go to yoga and read books and drug use doesn't cross my mind. On not great days, I notice I'm using coffee and wine as a sort of speedball. And on worse days, I look out the window from my basement apartment and see the sneakers hanging over the telephone wires and think about standing there and waiting for heroin. But then I think, *Would I buy heroin for the child me?* I use all my DBT tricks all day long. All. Day. Long. *What can I do to self-soothe? Can I use opposing emotion? Distraction? Mindfulness? How can I make this moment I'm stuck in better?* Besides the occasional pill, I've been clean for five months.

Recovery is heavy DBT therapy. It's NA meetings. It's walking around with workbooks in my purse: *The 12 Steps for Women* and *DBT for Anxiety* workbooks. It's telling my friends and family that I need support. It's learning to sit still in a room by myself. I roll off my bed and do this first thing every morning, sometimes for five minutes and sometimes for twenty: I set a timer and literally hold hands with myself while I sit. This is how I sit still in the only life I have, trying to love the only self I've got.

Depression is a Patient Stalker

RUTH PENNEBAKER

Go back with me—way back.

It's the mid-1950s and I am about six years old. My mother, sister, and I are hiding in closets while a woman bangs on our front door and screams for us to let her in. Outside, her pea-green car sits on our driveway.

The woman's name is Mrs. Schultz (back then, adults didn't seem to have first names). She is mentally ill, my mother says. How does Mother know? Well, Mrs. Schultz recently put her children in a rabbit hutch in their backyard.

We live in Wichita Falls, Texas, a small, desolate city close to the Oklahoma border. The wind blows dust most of the year, tornadoes bludgeon neighborhoods now and then, the sun blisters your face and arms, and the big red ants sting. It's not the kind of place where you'd want to leave your kids—or even your rabbits—in a rabbit hutch.

I don't remember what happens after that. Mrs. Schultz must

have finally given up and gone home. My mother, sister, and I must have cautiously exited the closets, relieved to have escaped the presence of someone who was mentally ill.

Mentally Ill: In my child's mind, it was always capitalized and related to rabbit hutches.

Two or three years pass. Mrs. Schultz hasn't been knocking on our door again. But a middle-aged woman in our small Methodist church—whom I'd once shared a hymnal with—has deserted her husband and their recently adopted daughter to run away with her boyfriend. She and her boyfriend even rob a bank together somewhere in Wichita Falls, and their faces are on *Wanted!* notices at the post office. Members of our church show up at the post office frequently, just to check on things and maybe buy a stamp or two.

In the meantime, my mother isn't doing well. She is very tired, she says. She stays in bed a lot. Sometimes, when my sister and I come home from school, she's still in bed. But she never sleeps.

One Saturday morning, Daddy, my sister, and I drive Mother to the hospital. She cries and tells us good-bye. She'll be back as soon as she's well. Afterward, Daddy takes us to get ice cream cones. He tries to talk to us, but he doesn't really like children—or maybe he just doesn't like us. We are all scared, we have all had a hole torn in our hearts, but we don't talk about it. What is there to say?

Years later, when I'm a teenager, I see a medical insurance form my parents have filled out. It refers to Mother's hospitalization in Wichita Falls, but it also mentions another, earlier hospital stay a week after my birth. I ask Mother about it.

"All I could do was hold you and cry," she says in a low voice. "I was very depressed then."

We had finally started using that word in our family: *depressed.* It gives us a little structure, but not much. It is a very private word. You have to speak it in a whisper and then only to members of your immediate family.

But what does depression mean? To me, as a child and adolescent, it means unmade beds and long silences and darkened rooms. Like all my childhood memories, it lies in the empty plains of North and West Texas, in a hard and hostile climate. I always wonder whether a certain kind of tough and unflinching people have been drawn to this harsh place—or whether the land has made them this way.

In any case, it isn't a world that's sympathetic to any kind of weakness. And depression, we all seem to know intuitively, is born of weakness.

After all, you can't see depression on an x-ray, can you? You can't remove it surgically like a tumor, you can't see it like a rash on the surface of a body. It's hard, even, to describe it in a way that others really comprehend it.

So maybe it's not even real.

Mother continues to be depressed off and on for the rest of her life. Her relationship with me is painfully bad—or just painful, period, for both of us.

All I know, in every inch of my being, is that I will never, ever be anything like her. I won't be a housewife, a mother who tells her children she's given up everything for them. I won't live in windswept, small towns that obviously turn women into depressives, bank robbers, and rabbit-hutch abusers. And I will do anything, I tell myself, not to be depressed like her.

So, I deliberately try to become everything she isn't and travel where she's never gone. I marry a smart, ambitious man. I go to law school and graduate high in my class. I ditch law and become a writer. I have two children but continue to work full time. I live on the East Coast, spend time in Europe, come back to big cities in Texas, all the time pushing and striving, writing books and newspaper columns and magazine pieces. Standing still would be like death to me.

But, you know, I am more like my mother than I want to believe. And depression is a patient stalker, waiting for its time.

Twice, in my mid to late twenties, I am blindsided by massive depressions. I wake up in the mornings, wondering if that black curtain will fall on me again. I spend my days wracked by pain and darkness.

Sometimes, I don't know if I can bear to live the next five minutes, since every second has its own agony. I can't sleep, I can't eat. I am too paralyzed to do anything.

I have an excruciating memory of stepping out on our back porch and looking down at our sleeping dog. I would have given anything to trade places with that dog—to sleep, to be free of emotional torture and self-loathing. Two decades later, I tell a friend this story, which I consider to be one of the lowest points in my life. She brightens immediately. "I understand!" she says. "I've *always* wanted to be a dog!"

But that's one of the many problems with depression: those who don't suffer from it don't get it. You say: *I feel terrible, I feel hopeless, I am wracked with pain, I can't endure this* . . . And they answer: *Hey, wait a minute! You're having a bad day, that's all! You'll feel better tomorrow. You'll be fine. Think of all you have to be grateful for. You have such a wonderful life; how can* you *complain?*

You then end up feeling worse, guiltier, for feeling bad. Since you already hate yourself so much that you wish you'd drop dead every second of the day, you really don't need more self-recriminations.

So you go to psychiatrists—or I do, anyway, and she listens to my many problems and watches me cry and prescribes pills.

The pills—old-fashioned tricyclics which were the best they could do in the late '70s and early '80s—make my mind fuzzy and my mouth dry. I'm looking at the world through rippling, filmy water. I don't care. Gradually, the drugs numb me and block my pain. I don't care if blocking my pain isn't curing my pain, if the pain is only masked and goes elsewhere. *I will do anything not to feel that pain.* It's in this place that I understand why people commit suicide; the psychic pain is unbearable.

Like my mother, I am also diagnosed with breast cancer. At forty-five, I get a bilateral mastectomy and go through chemo and radiation. I am very brave. I know this because everyone tells me this just about all the time. They also bring dinners to our house and presents and cards. I am their inspiration, many of them tell me. I join a survivor's group, march in pink-hued parades, and mention my bad breast cancer year on a regular basis. I also write about it in newspaper columns, a young-adult novel, and in my blog. I am so proud of myself for being a breast-cancer survivor that it defines me for years.

Breast cancer, like depression, used to be a disease of great shame, spoken of in whispers. Now, its on parade banners, and football helmets, and T-shirts. Its survivors are treated as heroines, but I knew the bravest I'd ever been in my life was summoning the sheer guts to get up in the mornings when I was wracked by depression. Of course, only my husband and a couple of close friends knew about that. It may have been almost fifty years after my mother's depressions first changed our family's life, but the stigma and shame of depression linger. No one brings you casseroles or calls you a heroine when you're depressed.

In 2000, the teenage son of one of my cancer survivor friends kills himself. I know Chase was depressed because his mother talked to me about it and asked my advice. She and her husband did everything they could to save him—therapy, drugs, advice from experts. But it didn't work.

At the memorial service, my friend and her husband publicly open up about the cause of Chase's death and the suffering their son endured. They hold nothing back.

Sitting in the church, witnessing the grief of Chase's family and friends, I realize how silent I have been about my own depressions. I have an op-ed column in the *Dallas Morning News*, for God's sake, where I have frequently written about my breast cancer and have been praised for my honesty—but my *depression*, never. Where's the bravery in that?

So, I write a column about Chase's suicide and my own depressions. I ask my husband to read it over, which is something I rarely do. I want him to ask me not to publish it. He won't. He thinks it's fine. He thinks I *should* publish it.

I get more response from that column than from any other I've ever written. *There are so many of us out there*, people who have struggled with depression. To look at most of us, you'd never know. We compensate so well, we look so normal. We've kept the silence. We've perpetuated the stigma.

Since Chase's death and that newspaper column, I try to write about depression and speak up about it whenever I can. I'm sick of the ignorance and lack of empathy about depression that crest whenever a famous person commits suicide. I'm furious that we're educated and living in the twenty-first century but we still cling to ancient notions about mental illness. So much suffering is endured silently and so many lives are lost or ruined because of depression. And all our silence and shame about depression? We need to lock them in the nearest rabbit hutch.

Allies in the Sky

DAVID LACY

After my ex-wife moved out, I flew to my hometown to visit family and friends nearly every other weekend.

This was difficult because I was terrified of flying. As soon as we reached cruising altitudes, I'd order two miniature bottles of tart airline chardonnay for the one-hour flight between Southern and Northern California. The wine, of course, chased the pre-flight Xanax, dusty pills that slid out of a bottle with a warning label that read, DO NOT MIX WITH ALCOHOL.

Some people who are afraid of flying will never voluntarily take the window seat. I needed it. As soon as the plane took off, I pressed my temple firmly against the glass and stared intently at the receding features of the earth. I somehow believed that if I remained acutely focused on the rattles and bumps of the flight, I could control it, thereby ensuring the continued levitation of a massive airborne cylinder of steel traveling at speeds in excess of 400 miles per hour. A teacher of mine once referred to this as magical thinking.

My psychiatrist has a different phrase for it: "a symptom of my generalized anxiety disorder." He's the one who supplied me with the Xanax, though, so I'll go with his terminology.

I desired the window seat for an additional reason: I wanted—*needed*—to scout for planes. Scanning the skies, I would search compulsively for little specks of metal crisscrossing the horizons. Somehow, and I still have difficulty explaining this to people, I found solace in the companionship of other moving airplanes. Their presence—along with the Xanax and the shitty chardonnay—steadied my nerves in a curious way. Clearly, they could be of no aid in case of an emergency, but spotting them out there—planes full of humans floating below, above, and around me—made me feel more secure. When one flew silently out of sight, I'd ball up my fists anxiously, my eyes frantically searching for the next plane. In my head I referred to them as airplane allies, and I didn't truly comprehend their powers until recently.

Even when you know it's coming, you don't *really know*.

I say "moved out," but if there were a more clinical way to describe my wife's departure I'd use that term instead. Before I left for a friend's house that weekend—a mutually agreed upon time where my wife's parents would help their daughter pack up without having to experience the pained and embarrassing confrontation with a son-in-law they had known for nearly a decade—we had drawn up a HIS and HERS list.

I didn't return until I was sure they had gone (confirmed with a text), and as I unlocked the same stubborn lock I had battled with daily for years, I stepped into an apartment that was *exactly* half empty. The surgical precision with which our home had been bisected and vacated was remarkable: There were exactly half as many electronics, half as many dishes, half as many Pottery Barn furnishings.

She was nothing if not judicious.

I walked slowly to the center of the living room, sweeping my head from side to side, seeking something, but unsure what. Suddenly, I felt a heavy pressure, as if I had been immured into the space between two repelling magnets, and I dropped to the floor. I doubled over, crossed my arms over my chest, and clenched my fists. I began rocking back and forth and breathing faster, sucking sips of air in increasingly quick, fierce intervals. When the numb tingling began prickling my face, neck, and arms, I knew a panic attack was imminent. The sips became gulps, and the tremulous sobs began.

The ugly, twisted, thick, labored sobs, each ending in a deep moan and mumbling lips that offered an incoherent plea over and over again in broken-record fashion: "Please no." Tears streamed from my eyes and merged with viscous snot.

What I remember most vividly is that no one was there. I spent the remainder of the evening completely alone.

I awoke in a daze, unmoved from that self-same spot on the floor. I reached out without lifting my head, grabbed my phone, and checked the time. It was 11:45 PM. I had slept through the entire day. Now I had the rest of the night to contend with.

I pulled myself up with considerable effort and went in search of Benadryl. I found two in my bathroom medicine cabinet (I didn't even bother looking on her side; I already knew what wasn't there), tossed the pink tablets in my mouth, stuck my head under the faucet, and swallowed.

I returned to nearly the exact same spot where I had passed out earlier and curled back up on the floor.

I've never stared at the base of a wall for so long. Memories played on loop in my mind: the intractable anxieties that had chipped at our relationship for years, shaving away small pieces of trust and security, one compulsive thought at a time.

More nights just like this came and went. Never reorganizing the furniture into a functional living pattern. Never throwing clothes in hampers, simply tossing articles into a corner of the room that quickly developed a stench. Never buying food. Never eating. Never hungry. It was as if the pendulum of self-restraint had swung in the other direction, from a fierce compulsion to regulate every minutiae of my existence to apathetic abandon. My therapist, Dr. Thai, had accumulated two decades of my crazy into a generic manila folder—my unconscious need to control bound together with notes chronicling anxiety, obsessive thoughts, and male anorexia.

I set the alarm on my phone, curled up on the floor, and attempted to make it through the next fitful night.

I would leave for work early, move through my days in a haze, and come home to repeat the same chores that felt more arduous than they truly were, which amounted to the bare minimum: showering and changing my clothes. My fridge remained stocked with a box of wine and a collection of half-used condiments.

In less than two weeks, I was practically climbing the walls in desperation. I needed to get the hell out.

"I love it. I want it. I'll take it."

"It" was a free-standing unit in Laguna Beach, California, built in the 1960s, and only minutes from the ocean. Original hardwood floors surfaced most of the home. The living room boasted a fireplace with brick mantle on one side and a long window offering glimpses of the sea on the other. Smaller windows cranked open with stiff, jerky motions, allowing the coastal breeze to circulate through. There was a back patio with potted oregano, basil, and thyme, and a garage in which to store pieces of my past life.

"It" was also the kind of place my ex and I had discussed renting on several occasions. When we had those occasional "fuck-it-let's-just-do-something-completely-and-utterly-fucking-different-just-for-the-fuck's-sake-of-it" conversations. The conversations that breathed the only brief gusts of oxygen into an otherwise exanimate marriage.

The conversations that went nowhere.

I launched myself into my work (I taught at three different colleges) and spent my limited free time exploring the quirky beach town. Soon, my neighbor—a colleague who'd told me about the rental the same hour the landlord had taped up a "For Rent" sign, and who lived in an attached studio the size of a walk-in-closet—began accompanying me on my regular jaunts through town.

"I want it. I'll take it."

This time "it" was a 2007 Mercedes Benz. It was also the lowest-end model on the used side of the dealer lot, but most importantly, it was about as far removed as possible from the family-sized American SUV I had traded it in for. Potential infant car-seat space was replaced by shiny black leather. Extra safety features supplanted by a sunroof and bucket seats.

My neighbor and I explored the town once again, this time racing up and down Pacific Coast Highway at night. The moon shimmered on the water, reflecting soft white light across the western edges of town. I felt alive for the first time in ages.

As I dropped her off and made the five-foot trek back to my home, my neighbor turned and paused.

"You're going to be okay, you know that, right?"

And she retreated into her walk-in closet.

They swept in from the east, west, south, and north.

Each time I flew home to Sacramento, friends would drive in from around the region to meet up. Though pockets of turbulence continued to rattle my nerves, I found myself glancing out the windows less frequently with each flight. Slowly, nearly imperceptibly at first, both my anxiety and grief seemed to abate, as if they were operating in some sort of strange alliance. Still, I breathed an audible sigh of relief whenever we landed, my childhood allies parked curbside, waiting to scoop me up.

Once home, we danced through the streets until three in the morning, kings and queens of our little empire.

In Southern California, several colleagues who had previously occupied mere acquaintance status evolved into close, personal friends. We traveled to Vancouver together for work and play. It was one of the first times I sampled seafood, and not just one or two items either, but dozens of pieces of fresh catch from the steel-silver waters of the Pacific Northwest. My friends also introduced me to Canadian whiskey and espresso martinis.

The socialization, the tasting, the laughing, the smiling, even the frequent flying, were working wonders on my soul. I felt like I was approaching some yet-unseen foundation, like a pilot coming in for a soft landing through dense fog. But I still could not make out the ground beneath my feet.

Nearly a year had passed since my wife left and there was nothing but radio silence between us. I was surprisingly grateful for this enormous gift, and I wished her no ill will. It was a healing quietude. I was in my campus office one morning near the end of a particularly exhausting semester when another colleague in the office next to mine walked over and began telling me about her upcoming trip to Holland and Belgium. She mentioned she would be spending several days attending a conference before sightseeing the two nations for an additional week.

"You should come," she offered, nonchalantly.

To this day I am unsure why I responded with similar nonchalance, as if agreeing to travel to Europe on a whim was a perfectly normal thing for people to do.

"When are you leaving?" I asked.

"Next Wednesday."

Twenty minutes later I had booked a flight to Brussels that would depart in under a week. Though it would be the longest flight I had ever taken, my anxiety barely reared its monstrous head in the days leading up to take-off. It had been replaced by an intoxicating excitement, a thrilling anticipation of the upcoming adventure.

Amsterdam and Belgium remain an astonishing whirlwind of memories: Dining each night on wine and tapas and chocolates and scotch until the summer sun set at nearly midnight; dancing in crowded clubs until four in the morning alongside people of every nationality; stumbling drunkenly through cobblestone alleys at sunrise in search of breakfast to stave off impending hangovers; racing bicycles across cobblestone streets, narrowly avoiding mopeds and pedestrians; screaming our lungs out at a carnival ride in the quiet town of Bruges—the type of horror "fun" house that United States regulators would have promptly shut down.

However, there were occasions amidst these adventures when I broke down. I might be staring fixedly at a particular piece of art in a Belgian museum and tears would trickle unexpectedly from the corners of my eyes. I stood at the top of a steep and ancient belfry in Bruges and felt an aching for something absent. And sometimes, I am ashamed to admit, when I was most vulnerable and overwhelmed with emotion, I would lash out verbally at those same people who allowed themselves to come into the closest proximity. But for the most part, inertia kept me moving, and I never slowed long enough to experience inertia's dangerous flip-side.

The side that could have sent me directly back to that barren apartment, locked in a haze of depression and dirty laundry.

I still have no clue where the idea to go skydiving came from. It set up residence in my mind one morning and refused to depart, until I was thinking about it almost daily.

I assumed I would have a difficult time persuading my sister to join me. To be honest, my invite was more of a tease than anything else. Brothers enjoy teasing their younger sisters. It's a scientific fact.

"I just have to be at work by eleven," she replied. Nonchalance appeared to be the new norm and I was beginning to love it. Rebecca was a barista at a coffee shop. "The clientele get irritable if I'm not there to hook in their caffeine IV drips."

"If any of them get grumpy with you, stare them square in the eyes and state in your most expressionless tone, '*You* just walked through that swinging glass door. *I* just fell from the motherfucking sky. Get in line.'"

She chuckled and agreed to meet me at the county airport on the appointed day.

The night before our trip, I camped out at the tiny airfield in the middle of the countryside with one of my best friends, Greg. We drove into town around sunset and purchased hamburgers and trimmings; on the way back we blasted the stereo as we sped across the empty back highways of rural northern California.

Greg fired up the portable barbecue when we returned to the makeshift camp. I chopped tomatoes and onions while he crisped slices of bacon and made sure the burgers remained a bit on the bloody side. He went to the trunk of the car and retrieved a six-pack of beer. Knowing I loathed beer, he leaned back into the trunk and re-emerged a moment later with a glimmering bottle of chilled chardonnay.

"It ain't the shitty stuff either," he said, handing me the bottle. I took a swig. It was indeed good. I was done with the shitty stuff. The next morning, the weather was perfect, but my nerves, which had been surprisingly calm until that point, were finally beginning to fray. My sister, along with family and friends, had arrived and we went up on the small plane together. As the plane climbed noisily, our instructors latched us in, buckled, clipped, pulled, and tugged taut the myriad straps and cords.

In that instant I was hyperaware of two distinct selves: one, who would refuse to budge, and who would remain obstinately affixed to the relative safety of the craft. And another, about to be loosed into the sky like one of those planes. One of those allies.

The door slid open.

"Ohfuckfuckfuckfuckfuckfuckfuckshitshitshit," I hissed. I'm not certain how long the stream of profanities lasted, but they sent most of the plane into a laughing fit and my instructor patted me on the shoulder reassuringly. As the person who had orchestrated this event, I was first. I felt my body lift against my will as my instructor stood halfway up and we began walking to the edge.

There are no words that describe the combination of sensations that flowed through me at that precise moment. *Terror, excitement, astonishment*—all of these terms are woefully inadequate. I stood thirteen thousand feet above ground and readied myself to jump.

And then I *did*.

The air blasted my cheeks, which flapped wildly as if attempting to flee from my face. Every movement, no matter how small, required significant effort, but after a moment I gained control of my body's position. I sailed through the air, staring open-mouthed at what looked like a cartoon checkerboard thousands of feet below. The sheer quiet of it all shocked me.

"This is amazing," I half whispered.

The feeling wasn't one of falling, but rather of floating. Below me lay everything: Every fear, every anxiety, every human I had ever interacted with.

And it wasn't a checkerboard below me, it was a puzzle. And in that moment the final piece had snapped, victoriously, splendidly into place.

I was alone in the sky, and I was no longer afraid.

Off With the Fairies

CHRISTINE KEHL O'HAGAN

I came to school one Monday morning in February 1961 to learn that Richard McGee, the smartest boy in my sixth-grade class, had died over the weekend, not of the stomach flu that had sickened his eleven siblings, but of appendicitis. I knew that children could die, for I'd found a photo in my grandmother's hall closet of two of my mother's three lost brothers, I just never expected it could happen to a boy who sat right across the aisle from me. There were no grief counselors in those days; there weren't even playground mats. For children in 1961—and adults too—there was little cushioning of any kind. Sister Francis, so very young, passed Richard's red pencil case around the room, his marble notebook, his spelling test from the previous Friday. He got a 98. "A grade Richard will never see," Sister Francis cried, the tears catching in her sheer veil.

There's a concelebrated Mass for Richard, three priests on the altar, baritone Latin, clouds of incense that smells like the Bell's Seasoning my grandmother dusts across the Thanksgiving turkey, all trussed and tied with twine.

Richard's casket, white with gold metallic flecks, rolls down the aisle past me, inside of which Richard, his blond hair, his blue eyes, his freckles, his bright white teeth, wears—according to my classmates, who weren't too frightened of his wake—a plaid sports coat.

Years later, when my own child dies, and I am digging through his closet for the navy blue blazer I'd put away specifically for the occasion, I'll think of Richard and his plaid sports coat.

Then, shortly after Richard dies, a little girl goes missing in Harlem. Her name is Edith and she's seven, as old as my sister. The story is in *The Daily News* and *The Mirror* that my father tosses on the end table every night when he comes home from work. When I grab the newspaper, my father stares at me through his gold, glittering eyes. "Would you jump in my grave that fast?" he asks, but I don't know what he means. I'm just so worried about Edith. My father says that all of my reading is what's ruined my eyes. He tells me to go and sell pencils on street corners, but I don't know what that means either. My mother buys pencils in Woolworths. My father says that instead of reading, I should be running around on the street with the other kids and getting some exercise. I don't see the point of running around on the street with the other kids when the library is only two blocks from home and there's so much I want to know. My father says that I don't run around enough, and that's why I'm so fat. Most people eat to live, he tells me, but you live to eat. I don't know what that means either. My mother says not to pay attention to him, he doesn't mean it—the "Irish flu" is on him, it's just his way, that's how men talk. She doesn't know what else to do: it's 1961.

While Edith is missing, our apartment building gets a new handyman who pays too much attention to my little sister. He pulls on her ponytail, takes her jump rope or her prized Baby Dear doll and puts it behind his back. He's got some sort of speech impediment, and he calls my sister something that sounds like "Miss Plint." It's *Miss Prim*, my mother laughs. "It's from an old-time comic strip. He's harmless," she says, but I don't believe her. My sister is in and out of the hallways, the cellars, and sometimes the roof where we kids, as plentiful as roaches, are not allowed but go anyway. Pam is small, the super is not big, but short and powerful-looking, with tattooed arms as big as Popeye's. I lay in bed at night, icy-cold yet sweating, unable to sleep, recite a hundred Hail Mary's with the blue plastic Rosary beads I keep under my pillow in my fist, begging the same God who took Richard McGee to find Edith and keep the super away from my sister.

When Edith's body is found in a cellar just like the ones we kids are in and out of, her uncle is arrested for her murder, but I think our handyman did it.

"You've been watching too much Perry Mason," my mother laughs, waving me away.

After Richard McGee died and Edith was murdered, Pam got a stomach virus that she just couldn't kick. She dehydrated. The skin on her feet peeled away. Her tongue turned black. Following the doctor's instructions, my mother was up all night pushing green beans and carrots through a sieve, but when my sister still couldn't keep anything *down* or *in*, the doctor sent her to the hospital. Aunt Nellie was recruited to climb the four flights of stairs and stay with me and my four-year-old brother, Richie. She sat on the sofa between us, and we all watched my mother cover Pam, who was in my father's arms, with her own coat. Then they were gone.

"You'll never see your sister alive again," Aunt Nellie weeps, and although I know she's a foolish old lady who takes cans of anchovies from the A & P and slips them into the deep pockets of her giant tweed shoplifting coat, I'm nearly destroyed. I love my sister, and everyone in the neighborhood knows what happened to poor Richard Mc Gee.

And although I *do* see my sister alive again, and in fact, a week after she gets out of the hospital, we are once again drawing battle lines down the center of our shared bedroom floor while my brother stands there watching us, chewing on the bars of his crib, the damage has been done. There is something very wrong with me. I cannot let my sister out of my sight. I watch her sleep, I follow her around the apartment, I knock on the bathroom door if she's in the bathtub too long and possibly drowned. If Pam leaves the house before I do,

running down the four flights of stairs, through the darkened hallways where the handyman lurks, I am in agony, terrified that by the
time I get downstairs, she won't be with the other kids and none of
them will know where she is. When I run out of excuses to visit her
classroom, asking her for a pencil, a pen, tissues, I ask her for "the
keys" that neither one of us have. Her teacher stands with her back
to the board, chalk held in midair, waiting. *What keys?* Pam stares at
me, confused.

When Sister Francis says that no, I can't go to the lavatory again,
when "going to the lavatory" means sneaking past my sister's classroom just to make sure she's still in her seat, my friend Kathleen helps
me out. Kathleen is living a life similar to mine, minus the obsession.
Kathleen's father, an alcoholic executive, is routinely carried through
the front door of their beautiful brick colonial by taxi drivers or truck
drivers. Her college-educated mother has a job going door to door
selling Melmac dishes just to put food on the table. Kathleen doesn't
question me. She leaves the classroom on a fake, risky lavatory run just
to walk past my sister's classroom and make sure she's at her desk.

I don't know where I would have been without Kathleen.

When Sister Francis finally meets with my mother and asks
about our home life, my Irish mother, used to keeping Irish secrets—
especially about the Irish Flu—gave nothing up, especially not to a
member of the clergy. My mother didn't tell Sister Francis about the
harrowing nighttime ride down Bear Mountain with my father drunk
at the wheel, my mother leaning over the back of the passenger seat,
pushing me, my sister, and little brother on to the car's floor in those
pre-seatbelt days. Or about the nights she threw her raincoat on over
her pajamas, ran down the stairs and through the empty streets, one
lone woman peering through the dirty windows of the Irish bars, while
my sister and I, in a jumble of vanilla-scented hair and long flannel
nightgowns, laid on our bellies on the cold Art Deco tile floor on the
landing outside our apartment door, our ears pressed to the top stair,
waiting to hear the door to the building open up four flights below,
our parents finally safely home while inside the apartment, our gentle,

oblivious baby brother—before the muscular dystrophy—slept on. Despite the private schools, the Buster Brown shoes, the cod liver oil, ours was a childhood filled with grief.

A more compassionate person, a more forgiving person, a kinder person, would let go of a father like mine. He came from a long line of alcoholics. He was orphaned young. He suffered concussions and a fractured skull. He could have had, probably did have, neurological damage. Maybe he was depressed, though depression doesn't cause a father to hurl a hot baked potato the length of a dining room table at his bare-chested little girl, sitting on the other end, or cause a father to stare at his own child in such a way that she drops her eyes, and for her entire life shrivels in front of him, filled with shame. Maybe he was just mean. How sad it is to remember him in this way, me older now than he ever got to be.

This first depression wasn't my worst depression, but it was the scariest, mostly because I was only eleven years old, sad all the time, anxious, confused, and I couldn't understand what was happening, and neither could my smart, funny, irreverent mother, who normally understood everything and was generally fearless—except if it had anything to do with craziness. My mother was terrified of craziness. She had panic attacks, unrelenting anxiety, fainting spells that, in her Irish way, she laughed at, thinking we children would never notice her clenched hands, her fingernails digging into her palms, the traces of blood she left on the newspaper, a hysterical stigmata.

When my mother was a child, she watched her beloved, Alzheimer-afflicted grandmother pace the screened porch of the family's rented Rockaway bungalow, screaming at invisible demons, while roaming packs of kids, with their bikes between their legs, stood outside laughing.

She threw her zombie-like uncle's "nerve pills" down the toilet, along with her own father's "red medicine" (phenobarbital), and my father's whiskey. On the phone at dinnertime, she frequently walked her alcoholic cousin through complicated recipes she was too drunk to attempt on her own, while our own dinner sat cooling on the stove.

In my mother's day, there were "nervous breakdowns," not "depressions," and "sedatives" or "tranquilizers" were the only available medication.

For a mother like mine, nothing could be worse than a daughter "off with the fairies," as the Irish say.

I know now that for months there had been fault lines leading up to that first terrible depression, that it hadn't just fallen from the sky, but I didn't know that then, and oh, if only for my mother, how I struggled to be "normal."

When my mother takes me to the pediatrician, he sends us home with a prescription for a thick, yellow liquid that costs $12—a lot of money in 1961—and it's a tranquilizer. My mother takes it out of the Mishkin's Drugs paper bag and stands it on the faux-marble table top. All I can think about while I'm staring at the bottle is that it will offer me relief, that all the worry that's killing me could be that simply cured by thick yellow medicine in a bottle.

But my mother, wearing her gray coat and melon-colored scarf, her nose perpetually leaking, has another idea.

"You can get through this hard life with medicine," she tells me, "or you can get through it by yourself. Now, which will it be?"

I pick up the bottle, and just as she (pill tosser, phenobarb dumper, whiskey drainer) intended, I take the bottle over to the sink, and I pour it away.

I was in and out of depressions for the next thirty-five years.

After my brother, my childhood's deepest love, died of muscular dystrophy, my younger son, Jamie, at age seven, was diagnosed with muscular dystrophy and soon confined to a wheelchair for the remaining fifteen years of his life, where pneumonia was a constant threat. As Jamie got smaller and sicker, my older son, Patrick, grew taller and stronger. At age twelve, Patrick was taller than most full-grown men, and yet Patrick was my life's jewel, and I was obsessed with the fear of losing him. If he was five minutes late coming home from playing hockey, I sunk to my knees on the front lawn, apron fluttering in the wind. I had to put away the walkie-talkies Patrick and Jamie shared, Jamie from inside the house, Patrick from somewhere outside. I couldn't bear hearing Patrick's voice weaken as he went further and further away. My husband, usually the voice of rationality, was rarely home, and I worried about him too. His job took him to dangerous places around the world.

My mother, on the other end of the phone, not only understood my anxiety but listened. She made me promise I wouldn't "succumb to substances," as she put it, and for all of those hard years, my mother was my only medication.

In 1997, at the end of a visit, what she called "a simple over-nighter," my mother suffered a massive heart attack and died on my kitchen floor, before my horrified eyes. So small she was lying there, too small for what she meant to my life. The night that she died, my husband wrapped me in a quilt and held me, like a child, on his lap.

Jamie, who will go first and make room for the other? my mother had written in a sporadically-kept journal that I found after her death. *I hope it is me, dear boy, for losing you would destroy all hope in my heart.*

She went first, and that is a comfort.

There she was, on my kitchen floor, the hope in her exploded heart strangely intact, yet destroyed in mine.

My mother's death changed things with Jamie and me. Although he was hardly able to move, he took care of me. "Did you eat?" he'd ask, rolling up to me in his electric wheelchair. "How did you sleep?' he wanted to know, while I sat on the sofa, staring at him, hardly able to speak, grief covering me in something like cement. After my mother died, I wasn't the mother I had been, and I knew it. I told myself that I would make it up to him. He was doing well, the doctors said, his lungs were no worse than they had been, and his heart, a muscle, was still strong. But it wasn't to be. Not quite a year after my mother died, Jamie caught a cold that became pneumonia. I leaned over his hospital bed as he struggled to breathe and inhaled as much as I could of his pneumonia-drenched breaths. I didn't want to live without them, my mother and my child, my alpha and omega, my beginning and my end.

When Jamie died, I looked up and saw my mother standing by the door. I was holding onto his chest when I felt his spirit leave, brushing across my knuckles like a feather.

For six years I wrote my way through grief with essays, journals, and even a memoir that hardly scratched the surface of what I felt about losing a child and was not the catharsis I expected. When grief started to kill me and I no longer wanted to die, I turned to medication. Though it's no cure, medication lets me put to one side that image of my mother on the kitchen floor and on the other side, Jamie's eyes locked on to mine in the last seconds of his life, just as they were in the first—and move forward.

Learning To Love
My Depression

SHERRY AMATENSTEIN

I am a therapist. When a patient expresses suicidal ideation, I invari- ably preach, "There is *always* another choice."

And I believe that to the bottom of my UGGs.

Still . . .

In my heart of hearts, soul of souls, I don't dismiss that one day I might down a bottle of pills. I have no imminent plans and don't foresee it happening, but I will never say never because never is a scarily long time.

Many times patients have cried in desperation: "How can you help me? You don't understand what depression feels like!"

I tell them: "I don't know exactly what *your* depression feels like. But I do know what it is to lose all hope."

I am eight years old, burrowed in my mother's lap in the shiny kitchen of our gold-carpeted house on Cruger Avenue in the Bronx. I am robotically eating potato chips from a Charles Chips tin. Mom has just finished telling me, for the third time this month, about being thirteen, escaping from the Nazis, and then allowing herself to be captured a few weeks later because she was going to a concentration camp eventually—why not go the same day as her best friend? My father, also a survivor, doesn't contribute his tales of trauma. It's not necessary; his hazel eyes are permanently haunted.

That night, and many nights before and after, in bed, I cry into my fat toy poodle's fur, "Fifi, I don't know how long I want to stay in such a mean world. If I didn't have you, I don't know if I could bear it."

All week I tick off the hours to Sunday night when Mom and I snuggle in her bed. (Dad is in the basement, listening to worn LPs of Madame Butterfly and Figaro.) Fingers intertwined, Mom and I watch Sonny and Cher exchange passive-aggressive banter, cherubic Chastity propped between them. I feel safe, light, whole, but darkness tints the edges of my psyche.

Tomorrow is school. I have friends at P.S. 96, even served as Class President, a position that rotates monthly. But to get there I have to go out in the world—a world that kills and maims and tortures. A world that often feels painful as a kidney stone.

When an optimistic thought burrows its way up my throat, I bite the words back. Voicing, *Adam Sherman will ask me to the school dance* is a "Kina Hora." This Yiddish term roughly translates into: *Who are you to expect fate to dish out something good? Fa—you will suffer now.*

Alas, refusing to believe Adam will ask me out doesn't deliver him to my door. However, not expecting my crush to crush on me is a win for a career depressive: less severe disappointment when the inevitable happens.

In these pre-therapist days, no one tells me that my ALL NEGATIVE ALL THE TIME mindset is a self-fulfilling prophecy.

My internal Debbie Downer, however, doesn't prevent me from being a rah-rah, find-your-happiness coach for others. The pleaser at home (how could I ever want to make trouble for my parents, who have endured the unendurable?), I'm the one classmates gravitate to for advice; the person who stays sober at frat parties so others can be reckless.

I even help my friend Ann sneak her stuff out of her super strict father's house—a plan that backfires when her father comes running after our car, scraping his bare feet on the gravel, crying and screaming, "Don't leave!"

Watching their fierce hug, the high of the reunion clearly making both certain their relationship will automatically be blissful, I experience what I have come to call "sad belly"—a pit deep, dark, and endless. People don't know how not to hurt and disappoint each other, I think. Ann and her dad's negative cycle will likely resume within a week.

I outdo even my expectations of doom and gloom when I marry a psychopath I'll call Bill. There are clear issues during the two-year-long engagement, like the time he pushes me out of a car. At least it was parked and I landed on grass. Yes, depressive positivity! We still made it to our appointment with a wedding photographer.

My parents know nothing of his violent side, though mom (the sharpie who snuck food from under the Nazis' noses to feed her ill friend) has suspicions there is something a bit off.

Still, Bill is Jewish so instead of saying, "Sherilah, you're nineteen. What's the rush?" my parents throw us a lavish wedding at Temple Torah.

I go through with the wedding because, well, Bill keeps saying how much he loves me and needs my help to become a better person. I need to be loved and needed, too, although I have no clue how to make him a better person.

Besides, the fog of depression is such an energy and clarity sapper, I can't fully grasp that I can call off the engagement.

During the three-plus years of our marriage, I lie in bed beside my snoring husband and think: *Is my life over? I'm so lonely I could die.*

On the plus side—yes, honing that positivity!—Bill never again pushes me out of a car. He is more into lying (passing off as his authorship a love poem by ee cummings) and the occasional verbal threat ("I

have Mafia connections. If you leave me I'll have your parents killed").
Okay, the latter boast from the string-bean boy raised in Co-op City
who still lisps when nervous is likely in the lie category as well. Only
I'm too naïve and ready to believe the worst to suss this out.

Despite the sturm und drang of my daily life, I am fortunate. My
depression is rarely *completely* debilitating. When sad belly and poi-
soned mind trap me in what feels like the bottom of a well, I retreat to
my place of salvation.

I am not an observant Jew. Indeed, I loathe the heinous inhu-
manities frequently committed in the name of religion. Thus the altar
I pray at is work, even if said occupation is neither feeding orphans
nor—my dream—being a staff writer at the *New Yorker*. My paycheck
is for editing a soap opera fan magazine called *TV Dawn to Dusk*.

Work saves me when the marriage finally implodes. As I now
tell my patients, it can be the hardest action in the world to leave the
familiar hell for something unknown. So I can't quit Bill until he is
nearly ready to quit me as well.

After enduring a three-day trial separation, with Bill staying at a
neighbor's apartment but stopping by every night for a round of let's-pin-
the-blame-on-Sherry, New Year's Eve morning I fill a plastic bag with
toiletries and take my shaky knees and sad belly into the rest of my life.

Becoming Sadie, Sadie, Divorced Lady without succumbing to
a total breakdown brings on an Oprah aha! moment—Perhaps I've
inherited a smidge of my parents' survivor makeup.

Ensuing crises are further tests of my spirit and spine. A car
accident leaves my ankle an inch from amputation, necessitating
three surgeries and moving back into my childhood home while I am
convalescing. The cherry on top: two weeks after car meets ankle, I
spend my thirty-fifth birthday in bed with Mom in my parents' bed
while dad is exiled to my sister's old bedroom because I'm not trusted
to sleep alone.

Then there's a live-in relationship with a man I'll call Bill No.
2, to whom I lend $10,000 to start a business. At the same time, I
put $60,000 into a startup homeopathic cosmetics endeavor with my

bestie girlfriend. Even I know this is a stupid move, as I recently left a soul-killing magazine job to freelance.

Shocker: Both businesses crash and burn simultaneously. Once again I want to end a love relationship; once again I'm too chicken. Bill No. 2 had given up his apartment to move into mine. He says, "I see your pain and that you wish I wasn't here. So I'll pack up and leave."

His departure, as well as the departure of the savings I meticulously built up after my divorce, creates an emotional tailspin that has me seriously contemplating suicide. But, as I tell my best guy pal, David, "I can't kill myself while my parents are on the planet. "

Instead I dive into work—reinventing myself with a 9 to 5 editing gig at ivillage.com, a part-time job at a magazine, and teaching journalism two nights a week. There is no time to think or feel. When sad belly threatens to upend my equilibrium also known as flatline, I pop an antidepressant and keep on keeping on.

The event precipitating my present incarnation—therapist, healer of souls, soother of my own soul—started on 9/11.

Volunteering at Ground Zero Food Services reawakens a need shared by many children of holocaust survivors: to help others in pain atone for being unable to erase our parents' pain.

Another pull toward more meaningful work is witnessing my parents' slow, aching decline. Mom develops heart troubles and dementia. Alzheimer's turns my opera-loving, *New York Times'*-devouring father into someone who stares and stares at the *New York Post* headline: "West Side Gory" with no comprehension.

David says to me, "Maybe you shouldn't kill yourself while your sister and her daughters are on the planet. "

My mother dies during my second semester at Wurzweiller School of Social Work; dad lasts four more years. His fulltime caregiver calls early one Friday morning—she walked into his bedroom (the one I'd slept in with my mother) and found him forever sleeping.

At the house, I cuddle next to his already icy body and whisper in his ear that I love him. Dad's hazel eyes are open, looking upward, beatifically, at mom.

It is surreal to be a fifty-something orphan. Once again surviving what I've long dreaded (can't kill myself while my sister and nieces are still around!) schools me in acknowledging and accessing my own strength.

By then I am seeing patients, many whose problems make mine look like a skinned knee at summer camp.

A millennial I'll call Sam whose father committed suicide asks at one session, "Dad was so weak I hate him, but how can I keep going with this horrible pain?"

I answer, "What he did is never something you're going to get over. But last week you laughed and talked about a great date you'd gone on. Pain isn't a constant. There's an ebb and flow. Looking out a train window there can be a gorgeous view you want to hold on to but darn, you whizz past it. Then there's an ugly sight out the window you don't want to see. The train whizzes past that too."

He takes a Kleenex from the ever-present tissue box on the sienna oak table between us and wipes his eyes. "If I'm happy sometimes, am I disloyal to my dad? When I feel good I tell myself I'm a horrible person."

I stifle a gasp. Sam's question sends a stream of light into the heart of my sad belly. I say to my patient and myself, "First off, every time you attack yourself, you dig that negativity deeper. It's emotional junk food; no nutrients. Second, you honor your parents' lives when you build something good and nourishing for yourself."

Sam reaches for another tissue, "That makes sense but how do I deal with my depression when it gets so intense?"

The question lingers in the air. I say, "Feel it here in the room with me. I can handle it. What is the pain telling you? Ask it questions. What can it teach you?"

The two of us lock eyes. He breathes slowly and I think about the Tibetan practice of Tonglen where one internalizes another's pain and sends back joy.

Sam says after some silent seconds, "I feel better. I guess running from depression doesn't make it go away. It just goes underground."

"Yes, life is a kaleidoscope. To live fully we have to embrace all the colors."

My patient leaves the session looking less haunted.

I feel heavy but also light. I've earned my depression. It still sometimes weighs me down. But it's a grounding weight rather than a bottomless pit of sad belly. I'd rather dance with my demons than drown in them.

One day I may commit suicide. But I doubt it. There is always another choice.

Skirting the Abyss

BARBARA ABERCROMBIE

When I was eight years old, I threatened to throw myself off my bedroom balcony into the backyard where my parents were gardening. They were nonchalant about this, which was unlike them. I was used to a lot of drama in my family—my mother's moods, my father's temper—but as I leaned over the balcony rail, they were calm about the possibility of my leaping off into thin air. I could envision my crumbled body below. The attention that would be paid. How sorry they'd be for ignoring me. The tears they'd cry. "Snap out of it," my mother called up to me.

I was a strange child, scrawny, with white blond hair, both shy and a show-off. All I wanted to do was to grow up so I could be in charge. I wanted to be an actress. I wanted to write stories. My favorite game was to make drawings of people, cut them out, then turn our living room into a town and act out dramas with my paper people.

Years later when I was in my early twenties, I attempted to throw myself off the balcony for real. However, I did it in the safest way possible: I took twelve over-the-counter Sleep-Eaze pills, then called a friend who lived around the corner. She came immediately and called a doctor. The doctor, who astonishingly made a midnight house call, was less than sympathetic. He said he found the paintings on my walls (my new hobby) disturbing and suggested that the looming black figures influenced by Munch might be my family members.

My friends rallied around me. The next day, I moved briefly into a friend's apartment so I wouldn't be alone. This was a friend who had made her own suicide attempt, one that was far better planned and more serious than mine. She had collected and then taped prescription sleeping pills behind photographs and artwork in her apartment, but I'd saved her life by dropping in on her unexpectedly shortly after she had un-taped and swallowed all the pills. And now it was her turn. She made sure I ate proper meals, and every day she'd see me off in a taxi as I went to visit my new shrink. All dressed up, I'd sail down to 62nd Street and Park, and to this day I can't remember one word that doctor said to me. All I remember is how fragile I felt, how important it was to dress carefully for my session; I remember that my head was buzzy and the feeling of being near the edge of a cliff—how easy it would be to fall over into an abyss and go completely nuts.

I held my breath a lot.

Here's what was really nuts: I was a working actress in New York, getting jobs on television and Broadway. It was the 1960s. I was healthy, I was pretty, and I had friends and family. But I was depressed and the word depression wasn't used or discussed in those days. I'm not even sure what set off my failed suicide. A boyfriend had left? Which one? Or was I simply sad? My feelings didn't make sense.

When I look back, I think of gray waves of loneliness, a kind of agoraphobia that would overtake me. I lived alone. I remember evenings in my apartment on East 90th Street, hearing people coming home from work, doors slamming, voices calling to each other. When I had an acting job, which actually was quite often—often enough to support myself—things were okay. I felt joy and excitement. When you're in a play you have a family, a posse, but then the play closes and you start from scratch again. Find a new job, a new play, a new family of friends—support, a new meaning to your life.

When I think of that depression, I think of paralysis. Which is odd, because I also took so much action in those days. I had dropped out of college at nineteen to make daily rounds as an actress, went to casting calls, never giving up until I finally got an agent and steady work. I was out there; I was brave.

But then this other thing—sadness, loneliness, and fear crept in like fog.

Depression felt like failure, a horrible character flaw rising up that had to be kept secret. I couldn't "snap out of it" on demand. It didn't make sense, yet it felt natural; many of my friends were in the same boat. I hung out with a lot of depressed people—not only my friend with the taped prescription pills, but a boyfriend who kept hitching rides on freight trains to get away from his life, and a friend who swore he had these mood swings because his mother threw him on the floor as a baby. In the late fifties and early sixties we all wanted to be cool, we wanted to be like James Dean who had died a few years earlier. We smoked endless cigarettes, we slouched, we drank scotch, we read depressed French intellectuals, and took Dexadrine pills— which we didn't really think of as a drug, just a little something to keep us awake.

What I finally learned was that the worst thing about depression is that it doesn't make sense, you can have it all and still feel hollowed out; still feel as if your mother threw you on the floor as a baby.

There was one more time in my life when I felt I could fall over the edge, into an abyss. I was married by then, with two babies. I remember standing in the shower instructing myself to breathe. I had given birth two months earlier, had given birth in fact twice in the same year; my girls were born eleven months apart. I adored my babies, and I was thrilled to have them. I don't think I had postpartum depression, but my hormones must have been on overdrive, and then a close friend's little boy died of an infection—suddenly, on his third birthday. He was sick, they took him to the hospital, and then he was dead. When he died, nothing made sense for a long time. Life was terrifying and dangerous. I was twenty-seven years old. My husband was in the Navy and got orders to move from Washington, D.C., where we had lived for two years, to Vallejo, California. We moved. We lived in a small apartment. All my energy went into trying to appear normal and taking care of my two babies who were both in diapers, one not yet walking. I was three thousand miles from my family and friends.

We had a small sports car, an Austin Healey, and I was afraid to drive it. Years went by on a roller coaster of emotions, the highs and lows of what I considered normal life. If my husband ignored me, I'd make dramatic announcements about leaving. We'd have huge fights, followed by lovely make-ups with sex and bouquets of flowers. We adored our girls, our large extended family, our dogs and cats. Though moody, my husband was the most honest and trustworthy person I knew. We fought a lot, but I was sure this was healthy. Things got aired out.

When I turned fifty, my mother and I were going through a difficult patch, not speaking. She lived in New York, and I was in California. When my father dragged her to the phone to wish me a happy birthday, she said, "Well, happy fiftieth. Maybe now you'll grow up."

I had believed that if my husband were ever unfaithful to me, broke the trust I had in him, I'd never again be able to trust anything in life, that I'd go right over that edge into the abyss I had managed to avoid for all these years. But when I did discover his infidelity, I went over a different edge—into fury. No woman on this planet was ever angrier than I was, dumped at age fifty-one for a younger woman. This was not some gray paralysis of angst: there was absolutely no slouching around in despair. If it's true that depression is anger turned inward, I was home free. I knew exactly who my target was, and it wasn't me.

Granted, I had spent a few previous years moping, weeping, and trying to get my husband into therapy, realizing I was in the middle of a marital car crash—but I hadn't admitted to myself that my marriage could really ever end, because there was only one way to end it, infidelity: which of course he'd never do. I simply hadn't realized how desperate he was to get out of our marriage.

Though crying a lot, I sprang into manic action. I hired a lawyer, bought a house of my own, and made plans to remodel it. I upped my teaching schedule because I now had to support myself, and found a therapist. I was a mess, but I was okay. I ran six miles every morning, I took tai chi classes, I joined a gym, I had three part-time teaching jobs, I filled page after page of my journal with rants and threats and regret. But I never got stuck. I ran circles around the abyss.

When my best male friend, R, who would become my second husband seven years later, took me out to dinner, I could not get to the entrée without crying. R had white handkerchiefs and would hand one to me as I sobbed over the treachery, the pain of being abandoned at age fifty-one! Twenty-six years of marriage and he had fallen for a younger woman with big tits and no brain! All that love and history and he had thrown it away! Tears falling into my wine glass, other diners averting their eyes, my nose running, R would just hand me another white handkerchief.

And then weirdly, six months later, my about-to-be ex-husband asked me out on a date. Equally weirdly, I said sure, I'd go out to dinner with him. "For God's sake don't have anything to drink," said my friend Nicki. "Excuse yourself and call me if you start to get emotional."

It was the first time he'd seen my house. He hugged me and commented on how skinny I felt. I resisted all the snarky responses that sprang to mind. *Yeah, but tiny tits.* I wondered what had happened to the other woman. At dinner we didn't discuss her or our separation. We talked about our kids. My anger had softened. Maybe we just needed space, some air in our marriage. During that dinner, I realized I was still in love with him.

A few weeks later, we drove to see old friends in San Diego. It was December. I was thinking maybe we'd work through all this. We spent the day with friends we'd known for years; we were comfortable with them, and were loved by them. It felt like we were moving back into our real life.

Driving home to L.A. that evening I asked him, "What are you doing New Year's Eve?"

"Oh, you know me," he said.

I looked at his familiar, handsome face illuminated by passing headlights. "Frankly, I'm not sure I do," I said.

"I've never liked New Year's Eve."

This was true. He was always a pill about celebrating. "We can just hang out," I said. "Watch movies." Silence. The air had shifted. Something was up. "Okay?"

"No, not New Year's Eve," he said.

We were off the freeway now, headed toward my house. There was an elephant in this little sports car. And I suddenly knew the elephant's name, the woman with the big tits. My husband's date for New Year's Eve, "She's coming to L.A.?"

Never forthcoming in the best of times, he was now silent.

"No, no, no!" I started to yell and then went totally out of control, sobbing as I beat on the dashboard of the Austin Healey, the car we had owned for twenty-six years, that I had been afraid to drive when we lived in Vallejo and our girls were babies. A 1964 green Austin Healey British racing car. The top of my head was about to blow off. If I'd had a gun I'd have blown off the top of *his* head.

Later, my therapist said my fantasies of shooting him or running over him or crashing my car into his or tearing his car apart with my bare hands were perfectly healthy as long as I didn't act on them. Every Tuesday afternoon I'd sit in her office and talk and talk.

About my anger. My pain. My parents. My past. My present. The rage. And about getting off the emotional roller-coaster of my failed marriage.

My grief over the loss of my marriage came in waves during that first year, and just when I thought I'd recovered I'd do something like go to the market to buy groceries and be flattened by memory and loss. C.S. Lewis wrote of being surprised that grief felt like fear, and that was part of it too; I was scared. But I knew there was a reason for the grief; it made sense. I had loved this person and shared my life with him for over a quarter of a century. I'd had children with him, made his family my family, and that's why this loss hurt so deeply. I was neither crazy nor self-indulgent. I had a right to be angry, to grieve.

My anger was such that it eventually healed me.

Weirdly, it was divorce that finally "snapped me out of it." Though I hated to acknowledge that my mother had been right, I finally grew up. The abyss was abandonment and loneliness, and I got through it. And when my father died, my mother got through it too and came to live in California. We became friends.

Terrible things happen—they go on happening all your life. But here's what I discovered: anguish, unhappiness, sadness, fear, loneliness, and grief are not the same as depression. It can all hurt as much as depression, but you are not paralyzed. You keep breathing. And the lovely surprise of growing older is that most of us get happier. If you're lucky and have decent health, friends, a roof over your head, food on the table, and something you love to get up and do every day—you calm down. You no longer want to throw yourself off a balcony.

God's Perfect Child

PATTI LINSKY

"Give him a banana."

Oh, God, here we go again.

I was driving the forty-five minutes from North Miami Beach to Boynton Beach so my parents could meet my one-year-old son, who sat quietly in his car seat for forty of those forty-five minutes completely content, and then just before we arrived, he totally lost it. Maybe he was picking up on the visit that was about to ensue. In those four words suggested by my mother, Blanche (may she rest in peace), I understood why I never learned to deal with my feelings.

Fix it with food.

Fix the never-ending emptiness within my being with *anything* that would cover it up. In my case, it was Fritos with onion dip, chocolate anything, and let's not forget the Three V's: Vicodin, Vodka, and Valium.

In those four words, it became crystal clear how her inability to deal with life, which was not an easy life, was transferred to me. And oh, how I blamed her for my inability to cope. Right up until her death in 2003, when I realized that she was simply passing down what she knew, nothing more, nothing less.

And that I had to forgive her as well as my grandmother, Sadie, for what they could not teach.

What my Mom did imbue within me was her love of music and her God-given talents. Beautiful singer, woman, spirit. She even received a full scholarship to La Scala Opera House, but her parents didn't allow her to go. Imagine, at seventeen years of age, the devastation she must have felt . . . as if she wasn't good enough, wasn't chosen by her own parents to fly and soar and achieve her greatness as was destined. Instead, she put all of her unfulfilled dreams and hopes and aspirations into me.

You see, I sing. I am blessed with an ability to hold pitch, interpret, touch, and inspire. All of the things she wasn't allowed to do. I inherited my talents from her side of the family. Heifetz was Blanche's maiden name (think Jascha Heifetz, the violinist). She lived vicariously through me, took credit for my talents, basically made me crazy.

I was God's Perfect Child. The part that Blanche left out was "with your imperfections." For if I had been allowed to embrace my imperfections and my vulnerabilities, instead of putting on the good front for appearances sake, my life would have been completely different. Mom was the one with the grand idea to move from South Miami to West Palm Beach, Florida, because the return address would look good on the envelope. There was tremendous pressure, self-inflicted pressure, to be the perfect girl, woman, wife, and professional. I had the need to please from a very early age. For as long as I can remember, I was striving for acceptance, to be noticed and loved and liked. I saw my face in the faces of others. Reacting to how someone talked to me, morphing into whatever they needed me to be, completely devoid of my own voice.

Perhaps it was because when I was younger, I was abused by my father. Not forever, but long enough to lose trust in myself and to look for Daddy in all the wrong places. My self-esteem was dependent upon any and everything except the truth.

It's so interesting looking back upon that time and how it played such a huge part in my development, or lack thereof. I am amazed that I am even alive to write this. I have had my share of close calls with death. Certainly I have experienced many emotional deaths: loss of self, loss of parents who weren't emotionally available, loss of integrity, dignity, and humility. Loss of being comfortable with who I was, feelings and knowledge of not being enough, acting out in a myriad of ways to find the balance within.

The truth is, there was no balance. I thought I would find my equilibrium as a wife, so I did what any nice Jewish girl would do—I married a rabbi, getting married right out of college to a man of stature in the community who gave me everything I thought I needed to be complete. I had a place of honor in the community, a new home on the West Coast (which was just far enough away from my mother), and became a Stepford Wife in the truest sense: appropriate, great cook, devoted wife, and cocaine addict. My marriage lasted two years and nine months. The reason it fell apart was because of a moment of consciousness with which I was graced one morning after the High Holy Days. We had decided to start a family. You know how sometimes you get these flashes of scenes within your mind, each lasting about a second? Well, mine went something like this:

> *We're going to try to get pregnant.*
> *I'm not sure that I want this . . .*
> *But he does, so we should.*
> *I don't think I'm going to be with him forever.*
> *So I'll be a single parent; my mom did it, and it wasn't so bad.*
> (Tires Screeching)
> *Wait a minute, being a single mom was really difficult. How can I knowingly do this when deep down I am sure I won't be married to him for the long haul?*

Then the discussion ensued.

Him: "When do you think you might be ready to have a child?"

Me: "I don't know if I ever will be."

By the end of the week I was out of the house. That was the beginning of the end of the beginning.

With the liberation of again being single, there was this gnawing feeling of incredible loneliness. For so many years I didn't know who I was. Yet, by the time I was in my late twenties, I had established myself as a cantor in a wonderful temple, leading the congregation in prayer and song, with warmth and enthusiasm that I truly believed to be authentic. I got remarried to a wonderful man. People would say to me, "I don't know how you do it all." Loving wife, mother of two beautiful children, working full time, singing all over the country, maintaining the illusion of Ms. Have It All Together.

If they only knew.

If they only knew how desperately—desperately—I was on the hamster wheel of wanting to be liked/loved/accepted/acknowledged.

The self-imposed prison of perfection was interminable. I felt like a pressure cooker ready to explode. It was at this time that God interceded and gave me the first of a series of what I now know to be gifts, namely of being in a car accident in 1996. "Slow down," God was saying. And I did. It stopped me in my tracks, giving me whiplash and a great excuse to begin my long waltz with painkillers—which I doubt God intended, but there you go. We mortals are a difficult bunch. They became my favorite food group, my best friend, my answer to not feeling anything at all

At first, it was a legitimate, prescribed cocktail to alleviate the excruciating pain I was in due to the accident. Over time, though, the medicine (taken as directed), became the drugs (which are not prescribed). It was a fine line, and I knew just how to finesse it to more or less function in my world. Vicodin, valium, and a plethora of other pills became a staple in my life. I became a functioning drug addict. It was also at this time, over a two-year period, that I experienced the deaths of four of the people closest to me. My best friend, Rikki, died of cancer. Soon after that, my stepfather passed away. Within the next year, I lost my mom and my stepmother, Ann, and it all became too much. The grief, anger, abandonment, and profound sadness was too much to bear. The pills became a lifeline to cope with the emptiness I felt.

One would think, I suppose, that it would be a temporary condition, to just take the edge off until things got better and life got more manageable. That never happened. I became a liar and led a double life, which of course, was coupled with tremendous shame. How could I, in good conscience, be a role model to my community, all the while living in the fog of addiction, and ultimately, descending into the disease of alcoholism?

Yes, I am an alcoholic. I cannot have one drink. It will lead to my physical death, and of this I am sure. It becomes a vicious cycle. The unmanageability of life, the shame of failure, the trying to get it right, only to find that the answers don't come. With each failure comes the desire to numb that reinforcement of feeling, as if I am never enough. Losing sight of what needs to happen rather than being more than alright with any progress at all . . . the futility was constant and too much to bear. Fortunately, even with coming close to death more than once, it wasn't my time yet.

But I sure came close.

We were having a garage sale. I was organized, ready, and willing to give it my all. The kids and our nanny and some friends helped with the meticulous set up, and I took my "medicine" so I would have energy and calm and sell everything.

I was all that.

Yes, I was.

I was in complete control.

Until I went back into the house for a minute and forgot that I had taken the meds. I proceeded to take a second helping, and instead of drinking apple juice to swallow the pills, I took a large swig of chardonnay instead: God's Intervention No. 2.

I never returned to the garage sale. Our nanny found me slumped over the computer table, unresponsive. She tried to walk me around but I was totally out of it, and who wouldn't be during an overdose? Now picture this if you will: two children, ages eight and twelve at the time, watching the chaos and panic and not knowing how or if their world would ever be the same. My son was asked to call 911 as my daughter held tight to our nanny, and then they watched as the paramedics wheeled me away to the ambulance. The paramedic, of course, had to ask the question that haunts me to this day: "Ma'am, is this what you want? Do you want your children to be taken away from you because of what you did?" I hated him for that. And I hated myself more. My last memory was of my children—their innocence in that moment being stripped away, staring out the window, watching me go, and saying to me, "Mommy, please don't die."

Mommy.

Please.

Don't.

Die.

I have permanently reserved those words and that moment as the devastating marker of my alcoholic, drug-addicted bottom.

To this day, tears come to my eyes just thinking about it, what I did to my family, how selfish and entrenched with my disease I was, the disease that comes between the love of a mother and her children, a husband and a wife.

Thankfully, I went into recovery and remained sober. But there was still a gaping hole within me, one that I could not fill.

It was on the way to a Bar Mitzvah about ten months later that I began crying and could not stop. *Could not stop.* I called my Rabbi from the car and told him that I thought I was losing my mind, and that I needed to talk to him when I got to temple. Thank God he is who he is: compassionate and understanding, and willing to give me space and support as I was beginning to go down the road of a nervous breakdown.

Three days later I put myself in rehab.

For thirty-one days I was in rehab. I turned fifty on Mother's Day while I was there. It was the best birthday of my life. You may be shaking your head at this point wondering how in the world someone might say that, but truly, it was. I was grateful that my husband and two children came to visit me, as difficult as it must have been for them. My heart was filled beyond words at this strange dichotomy, with the surrealism of it all. But deep down I knew that I was in the right place to heal the wounds and incompletion that had permeated my soul for a lifetime.

And of course, there were two cakes—one for the birthday and one for Mother's Day—so that helped a little. It was not devoid of pain or shame. However, I am eternally grateful for the courage it took for them to make the trip to tell me that they loved me. I was actually beginning to even love myself again.

I wrote and journaled and cried. I sobbed and detoxed and meditated. And I talked about the crux of my issues—the deep, horrible, painful feeling that I'm not enough. Slowly, I began to piece together the dysfunctional pieces of the puzzle that was my life. I started seeing how much drama I infused into every fiber of my being, trying to be more than okay, wishing I was who everyone thought I was.

In rehab I came to terms for the very first time with my father's abuse. Things started to make sense. I realized that my inability to speak up for what I needed and wanted, unapologetically, stemmed from my shame. It wasn't until a couple of years later that I truly came to terms with the preciousness of life and the importance of voicing my needs.

Cue God Intervention no. 3.

It was the summer of 2009 and I was experiencing abdominal pain and flu-like symptoms. I decided to see my doctor, who ordered a CT scan, which found a stone in my bile duct. We decided to take care of this with a minimally invasive endoscopy after the High Holidays. I sang my heart out, asking God to break me open so that I could inspire our congregation to feel the Divine within each of them. Words of praise and thankfulness for my gift were overflowing. My ego soared. I had succeeded. I was loved and praised and made a difference in the lives of so many.

What a perfect time to get the procedure.

What was supposed to be a two-hour outpatient experience led to a three-week stay in the hospital. During the endoscopy, my pancreas was nicked, sending me into sepsis and pancreatitis. Two days later I had an open surgery to save my life. Awakening in ICU with twenty-six staples in my stomach, I knew that something went horribly wrong. And yet, I knew nothing. I was in shock, terrified, higher than a kite on morphine, and completely at a loss for words.

And my belief in God had vanished. Completely vanished.

You see, in life, I had always had a close relationship with God (or whatever you may wish to call something larger than yourself). Because I came so very close to meeting God in death, I couldn't find God's presence and bigger plan in this mystery that was unfolding with my body. To even entertain the notion that God was with me the entire time, guiding and sustaining me until I arrived at my next chapter's destination was unthinkable. I wasn't able to understand this until several years after the operation and hospital stay, which would forever change and affect my life and its path.

My recovery from surgery was close to four months. When I tried to go back to work as temple cantor, I simply couldn't muster up the energy and strength required for the position. It would have meant sacrificing my family for my temple community, and due to my disease, I had done that for too long. It was time to retire, and trust in the things that I could not see.

I had been a cantor for thirty years. It was in many ways my identity, or so I thought. What I could not fathom was what I would do for the next chapter of my life. It made me crazy to be dependent upon anyone. After all, I was God's Perfect Child and could and would not ever want to be in the position for asking for help, from anyone, ever.

The vulnerability and fear that ensued were like nothing I had ever experienced. The pills beckoned on a daily basis for a very long time—anything to aid in not feeling. But I knew there had to be a greater purpose in the operation gone horribly wrong.

By the grace of God I found the answer.

It was in the form of a four-month women's empowerment workshop. We met one Sunday a month, for five hours—ten women who were searching for their passion, their direction, and their purpose.

We were taught by two gifted women who became extraordinary life coaches, Michelle Bauman and Carolyn Freyer-Jones, who had embarked upon their own journeys. We listened to one another, gave feedback when asked, did bucket lists. It was there that I found the courage to tell my story in the format of a one-woman show, *Altar EGO*. It is brutally honest and funny and human and I am so proud of it. In some ways, God knew that this was supposed to be a part of the journey I am on. I sing and tell stories about the things we do to fill us up . . . make us feel supposedly whole, be it with relationships to food, people, religion, addictions, little games on our phones, etc. But truly, the play is about the journey back to myself and feeling that I am enough. And it's something I believe I was meant to share to inspire others to find their own second chances and forgiveness.

We all have something.

We are imperfectly perfect.

I had to accept that, and that I am here for a reason. The addictions and pain and severe crippling depression I have experienced are what have made me the woman I am today. If I can help just one person know that they are not alone in their struggle, that second chances are possible and mistakes are just illusions, then the journey has been more than worth it.

Irish Wake-up Call

KITTY SHEEHAN

"The Irish cannot be psychoanalyzed, because they're chronically unable to tell the truth about unfortunate matters."

Frank McCourt's audience howled when he said this at a 1998 lecture in Minneapolis. I laughed along with them. I knew it was true and was happy to make it a joke.

After McCourt's rollicking talk, I waited in line for him to sign my copy of *Angela's Ashes*, the Pulitzer-Prize winning account of his Irish childhood in the slums of Limerick, featuring his complicated and somewhat ruthless mother, Angela Sheehan McCourt.

"I'm a Sheehan," I told him when I reached his table. "My grandmother came from Ballyporeen." He responded by bowing his head and making the sign of the cross. Once again I laughed, silently congratulating myself upon sharing a joke with Frank McCourt.

"We should find out if they're pourin' the Bushmills nearby," he concluded, as he handed me my book.

The signed copy was a gift for my mother, Betty. When she read it, she laughed out loud at almost every page, read passages to me, and used phrases from the book like, "Oh your bladder's all up in your eye" when they fit the occasion. I'd never seen her enjoy a book more.

"It explains everything about Tom's family, Sheehans or not," she told friends when describing the book.

Tom, my father, didn't agree. He didn't believe a word of the book and found no humor in it. And he usually found humor in anything. His parents, Thomas Sheehan and Bridget Cull, were sent to America from Ireland as teenagers and never saw their own parents again. He'd grown up hearing stories of the crushing poverty they'd left behind, and to him there was nothing funny to be said about it. Many of McCourt's countrymen back in Ireland shared these views.

This made the whole thing even funnier to my mother, whose parents, Lewis and Florence, were English, Scottish, and Irish. You had to go back a long way to find their roots, and no one had really bothered. Both were born in Iowa.

So, we have a bittersweet Irish childhood memoir that may or may not be true, but certainly portrays its author as a victim of indifferent parents: a mother too busy gossiping and doing unsavory things to care about her children, and a father who can't hold a job, spending every cent he finds on alcohol.

A book about the Irish and their alcohol. But not a word in it about any of these people being *depressed*.

My mother finds it hilarious. My father declares it all a lie.

Denial. Not just a river in Egypt, to paraphrase Stuart Smalley.

When *Angela's Ashes* was published in 1996, my parents had been married for forty-three years. She was an alcoholic; he was depressed. Neither would acknowledge either. To the outside world, both were funny, smart people.

They were the perfect guides for teaching me how to mask pain and transform it into depression.

Almost as soon as they'd met in 1950, a kind of mayhem began: a succession of sudden deaths in their families.

The first was my father's older brother, Edward "Red," on July 26,

1950, at age thirty-two. He was a strapping athletic hero from New Haven, the most talented of the trio of Sheehan brothers. My father was playing ball in Iowa, at age twenty-eight, when he learned of his adored brother's unexpected death from a brain aneurysm. I think it was an aneurysm. I'm not sure. No one has ever really explained it to me. His brother left behind three sons and a wife, all in Connecticut. My father had very little contact with any of them after the funeral. I'm not sure why.

My parents were married in Nevada, Iowa, my mother's home-town, on October 10, 1953. Six days later, my father's father died in New Haven without warning, from a heart attack. I think it was a heart attack. I'm not sure. No one discussed it.

Two years later, in 1955, my mother's only sister, Janice, died at age twenty-eight. She'd been born with a "heart condition" and that's what eventually killed her. I only knew her as the pretty woman in the burgundy organza dress, standing beside my mother in wedding pictures, with a softer, somehow more refined smile.

Janice was married to a sweet man named Stan. Stan had given my mother the two place settings of wedding china he and Janice had received, a pattern called Westvale by Syracuse, still in their boxes and tissue paper. My mother later gave them to me, along with the two place settings of her own china she'd received, Olympia by Lenox, also still in boxes from the same store. She offered no explanation.

My brother Dan was born on December 26, 1955. He was named after my father's favorite song, Danny Boy. His middle name was Edward, after Red. My parents adored him. He was sick with fevers and odd viruses almost from day one. I came along May 1, 1957. I was named Ann Marie. Six months later, my mother decided I somehow wasn't an "Ann" and had my name legally changed to Kathleen Ann Marie. The plan was to call me Katie, but Dan pronounced it Kitty, and that's what stuck.

My brother and I had fun together, playing outside with neigh-borhood kids, riding bikes, and hanging out with the adults who came to our house often for parties. We were always there for the beginning of the parties, as the men and women smoked and drank and told stories, making each other scream with laughter. My parents often took us with them on weekends when they went to their favorite bars, the Amvets, the Lincoln Club, and the Country Club.

Friday night, July 10, 1964, we were all at the Country Club when my mother got a phone call from her brother saying she needed to come to Nevada immediately. Her father, Lewis, had a heart attack at home. He died instantly. I think. I was seven. My brother and I didn't go with our mother that night. She was crying when she hugged us goodbye in the front yard, still in her purple summer party dress and dangling gold earrings. I'd never seen her cry before.

My grandfather chain-smoked and gambled, losing huge sums of money more than once. He never drank. He gave me dice every time I saw him, which I put in my pockets and then into my white leather jewelry box with the twirling ballerina inside. He was a livestock auctioneer and wore a grey fedora all day. He delivered pigs to farmers in the back seat of his Cadillac. No wonder he had a heart attack at age sixty-one.

At home, my mother was angry or sad most of the time after my grandfather died.

A year later, on October 12, 1965, my father's mother, Bridget Cull Sheehan, died at age seventy-five from cancer. I have no idea what kind. It wasn't discussed. My father flew alone to New Haven for his mother's funeral. He brought me back little salt and pepper shakers from the airplane and a board game of the New York World's Fair. The trip for his mother's funeral was the last time my father went home to New Haven. I don't know why.

After that, he spent many nights sitting alone at our kitchen table with a beer, listening to big band music on the radio.

So, by the time my parents were forty-three and thirty-eight, each had lost an idolized sibling, both their fathers, and one mother. Since no one was talking about it, I still knew nothing of death, funerals, grief, or why the adults in my house didn't say much to each other anymore.

We sailed along this way for the next twenty years. Denial is a powerful wind.

Outside our house, my parents were the life of every party. When I was old enough, I was too. In Iowa, you're old enough to drink whenever you decide you are. For me, that was eighth grade. Alcohol was readily available in most of my friends' houses. Our parents didn't know we drank until we were in high school. The legal age was eighteen then, and since I'd had a few years experience, I took my place at the bar beside my elders fairly easily.

My parents were only in good moods if they were drinking. When my mother wasn't drinking, she was exasperated with life. I drove her nuts with my adolescent bouts of brooding, sassing, and knowing it all. My father drove her nuts, and she let him know it. The only time she was nice to him was when they were out.

In 1977, my brother Dan was diagnosed with cancer. I was twenty. Within a year, on July 27, 1978, he was dead. The first thing my mother said after he died was, "He never saw me cry." Earlier, she had bolted when the priest came in to perform last rites, saying, "Well, I'm not watching this." My father and I were left to witness my brother's last sacrament.

This death I *can* tell you all about. I was there. I made all the phone calls to my parent's bosses and friends that night, telling them what had happened. I planned his funeral because my parents could not.

I don't know how my parents felt about losing their young son to cancer before he had a chance to become anything but their son. I couldn't bear to make them sadder by asking them about it. The silence flooded every corner of our house: the empty chair at the dinner table, his boyhood bedroom, my girlhood bedroom which was used as his sickroom, the couch he'd spent most of the summer on, covered with a flannel hospital blanket, not talking. All the places he no longer occupied were wrapped in a cottony web of quiet sadness and isolation. I fled back to Iowa City for my senior year of college at the end of August.

As soon as I could, I filled the emptiness with another male, one I married. I was desperate to bring gaiety back into our family. That was the main qualification for a husband, to make me laugh. And even more importantly, to make my parents laugh. For a while, this plan worked.

One day, my father decided to stop drinking. He didn't talk to anyone about it. He just did it. As he'd gotten older, he wasn't that much of a drinker anyway. My mother had surpassed him long ago as the real drinker in the family. I was a close second. I knew he was hoping his sobriety would magically make my mother stop drinking. It didn't.

Her drinking became my problem. I hosted an intervention at their house. After the few people who were brave enough finished speaking, she told us all to get the hell out unless we wanted to stay for a drink. We left and went to a bar to debrief.

She didn't speak to me for a couple months, and when we spoke again it was as if nothing had happened.

My father's anxiety began to eat him up. It presented as a kind of dementia, and that's how my mother treated it. He began repeating himself incessantly, asking the same questions over and over. He didn't want to leave the house. He couldn't focus on a book long enough to read a page. None of us mentioned the possible reasons for his anxiety.

Eventually, predictably, but entirely out of keeping with family tradition, I found myself single and sober in a therapist's office for the first time. Both of my parents were now dead.

As I described my parents to her, the therapist listened intently.

"We're Irish," I began, with a wry smile. "So, you know, no one talks about anything. You know, whatever bad can happen, will happen. We whistle in the dark, as my father always said. We expect the worst, so when it comes, we're not surprised. Nothing surprised her, my mother always said. We panic if we have nothing to worry about. My family is the ultimate contradiction, like all Irish families. Creative and colorful, and wildly self-destructive. My father used humor to shield his pain. My mother's weapon was booze, with a chaser of anger."

I went on, trying to get her to laugh.

"I mean, my mother's modus operandi was to not talk about things, laugh them off if pressed, drink, and deny," I explained.

I didn't add that this was also my former personal roadmap.

"Do you realize a lot of what you're describing fits under the heading of depression?" the therapist asked me.

"Yes," I ventured.

And with that *yes*, I changed the course of the rest of my life. I had a name for my family's affliction of the mind and heart: depression.

I no longer wish someone had told me about depression sooner in my life. I cherish the wisdom gained from learning how hard it is to pin it down. It's stealthy. It can spend years patiently sneaking up on you. Then it may hide itself in a bottle. It doesn't care how long it has to hang around; it waits. If you ignore it, it busies itself by spreading its web into more corners of your life, blotting out light as it goes.

But you can get a broom and knock it down. If no one has helped you name this feeling, say it to yourself. It's okay. There is help available, so much help. Tell someone, and *boom*, just like that, you aren't alone, which can be a miracle.

You can still be the funny, self-deprecating life of the party. But now you have depression to use as material. The possibilities are endless.

Back to the china I inherited from my mother and my aunt. Last year, I searched the Internet, bought additional sets of each, and combined it all to make enough place settings for eight. I took the beautiful cream dishes with silver rims out of their boxes and threw the boxes away. I washed and dried each piece carefully. I set a sparkling table. I lit two candles, and sat down with my husband and friends to use those beautiful objects, the ones that had been stored away for more than fifty years, for the first time.

The Dialectics of Suicide

SAMANTHA WHITE

My mother's hobbies were running away from home, cutting her wrists, and overdosing on pills and booze.

The first time I called an ambulance for her, I was seven years old.

By the time I decided to take myself out, I'd had lots of time to study her and her failed techniques.

I was pretty sure I knew how to do it right.

It was my twenty-ninth summer. I had been in and out of depression and manic episodes for as long as I could remember. As a teenager, I didn't have the words "depression" or "manic," but I knew that the extreme highs and lows I was experiencing were different than the adolescent angst my friends were going through.

What was happening inside of me was different.

After periods of insomnia and fiery creativity, my biochemistry would shift; everything slowed. I wanted to sleep forever. I snarled and threw things at anyone who tried to rouse me. I couldn't hide the sleeping from my aunt and uncle, who cared for me when my mother was "away," but no one seemed to notice the times when I was awake for weeks. I shifted from feeling like a light, creative genius to being weighted down by shame and self-disgust. I was paralyzed by the certainty that nothing about me was good enough and never would be. There seemed to be no point to anything, especially my life.

The most terrifying aspect of these episodes was how much I recognized my mother. I was terrified by the vivid stories of what would be done to me if I ended up in the state mental hospital like she did. She was blank and distant when she came home after undergoing electro shock. The doctors said it would help "calm her". It seemed to erase her. I looked at my mother and saw an ugly future. I kept silent.

By my mid twenties, the manic episodes had almost disappeared and I was left with just the lows. I referred to it as "being in the cave." Everything went dark. The depression that owned me the summer I tried to kill myself was long and deep. There were so many days I could not function that I had used up both my sick time and vacation time at work. People would say, "Hope you're feeling better," when I returned from having "the flu" again or, "Did you have a nice time?" when I used my vacation days. I'd reply affirmatively that I was all better and say that I spent my vacation "relaxing at home."

I didn't have the energy to invent a better imaginary vacation. How could I explain that I spent my time off trying to muster enough will and focus to wash my hair? Or that I had clean clothes when I returned to work because I had lived and slept in the same ones all week?

People didn't talk about depression the way they do now. It was a shameful secret. I was frightened that anyone would find out. Even my therapist did not know how bad it really was for me. Without any family or anyone to back me up, I had to keep going, had to keep it together by myself, and struggled to seem "normal." I felt like an alien, studying and mimicking the behaviors of the locals. It was exhausting.

There was nothing special about the night I drank most of a quart of scotch and took a handful of valium. It seemed almost spontaneous, but the plan had been percolating for some time, possibly since the first time I called an ambulance for my mother.

I had cut my wrist a few years before, but that was such a disaster, I knew I would never try that way out again. My plan had been to cut both wrists to speed the process, but when I saw all the blood coming out of the first cut, it was over. It made me sick. Literally. Before I could stop myself, I was scrambling around the bathroom, trying to manage vomiting and bleeding, frantically trying to clean the white tile floor. I was so freaked out, it took me a minute or so to realize I needed to bandage my wrist first. Getting the bathroom cleaned seemed the most urgent thing. Apparently, I was okay having my boyfriend come home and find my bloody dead body, but I was ashamed to have him find that I had tried, failed, and made a revolting mess in our bathroom to boot.

After I bound my wrist, I brushed my teeth, scoured the bathroom, and washed the towels I had used to clean up the blood. When my boyfriend came home and asked me about the bandage on my wrist, I said I had burned myself cooking. "See," he said, "aren't you lucky to have a guy who keeps the first-aid kit stocked up?" I agreed that I was so, so lucky. But I also knew that I would try to kill myself again and knew my weapons of choice would be pills and alcohol, not sharp objects. `I always thought of that episode more of a reenactment of my mother's story than a serious suicide attempt.

This time, I was taking my lead from Hollywood. I would swallow too many pills with too much booze, fall asleep, and not wake up. Done. Dead, But I discovered that it's not so easy to kill a healthy body. Aside from having alcoholic blackouts, a somewhat perpetual hangover, and clinical depression, I was pretty fit. My body was not going down without a fight.

I bought a quart of Glenlivet, my favorite single malt. Ordinarily, I would buy the cheapest scotch I could tolerate because I was after the most high for the money, but I figured my last binge should be with the good stuff. About halfway through the quart, I swallowed a handful of valium. It was the 1980s and everybody had valium.

This was not a drill. It was not meant to be a call for help. I had no belief in an afterlife at the time and was not looking forward to some heavenly post-mortem experience. My idea was that death was nothing. The absence of everything. That was what I longed for and was willing to murder myself to achieve. After I took the pills, I lay down on my bed with towels underneath me because I had read that when people die the sphincter and urethra let go. I wanted it to be an easy clean up for whoever discovered my body.

I knew it was critical to keep down all the pills and alcohol. If I'd had more mind-over-body training, it might have worked. As a binge-drinking alcoholic, I was an expert at vomiting. But this was something different. My body violently rejected the poisonous stew of valium and scotch. I barely made it to the bathroom. I thought, *Oh, fuck, I'm not going to die from an overdose, I'm going to die from choking on vomit!*

That was when I started to really panic. I had swallowed all the pills; there was no second chance. I had vomited so much it seemed unlikely that there was enough left inside to kill me. What if I ended up with some kind of organ or brain damage that would leave me hooked up to machines, paralyzed but still aware? Alive but even more messed up? I knew I had to get myself to the hospital.

I began to actively try to save my life. Trying to murder myself was a lot more painful than I had anticipated. The sound in my head was like fifty jets taking off at once. The intense roaring felt like a physical assault. There were tiny electrocutions going off in my muscles and nerves. This was not the numbed-out, drifting away into the nothingness of death that I had planned. It hurt. A lot.

I was starting to feel kind of dreamy and disconnected but was terrified that if I fell asleep, I'd wake up disabled in some horrible way. After I called a taxi, I threw up some more. I hoped to be done purging before the cab arrived. Understandably, taxi drivers really do not like for people to vomit in their cabs. If they even *think* you might, they will put you out.

The taxi arrived. As we were driving away, I discovered I had no cash. These were the days before ATM cards. I had checks, but the driver would not take a check.

He offered to drive me to the dispatch headquarters and ask if the night manager would cash a check for me. Very sweet guy. We drove to the place where all the cabs come from. It looked just like the television show *Taxi*. The night manager was a bit reluctant, but I seemed like "such a nice girl," he cashed a check for me so I could pay the cab fare.

The kind driver let me get back in his cab even though I had made him stop once on the way to dispatch so I could throw up on the side of the road. He expressed appreciation that I didn't vomit inside the car and said, "You let me know if you need to stop again." I had him drop me off close to San Francisco General Hospital and walked myself into emergency. I did not want the driver to know where I was going or why.

A lot of what followed is blurry because once I got to the hospital, I was able to let go and surrender to the effects of the drugs and alcohol still active in my body. Like in a story I had read about a guy who drove for miles with a nail through his brain, I kept it together until I knew someone else could take over. I remember being on a gurney and in a wheelchair. I remember people rushing around, asking me questions, but it seemed like it was all happening far away. The intense roaring in my head made it difficult to understand what they were saying, but I tried to be helpful and cooperative. I'm pretty sure I threw up some more.

Someone made me drink something disgusting, which I later found out was activated charcoal, meant to absorb any remaining poison. After a few more people observed me and asked questions, somebody took me up to psych intake where I waited. And waited. It was a busy night for despair in San Francisco.

By the time it was my turn to talk to the intake intern, it was obvious I was not going to die. That meant I had just a few hours left to get myself together and get to work. I could not afford to be held on a 51/50, the code for someone who was considered a danger to herself or others and would be held 72 hours in the psych ward. I knew I would definitely be out of a job if that happened. Not only could I not afford a break in income, I knew I did not have the energy or attention left to go through a job search and interviews.

My mission became convincing the tired, overworked, underpaid, intake intern that my overdose, while maybe not exactly a complete accident, was not a serious attempt to kill myself and that I was not now, nor would I ever be again, a threat to myself or others.

I called upon everything I had learned in my training as a volunteer on the San Francisco Suicide Prevention hotline about establishing rapport and using empathy. I remembered everything I heard from my friends who had been intake interns in psych wards. I expressed gratitude for being alive, for all the people who had helped save me, said I was sorry to have caused everyone so much trouble and concern.

Yes, I assured the intern, I would call my therapist and make sure I saw her right away. I called on every acting skill and talent I had.

Not only did I keep myself from being held on a 51/50, I ended up counseling the intern. She was overwhelmed by the number of people coming through the hospital, dismayed by the poor facilities and treatment that were available and wondering if anyone was really being helped. She was wondering if she had chosen the wrong career. I listened carefully to her story and assured her that she was helping people because she had helped me. She signed my release. We hugged when we said goodbye.

Then I took the bus home from SF General psych, showered, brushed my teeth a bunch more times to make sure there was no charcoal residue, changed into my downtown office-drone costume, and showed up for work early. I never told my therapist about that night.

That night happened over thirty years ago.

There have been no more overdoses or razor blades for me since.

Almost exactly one year after my night in the emergency room, I got sober and started learning how to save my life every day.

But this is not one of those happily-ever-after stories.

I still cycle in and out of depression.

Last year I had one that came on so slyly and slowly, I hardly realized I was in it until I caught myself with a plan to take myself out. As I was sorting through the details and making sure I had everything I needed, my internal observer, developed through years of meditation practice, woke up and set off an alarm. I became aware that I was in a depression cycle, and the plan to kill myself, which seemed so reasonable and such a good solution, was the illness talking, not guidance.

I have lived with this illness for a long time. Over the years I have developed skills, behaviors, networks, and a toolkit of coping strategies that make it more manageable. It's likely I will be spending more time in varying shades of darkness inside the cave. Having a regular spiritual practice and community helps. Friends with whom I can be truthful help. Dogs really help.

I still feel the despair, dormant, pressing on the edges of my awareness. Sometimes just opening my email is dangerous. According to my inbox, it's up to me to stop fracking, save salmon, whales, dolphins, wolves, and hundreds of other animals; stop global warming, find all the missing children, and cure Ebola.

It seems probable that everything that could possibly happen is happening somewhere right now, so I choose carefully what I focus on. I have trained myself to practice keeping most of my attention on what is beautiful, kind, and uplifting as much as possible. Nurturing my awareness of what I love, what I am able to contribute, and letting go of what I can't control is a lifelong practice.

Cruelty and chaos will kidnap my mind again. I may feel it coming on and it may ambush me. I could be thinking about puppies and kittens and notice that instead of imagining their cute, furry faces and charming antics, I'm obsessing about the thousands of them that will die because they have been abandoned. I will feel their terror and confusion as if it's my own. That thought stream expands to include wolves being run down and murdered by men in airplanes, manatees scarred and maimed, drowning polar bears, homeless children. Instead of going around taking photos of beautiful trees and clouds, I'm paralyzed with grief over the destruction of the rainforest.

Depression pretends that it can predict the future, insisting that I will feel hopeless and ashamed forever. It pretends to know me better than my best friend and tells me hateful lies about the true nature of things. When it happens again, those messages will seem very real. Then I will try to stay awake, use my skills, lean into my network, and wait for it to pass.

What is really different now is that I don't have to hide when it gets bad. There are more and more places where I am free to tell the truth when someone asks, "How are you?" As more of us "come out," I am reminded that, not only am I not alone, I'm in really good company.

Forty-four Steps

KATHRYN ROUNTREE

It has not been quite six months since I lost my brother to cancer. I am still new at living in this world without him.

Michael was my younger brother, my only brother. He was my playmate, guinea pig, confidant, and at times a huge pain, as all younger brothers can be.

Once when we were little and in the middle of a childhood squabble, I told him he was adopted. He cried and cried until I finally relented and had him look in the mirror to show him we had the same green eyes, the same wavy brown hair, and the same crooked front teeth, making us true-blue brother and sister.

We had an unusual childhood to say the least. Ours was a made-for-TV movie: Father walks out on family leaving no forwarding address. Mother is left alone to raise three small children in New York City. Baby boy of the family lands a part in an off-Broadway show at age four and becomes a child actor and the sole breadwinner of the family. Fifteen years later, mother sees the father on Mission Impossible TV show and eventually he and the mom remarry. True story.

Michael grows up and earns a scholarship to drama school. He is dangerously handsome, with emerald green eyes and a smile that draws everyone to him. The list of girlfriends is long and at times overlapping. He starts to paint and becomes an artist. He plays baseball like a Hall of Famer. He is an enthusiastic amateur magician and is side-splittingly funny.

Still, his story has many edges to it. His life was like a prism with rays of light that dart off into moments of staggering beauty and unfathomable darkness. There is the depression that haunted him most of his life and had a vice grip on everything he tried to do and accomplish. It began when he was nine years old, when he told us he felt like a cloud of darkness enveloped him. His moods would be unpredictable and often manic. But there was also the kindness that he showed to everyone in need and brought him to tears if an animal was in distress or hurt in anyway.

I would have done anything to help my brother. Walked a thousand miles to cheer him up, battled a dragon, crawled through the mud, fought the unbeatable foe, but the foe was depression and that enemy was ruthless.

Depression was a coward. It hid itself behind my brother's defensiveness; behind his anger and aloofness. It was also depression that fueled my brother's alcoholism. The two debilitating diseases had a strangle hold on him, slowly killing him, holding him hostage and keeping him from his family.

Depression stole his ability to be a son, a brother, an uncle, and a boyfriend. Every time he got close to happiness, depression came sneaking in and took him down at the knees. It beat him to a pulp until he finally let go of everyone and everything else. He was shackled by depression but not defeated. Courage became his shield against the dark knight. He'd slip out though the door of his apartment facing the onslaught of New Yorkers scurrying to wherever they go and come to meet me in the park where we would sit on the bleachers and laugh, talk, and watch our beloved baseball. He was like a phoenix emerging from a black hole that let in no light or life, fighting his way back to joy.

Michael made everyone around him laugh. He did magic tricks, loved little children, and the Yankees. He had a little kitchen in his studio apartment and could cook up a one-pot meal, which had five-star gourmet flavors blended into each bite.

On Sunday afternoons for as long as I can remember, I would call my brother in New York and we would spend time on the phone just catching up on the week and our lives. He never married nor had kids, so week after week I would hear about new people coming and going, jobs started and lost, and about new ideas he had for the invention that would finally make him a millionaire.

When he would fall into the deep hole of alcoholism, mixed with a dose of depression and a dash of self-loathing, his life ceased to exist. I would call and leave frantic messages on his machine. "Michael, I am so worried about you. Please call me or I am going to call 911."

I made threat after threat, fully expecting a call from the landlord informing me that he had found him dead in the apartment. I braced myself time and again for this call over the many years of this pattern. Each time I was certain that it was the end, my phone would ring and there he would be on the other end. "Hi, what are you up to?" he would ask me, as if nothing was out of the ordinary, and I could suddenly breathe again.

After these scares, I would try to come to terms with the knowledge that one day the depression would finally crush his soul beyond reasoning and he would be lost forever. But always, I vowed to fight for him. I would not allow this monster to take my brother from me. When I felt he was in danger, I made him stay on the phone with me, talking all through the night if needed, just to give him a lifeline to hold on to when the demons seemed so strong and his will so weak. As it turned out, depression was not the only enemy he had to face.

The call came on our usual Sunday afternoon catch-up conversations. He sounded stressed and distracted. I asked him what was wrong and he said he had been having stomach pains and thought he had food poisoning. I encourage him to go to the doctor. He had no insurance and ended up going to the emergency room.

The pain turned out to be stage-four colon cancer. He went into surgery before I could even make a plane reservation to get to New York. He had most of his colon removed, along with a gaping hole for a colostomy bag. He woke up alone in a strange hospital room where they told him he had two years to live, maybe.

I was struck by disbelief, devastation, denial, and utter paralysis when he told me, but he seemed to take it well. At least that's what I thought in the beginning. His world, our world, shattered under the weight of endless treatments, unbearable pain, and the everpresent ticking of the last years, months, and then days of his life.

There are forty-four steps up to the third floor of my brother's studio apartment on 85th Street and Second Avenue in Manhattan. He would now have to climb these steps, getting weaker by the day. He lived in the same apartment for almost thirty years. The walls are covered with his artwork. Working with pastels, he created beautiful images of seascapes and brilliant green and gold tree-lined paths and images of New York. He created amazing 3D replicas of the cartoon characters Popeye and Olive Oil in minute detail. In them, Popeye is fighting off Brutus for the love of his gal, Olive.

When I first arrived in New York from my home in New Mexico to care for him, I climbed those steps, huffing and puffing and wondering how on earth he was able to get up those steps after such a debilitating surgery. Forty-four steps up, forty-four steps down, no matter the purpose.

I lived in two worlds for the next couple of years. I flew back and forth to care for him after a procedure. Left my family in the middle of vacations, if he was in a crisis. Dragged myself up and down the forty-four steps wondering how long he could possibly stay in his apartment, hoping I could convince him to live with me in New Mexico where I could take care of him.

For the next couple of years, he rallied, he faded, was silent at times, but every once in while, we would talk for hours. Fighting cancer, it seemed, gave him an excuse for his depression. Now when the blue moments engulfed him, he blamed the cancer instead of himself.

Eventually, he was moved to a hospice facility in upstate New York, which was like being on another planet to a guy that had never lived outside of the city in his entire life.

Michael was a complete rascal at the beginning and gave the staff fits. He was still strong enough to sneak out the back door and walk to the small town. He often encountered deer on the road as he walked to and from the hospice facility. He tried hitchhiking at times. He asked the ambulance driver in front of the hospice center to give him a ride. The guy looked at him like he was crazy and maybe he was, just a little.

He couldn't understand why anyone would want to stop him from doing what he wanted with the little time he had left. He wasn't about to let cancer, doctors, doors with alarms, or even death dictate how he would spend his remaining months.

I was fortunate enough to be with him during the last two weeks of his life. Our time together was bittersweet. We both finally faced the reality of his situation and no longer pretended that remission might be possible. We knew the end was near. During those final days we acted like kids again. We laughed at the same jokes we had been telling each other since childhood, watched our favorite shows on TV, and ate grape popsicles.

Luckily it was spring and the Yankees were playing. His love for the Yankees pulled him through many episodes of depression and now, so close to the end, watching the games on TV made us both feel like it was just another normal Saturday afternoon.

He fought with me about shaving. "I can shave myself," he would say and take the razor out of my hand. He was so sure he could still use a straight razor and I was afraid his weak hands would slip and he would slice his cheek open. I begged him to let me help him, but stubbornness and independence won out, so I let him shave himself thinking about all the stitches he might need.

When the pain became too much for even the Yankees to distract him, he would push a button that released morphine into his system and then he would drift away from me into a deep, unnatural sleep, and I would lose those precious moments with him.

The last words we said to each other were "I love you." In the end of everything, I guess that is the best anyone can ask for out of life, in spite of everything. *I Love You.*

I love you Michael.

Upon Being Told to Be True to Myself

JENNA STONE

I am weak
        pliable
Unlike the gods
        the masters
                the voices . . .

I will crumble
        when it is time to stand tall
                spineless.

I will take the road most traveled
and still trip
over both of my feet.

I will drive peering back through my rearview mirror
only to crash into the school bus right in front of me.

I swim in my own pool of pity.
Ashamed of who I am
    of who I was
        of who I've never become
            and never will.

Speak to me.
I will listen.
And change
    my words
    my voice
    my ideas
until . . .
they are yours.

I am a liar
    a coward
        a thief

hiding in the tumor
of someone who is real.

I am a scared box
of teeth and hair
    waiting to be noticed
    and ultimately extracted.

Plucked out by
    Saviors
    Doctors
anyone who will finally notice me.

Slow down?
You want me to be true to myself?

Fuck you!

I don't even know that Girl anymore.

I have traveled
and hidden, shivering,
under cum-stained mattresses
discarded in the wash
by happily married politicians.

The cold
makes me forget
    the heat
        makes me want to.

And in the end
there is just this:
    a piece of paper
    and these words.

I woke up today
not really sure
    if my eyes were wide open
    or shut tightly.

When does it cease to be life
and begin to be
    a painless
        mere
            existence?

Show me the morphine
    the heroine
    the elixir
    the anti-life . . .

The room is spinning
as I lie shackled
hard to the earth
in the lies
    the sweat
        the sex
            the torture.

Disappointments.
    Betrayals.
        Abuse.

I've had enough.
I am alone.

There is nothing here
left to save me.

I have nothing
    own nothing
        and will be nothing.

Lost and discarded,
used and abandoned.

How diabolical
    to be shoved
    into this prison.

An assembly line
    of empty bodies
waiting for a soul
    to be squeezed in.

Eyes bright

hoping to conquer
    an already conquered world.

What is at risk?
    Only this:
    An apology
    for being me.

Viral Goodbyes

MATT EBERT

Have you ever tried to commit suicide and failed? I have. The last time it was so laughable, I told it in joke form when I laid it out to my friends. Truthfully, suicide is a deep-inside bone-crushing thing. That rain-slicked Seattle bridge, the poison sumac and the blackberry bushes, a can of gasoline and a lit cigarette, all the dope in my system, the fact that if I hadn't already been half-crocked on booze and pills, I would never have bounced and tumbled and lived.

And before that, several attempts at suicide by overdose, all misfires, they will never go away no matter how many times I land that "funny punch line." I swung and I missed. The pills will be no lesser, the bridge won't shrink, the cars I smashed will not reemerge from their automobile graveyard, the emergency-room red bracelets will not decay in the town dump, and the NA newcomer chips I strung together to make garland to decorate that pitiful tree one holiday season in rehab—they won't get any less Charlie Brown shitty. When I was kicked awake, I walked three miles and ended in a friend's back yard. I was shrouded in my gasoline-drenched coat, and the first thing I did was light another cigarette. Thank God they tossed me out. Thank God they handed me an ashtray first.

In my circle, suicide among long-term HIV survivors is higher than average. Depression and long-term HIV go hand in bloody hand. And if you say to your doctor, "I am contemplating suicide," you get a short trip to a jail cell, or in my case, the psych ward. But if you say, "I am going off my AIDS meds," you get the patient bill of rights, a DNR, and a blank sheet to list all your assets. Hopefully, they'll add some state-sponsored hospice care for the end game.

Two of the five friends I have known who went off their meds and died from AIDS in the last decade both tried suicide first. And they failed. And when they failed—when they awoke with a vomit-filled plastic bag taped around their necks, or a heavy-duty hangover from the wrong cocktail of painkillers and benzodiazepines—the decision to incant a death from AIDS was a whole lot easier to make. Pray someone hangs in the shadows to hold your hand those last days. I'm good at caring for the dying; I have bathed the dead—it's a skill I've honed without ambition.

I have bipolar disorder, type I, which manifests as a rapid cycling mood disorder. I feel things as deeply and as swiftly as the Susquehanna. My moods alter me—I hurt physically when I hurt psychologically—I walk with a stoop sometimes, and my body cramps. This has been true since childhood. And these moods: rapid cycling, crests and troughs, crippling and immobilizing depression, euphoric and destructive mania, or worse, both at once—hypomanic suicidal—there's no pill, no treatment, nothing but a footstool and a tight noose. I hold out my hand—is it shaking? Am I peeing too much? Am I thirsty? The elixir of stability eludes the genie and coaxes a deadly response from the bottle and dreams of lithium—extended release.

Left untreated, and by my own hand untreated for many years, I enjoyed a slew of narcotics and hard liquor to normalize myself—until booze and dope normalized me right out of society and into institutional living. Jails, rehabs, Salvation Army cots, and hospital wards—those years are lost to me now. Relief came in a big western city. I hustled to my psychiatric appointments like I would a hot date. In two or three years, pharmacology and psychiatry did for me what I couldn't do for myself, but nothing works forever. Bipolar disorder is a notorious shape-shifter, either you're in the game for life or you're out of the game for good. In a very real sense, few people survive severe mental illness because few people engage in lifelong psychiatric care. From the perspective of this patient, it is a delicate balance, and maybe a lofty expectation, to think a person with severe mood disorder and suicidal tendencies will get to the doctor on time.

I contemplated suicide, and that moved quickly to action. I checked it off like a lemon on a shopping list. Doesn't everyone think about suicide all day? It was all I thought about. By age twenty-nine, when I learned I had AIDS, I felt the urge for suicide so strongly, but I never attempted it. A jump off a bridge with a lit cigarette and a can of gasoline fifteen years later shook the dust off my to-do list. And though I failed—I bounced; I rolled in blackberry bushes and lacerated myself on nature's thorns, this natural world of tiny shark fins and berry blood—pulled my head just left of the concrete pylon—my failure a marked glass of blessings.

I have yet to fully understand gratitude, but I know a sumac saved my life, and when someone asks me to remove one from the garden, I hesitate. Life changed. I moved away from the western skyline, where I was receiving great therapy, to the banks of the Susquehanna River, where I received no therapy. Moving away from good care was a disaster. I got suicidal again. But I did not forget, as I shall never forget, the seven other near misses—a bell jar full of narcotics, painkillers, and benzodiazepines. Add alcohol, mix it into a breakfast shake, and you're off to the gym. Or, like me, you wake up in the ER a day or two later, the leftovers in the blender, an ambulance screaming outside the sliding glass doors.

A friend, now dead, once told me, "When they invent a pill, the one that will strip away the stigma of AIDS, the one everyone else must take, then I'll take my AIDS meds." He didn't want to walk this line, so he walked out. And what does my ear tell me when it rests on the unfinished track of a rail line aiming for a station marked "End of AIDS"? This is quite a long train, and many have jumped from the caboose. The train took thirty-plus years to build, and it stops short of a final destination: the cure. Where the tracks come up short, we've made a resort out of a deserted landscape. We've found ourselves the only oasis without water, and we've celebrated the end of something that has no end in an environment not meant for unprotected access. We are so relieved that AIDS is marginally over, we failed to comprehend AIDS is not over.

Lifting my head off the tracks, I see the train coming for that mirage. The functional cure for a chronic manageable illness, a design for living with AIDS. It's the middle teens of the twenty-first century, and AIDS now affects over forty million people worldwide. I think of ways one can commit suicide by AIDS, and one of them is to be silent. Another is to ignore it—never identify risk factors or get tested. You can test at home, anonymously; you can know, and in knowing, protect others. By not knowing, you are harming yourself, and by extension you are dramatically affecting others people's lives as well.

You want to get a man to use a condom? Put me in the room like a dead air freshener. I'll scare that rubber right on him. Maybe instead of pushing prophylactics, we should try talking about the realness of living your life on disability, with no career options, and no life savings. Maybe I can walk young, clean, temporarily drug- and disease-free men and women to my stack of unopened social service letters and they can help me read through them. We can try to find the ones I am most terrified of, like the one that says my prescription plan has just expired, or the one that says I don't qualify for Medicaid. Maybe instead of a billboard with sexy people using dental dams, we can have me, twenty years positive, telling my dogs how I haven't had sex in years because I am neither drug nor disease free, and my testosterone levels are in the toilet thanks to an abundance of narcotics and antiretroviral to suppress AIDS. I want to tell people at risk that their lives will be tied to a pharmacy and an infectious disease clinic. Your career you can toss in the can, because no matter what you think, by year ten you are going to be fatigued. Your fatigue is going to be fatigued. You'll be socially ostracized whether you know it or not. And every time you get a bruise, a skin rash, a bad headache, or a stomach problem, you're going to think: *Is this it? Is this what's coming for me now?*

There is no reprieve from my anxiety or my depression, and there is no drug effective enough to stop these tremors—the shakes not caused by alcohol withdrawal or lithium. No, most people are not thinking about fifty or even thirty years old. They're thinking about now—their latest tryst. I was a kid once. Sex is a powerful elixir, but it dilutes common sense. Until there is a cure, there will always be AIDS sitting there like a wet stain on the duvet. You'll just be scooting around it, trying to ignore it and get off at the same time.

Many of my friends who died later in the pandemic, they died of depression and this immovable wall of stigma. Our lives shifted in ways I never expected. I tried very hard to kill myself, but not hard enough, I suppose. A few times a year I wipe my brow and say, "That was a close call." But it never leaves me. Suicide is truly aimless where I am concerned. There's blowback that comes from surviving suicide; there's a kind of post-traumatic stress. I don't know how I survived it. All I know is that I did. Maybe that's all I need to know to move on from that empty, rain-soaked bridge and those expired pill bottles.

Someday This Pain May Be Useful

JENNIFER PASTILOFF

I'm tired. I just spent a week leading a retreat with twenty-two women, a yoga retreat in which these twenty-two women and I talked and wrote and laughed and celebrated our capability to make the most of our lives, and our desire to own our own happiness.

I love what I do, but I am also exhausted. I'm awake and filled with gratitude, but at the same time I'm drained. It's my job to inspire others to reach for joy, but I can't help but be very aware, in this moment, that I'm more than a yoga teacher, and a retreat and workshop leader, and a writer. I am also a depressive.

I've suffered from depression and anxiety for as many years as I can remember; many of those years I was anorexic as well. I hit my worst in around 2007. I was desperate, as in crawling-on-the-floor and eating-food-in-my-sleep desperate. At the time, I was working as a waitress in LA. I'd been working at the same restaurant for eleven years, even though I was miserable there. There were days when I would do almost nothing but read over and over again instant messages (still so novel back then) from my ex-boyfriend, messages like: *U just gotta get your shit together. U gotta get out of the restaurant. U gotta make moves. You've gotta decide what u want to do with ur life!*

As if I didn't know that I was drowning.

As if this were what I wanted for myself.

I finally had my nervous breakdown behind the restaurant. That's where everyone went to smoke once the tables had their food and seemed to be as happy as they would ever get during their meal. In that little secret cove for the smokers, I leaned against the red brick wall and slowly slid down to the ground. My chest heaved, desperately wanting air and not finding it. About a hundred years passed. I was surrounded by cigarette butts, millions of them, and they were staring at me with their ash and nicotine and lipstick stains and sticky bird shit that also had been on the ground. There might have been bubble gum too, but when you can't breathe you don't pay attention to anything except oxygen, and that is what I couldn't find anywhere.

Somebody help me my brain told my mouth to say. But nothing came out.

Except one word.

The word *enough.*

Enough.

Enough waitressing. Enough guilt. Enough anorexia. Enough numbing myself with sleep and food and drinking. Enough saying what I don't want instead of what I do want. Enough sex with people I don't love or even like very much. Enough living in the past. Enough worrying about the future. Enough wearing six-inch platform shoes because I feel being short means I am inadequate. Enough self-hatred.

Enough.

That one word slipped out and traveled down Robertson Boulevard in West Hollywood, past all the shops and the traffic, and I saw just for one brief second where it was headed—before I lost sight of it behind the roller-skating homeless man.

At this point I realized it was it was either sink or swim for me, so I decided to go on antidepressants. Cymbalta was the one I found worked best for me, especially with the obsessive anorexia thoughts.

It took some time to help, but it did. About a year later, I quit the restaurant. I started teaching yoga and I went back to my first love, writing. When I started sharing my blogs and personal essays I developed an online following, and then I started leading transformational workshops called *The Manifestation Workshop,* which quickly turned into sold-out events and retreats all over the world!

It all happened very quickly—in the course of two years, I went from serving tables to traveling around the world and being on *Good Morning America* and featured in *New York* magazine. This was my life! I had found successs! It was thrilling.

But there was a caveat: I was still taking meds, and I felt like a fraud. I felt like I should be able to be who I was, and to use the tools I taught in my workshops, without chemical assistance. So after a few years I thought it was time to see if my depression was "circumstantial." I also thought I might want to get pregnant. So in the summer of 2014 I went off my anti-depressants, and about five minutes later got pregnant.

This did not work out well.

The hormones from being pregnant, combined with the emotions and brain freak-outs from going off medication, made me feel like I was going crazy. I was scared all the time—even before I began hemmoraghing, even before I learned that the pregnancy was ectopic, or "extrauterine," meaning the fertilized egg didn't implant in the uterus, and was thus unviable. Even as I put on a happy face to teach workshops in New York, and Lenox, Massachussetts, and Seattle.

I was desperately miserable, but I kept going, smiling for women and reminding them that life can be joyful and complete.

I'm not sure I can pinpoint the moment that I first earned the repu-tation for being "positive" or "inspirational," but I can tell you that the irony isn't lost on me. This is my dichotomy: It is in my life's work to be asked how I got over my own depression and sadness, when some days I haven't even managed to brush my teeth because I am sitting by the front door with only one sock on and a bag of trash and I can't find the will to move.

But what I'm learning is that this isn't so ironic after all. And that being depressed while embracing joy is not so strange. To pretend to be always perfectly content would be a lie, the same lie as when we believe our own illustions about the people we admire. While we pine over their "perfect lives," behind their closed doors, they may be silently weeping into a coffee mug.

I no longer feel like a fraud for having taken meds, either. I have finally come to understand that my success was not owed to medication, but from being myself, being real, and telling the truth about who I am. I like to say I have a no-bullshit clause in all that I do. I think people need that—it's refreshing in a time with so much perceived perfection on social media, and in yoga classes.

I am willing now, in ways I wasn't before, to be honest with others. I'm willing to talk about masturbation, or what lies in the bottom of my closet, or how I drink too much wine. Honesty is important because it keeps us fromg being stymied by trying to live up to the expectations of others.

Honesty is important because if we don't face our truths head-on, they will come back to get us in other, more insidious ways.

I've carved out a beautiful life and love what I do, but sometimes, especially lately, I feel the old tug of depression. It's a magnet of sadness, buried somewhere next to the grief of losing my father at a young age—though not relegated to just that grief.

The sadness can appear out of the blue—when I'm leading a retreat to Costa Rica, on a day when I receive a plethora of praise and validation, when everything seems to be on the upswing. No matter how "positive" my situation may be, or seem, the blueness can still come.

If depression is a thing in your body, as mine is—some days it lives in my throat and gives me migraines; others days it makes me hide out in my apartment all day—then you have to deal with it. Pretending it doesn't exist, like by saying affirmations or posting happy quotes on Facebook, isn't going to help. And to start dealing with it, I say let's talk about it.

Let's talk about how hard it is to keep going when you can't move, when you want to get down really low to the earth and see if you can hear it hum and when it does, you want to stay there—all flat like that, pressed to the floor.

Let's talk about how that nothingness feels.

And let's talk about how, for some, facing depression means taking anti-depressants. Lord knows, there are people who cannot exist a day off medication, literally. Not a day. And while I'm not taking medication now, truthfully, I feel far more emotionally tentative now than I was when I was on them. Even though a lot of my days off them are good, if my depression again gets too much to bear, I might take them again.

I also might try to ride it out. (Or, rather, to write it out.)

It's complicated, the circuitry of the brain and the things we are hard-wired to believe. I know we have the power to change our thoughts, and I teach believing in ourselves, and who we are in the world, and who we are surrounding ourselves with, what inspires us—how all of that creates the lives we want for ourselves. And it does. But if we hit times when we get so low to the earth, skimming for love by any means available, when we are literally jonesing for something that is dead, well, sometimes the pain is no match for the affirmations.

The fact is that I am struggling. It's real. It's in my body, possibly from who-knows-when, carried down from my ancestors, passed on through my Romanian grandmother or my Native American great-great grandfather.

Or maybe it came when my father died in the night and left something broken inside of me.

I don't know.

But in my mind I keep hearing a quote by Ovid: "Be patient and tough; someday this pain will be useful to you." And so I'm trying: I'm trying to be patient, I'm trying to be tough. I'm trying to imagine a time when I will have greater perspective about my pain, that I'll be in a place where it could be useful to me.

And I also keep thinking that, instead of hiding who I am, I should share it: I should tell you about what I'm experiencing, the full truth of it. And then, maybe my pain will somehow be useful to you, too.

Riding Shotgun

judywhite

Sometimes when I'm driving the car, suddenly he's there sitting shotgun.

Damn. Here we go again.

Well, geez, let me at least move my bag.

Sometimes I yell. I've finally got him where I want him, trapped in the passenger's seat so I can scream how pissed off I am that he's gone.

Usually he takes it. Sometimes he leaves.

Sometimes, most times, more and more often, I tell him I forgive him. I know if I say it enough, eventually it will stay true.

The second time we lived together, the first day we moved in, he brought the shotgun his dad had given him when he was twelve and put it in the hall closet while I stood there with big eyes.

"Are you crazy?" I said. "If you leave that there, someday I will probably shoot you with it."

He just laughed.

Ha.

Usually it's a song on the car radio that makes him appear. I never know which one will do it. Always a surprise. That's one of his dead-guy powers, materializing out of nowhere to punch me in the stomach with grief and all its magical ride-along emotions. And he gets to stay thirty-five forever, unlined and lovely, beaming out of that great photo at the funeral. Not me. Silver hair and countdown to Medicare.

Sarah Mclachlan's "I Will Remember You (Will you remember me?)" can usually do it. Or anything from Linda Ronstadt's *Heart Like a Wheel*—I wore out the vinyl in college during our many break-ups. Technologies change. Sadness, however, has a perennial sound.

So here I sit, still wrestling with the ghost of my love at nineteen.

That's more of his dead-guy powers. He got the last word. You put a shotgun in your mouth and presto, nobody else can answer back. Nobody can ask you why, nobody can talk you out of it, nobody can help you see this might have been just one of those moments over the edge. And nobody gets the chance to try living with you a third time and maybe this time get it right. Boom. Presto. All gone.

So. That shotgun in the closet. Only one percent of suicide attempts are by trying to blow your brains out with a firearm. One percent. But because guns are so good at what they do—close to 90 percent kill-good—shooting yourself is the go-to method for well over half of all "successful" suicides. Can't stomach-pump a bullet. Guns also make suicide horrifically impulsive. Instead of pondering the act for days or weeks or years, 70 percent of those who tried with a gun, and then managed to survive, said they'd thought about it for less than an hour. Twenty-four percent gave it only five minutes before pulling the trigger.

Yikes. Tell me we haven't all had five minutes over the edge at one point or another.

Which may explain why he left the bedroom door open so the dog could find him. The dog he adored so much it used to make me jealous. The police discovered Razz going berserk in the house all alone, bedroom door open. That's the part that made the least sense to me out of all of it, but it's the part that ultimately made me realize the desperate psychic agony, the terrible black hole he must have been in to do that to a goofy yellow Lab. Not even to close the door first. Totally and utterly over the edge, if only for five minutes.

I know our fifteen years of ridiculous, mecurial back-and-forthing had something to do with his decision, in the mix with all the other things that contributed to a perceived lack of options in his prison of perception. It drove us both crazy, our inability to make such a huge and passionate love work for any length of time in the real world. And then, boom, presto, he does this, six weeks after I finally marry for the first time, to someone else. (A marriage, you might guess, decidely doomed.) I refuse, mostly, to be guilty about it. I know in my head that I can't take the blame for someone else's hopeless choice. But suicide is a vacuum cleaner, endlessly sucking you in with the pull of guilt as you sift for clues amid the debris.

"Who would play you in the movie about your life?" I once asked, one of those iconic questions in the relationship game.

"Bruce Dern," he said. "You know, the Bruce Dern in *Coming Home*."

Bruce Dern? Bruce Dern? I would have cast James Garner, from the *Rockford Files*.

"You're nothing like Bruce Dern! You mean the guy who walks into the ocean at the end of the film and kills himself?"

"Yeah."

Big clue.

Suicide leaves a long memory—a complicated grief, they call it. It is thought-rape, a complete and utter rape of the senses.

My first suicide was our next-door neighbor when I was fourteen. He was seventeen, funny, handsome, and smart. And evidently, though not to the naked eye, very, very sad. He took some pills, put a plastic bag over his head, and didn't answer the phone when my older sister's best friend kept calling. So she went and found him and ran down the street screaming at the top of her lungs. My sister ran with her, both engulfed in grief. I can still hear them. My mother ripped off the bag, got down on the ground, and started blowing into his mouth. I stood there over her, watching, listening to the indescribable sounds of air rattling in and rasping out of dead lungs, greenish tinge already around his hairline, pretty clear it was too late, but she tried for a horrible eon before the paramedics arrived. I can still hear that too. My second and third suicides weren't successful, a roommate I couldn't wake up, whose stomach pumping was in time; then an ex-boyfriend who called after he'd taken pills; and I had to hang up on him and dial to negotiate the ambulance and his rescue.

No one ever knows the heart of anyone else.

I know about death, "regular" death. My parents decided early on to expose us kids to death, to defuse its power, taking us to open-casket wakes even of people we hadn't known very well or at all. We were half-Irish, and wakes were often full of laughter amid the sobs, with boozy great stories and gallows humor. We got comfortable with death, in a way. It was a good thing, I guess, a preparation. My father died too young of war-related heart disease. My older sister died way too young of a brain tumor. Both were lingering deaths that had a sense of closure, even relief, to those of us left behind, and we learned to integrate those heartbreaking losses into going on with life.

But suicide has no closure. It's complicated, with the usual grief and bereavement jumbled up with the shock of sudden death, topped with layers of guilt and post-traumatic stress disorder and stigma and trying to figure out why, sucker-punched with your own complicated ensuing or ongoing depression. And anger and blame at the very person who stole away that person you loved. You don't "get over it." There is no closure. The best you can do is dilute its power, learn to push that ungainly and wrinkled parachute back into a pack that is impossibly small, where some bit always refuses to behave.

I was so mad at him that when his mother asked me for suggestions on what should be read at the funeral, I gave her a poem I knew he hated.

Not that I don't understand about depression. I know about careening from low to high and back again. And I have often gravitated to people who do the same, attracted, perhaps, to some sort of mirror. I don't know when we stopped calling it manic-depression and changed to bipolar, a linguistic loss since the manic highs and lows are truly descriptively manic, but that kind of thing runs in my Irish side of the family.

And I know about wanting to die. I know about wanting pain to just go away, any way you can make that happen. Alcohol, sex, drugs, any dumbing numbing excess or escape will serve when you feel that anything is better than *this*. As effective as slamming your big toe with a hammer to stop thinking about the pain in your spirit. The temporary fix to what feels hopeless, instead of reaching for a more permanent one. Knowing what suicide does to the ones leftover—that knowing has kept me safely from the edge more than once. But it's not a guarantee. The thought-rape of someone else's suicide, especially of someone you knew well, with whom you weren't finished, makes you think about suicide far more than you might have done. It becomes a terrible viable option.

Once upon a time, on a perfect summer day, a boy and a girl walked barefoot on a perfect sandy beach, making up a fairy tale about themselves, falling into each other's souls. All I have left of that afternoon is a piece of sea glass found on the shore, a smooth and tumbled piece of loveliness in a particular shade of turquoise blue that you can just about see through, but not quite. When I want to touch the past, I pick it up, fingering little flaws on its surface, a magic time machine. My memory is terrible—just ask my little sister, who can't believe the amount of detail I have managed to forget over time, and who has taken it upon herself to remember all the stories of our childhood for me. But there are moments in my life that are indelibly etched upon my being, that can transport me instantly with acute and perfect recall of how it *felt*, how it *still* feels. I don't quite know who that person was back then, but I do admire the reckless way she loved.

I began to wear that sea-glass color so much and so well that he dubbed it "judyblue." It was a running joke. All these years later, I still look good in it. Goes great with silver hair. Sometimes even now when I see that shade, without consciously knowing why, my heart will stop, and a hunk of anguish will appear, sitting in my chest, riding shotgun.

With age we actually do get wiser. Our coping mechanisms improve. We get different, able to weather better or longer. Generally the highs get lower, but the lows get higher. Modern drugs can help, other people can help, you learn to help yourself. Most suicides and attempts and thoughts are by people under the age of thirty-five, people who haven't had the chance yet to see that paradigms shift, a lot of stuff passes, changes, morphs into tolerable or good or even disappears. Or maybe it doesn't, maybe something so awful gets in your way at any age, because anything can happen to anyone at any moment. Everyone's broken. And sometimes the burden of trying to not be broken, trying not to be sad, for all the innumerable reasons that can cause you pain, or perhaps unable to keep living up to what you think is everyone else's expectations, or maybe of trying to always make everyone laugh, like the comet that was Robin Williams—it can all just get to be too much. Or the chemistry of your brain wreaks an unmitigated havoc for no reason at all. And all you need is five minutes over the edge. And then, oh, you miss so much that lies ahead.

He would have loved the Internet. And Ireland. And knowing I wrote a movie.

Yearning, one way or the other, can do you in. Memory torments when the old images are bad ones, the moments you were glad to be shot of, but that can return to stab at unexpected times with unexpected pain that you yearn never was. But memory can torment even when the flashbacks are good, because you can yearn too hard and too long for those moments to return, to be equaled, to be surpassed. I will mourn those moments of passionate totality all my life, if only at this point in widely spaced intervals. Time doesn't heal. It just makes the spaces in between pain grow longer and longer.

So. Coping mechanisms. Mine is humor. Because life is still funny, even amidst loss and grief, if you can just let it. Laughter is the tool that can jumpstart me out of sadness sometimes. Even when

I don't feel like it, because even a fake hearty laugh has been shown to change your brain chemistry, an inner pharmacy proven to reduce pain—or at least raise your pain threshold—that seems to increase the happy endorphins, decrease stress hormones, load you up on oxygen at even the cellular level. Einstein famously said that you can't solve a problem from the same plane of consciousness on which it was created. So I break the sad relays when I remember to, when I can, with belly laughs I don't initially believe in, but that end up getting me to a different level, out of the blue.

We color memory. It's not a fine-tuned ability. We color it bluntly with crayons, coloring outside the lines, or only partially filling them in, usually with broken stubs, old, melted and misshapen, coloring as if our lives depended upon it. All we have are our colors, and the power to choose the hues.

And with those colors comes a revisionist history to suicide. Even though he seemingly got the last word, I have the control in the end. I am still here. I can rewrite what happened and skew it to my heart's content, try to make more order, color it however ineptly with my assorted tones, change the shading when I need, and when I want, when I can. Because the only thing I have any power over, though I have to remember it over and over and over again, is how I choose to react.

Sometimes, when he's there riding shotgun, out of the blue, I tell a joke.

> *Knock knock.*
> *Who's there?*
> *Boo.*
> *Boo who?*
> *Just boo, you dope. You're a ghost.*

And sometimes, every once in a while, the complications drop away and my memory is simple and pure and uncluttered, and all I remember is love.

And color it, judyblue.

Surviving the Spiral

REGINA ANAVY

Picture a spiral. You are on top, going along in your usual pattern. A thought intrudes, a moment of doubt, guilt, or self-reproach. Your spirits drop. You move lower, to the next rung of the spiral. As your mind turns inward and your thoughts become more constricted, your options seem to narrow. You suddenly flash in vivid detail on every error committed in your past: spiteful words uttered on impulse that you cannot take back; impulsive acts you cannot erase. You begin to obsess about relationships that have drifted away—all your fault, of course. And you weren't always the perfect child, the perfect sibling, the perfect worker, lover, or friend. Oh, the mistakes you have made. Your life is one big mistake, from the minute you were born. You spiral down and down into the blame and shame of your life.

This negative-feedback loop of depression had been a familiar part of my psyche for as long as I could remember. Usually, I would find my way back up and come out on top of the spiral. However, in 1971, my luck ran out and I had a full-blown breakdown.

I was twenty-eight years old, Jewish, middle-class, and college-educated. I was living in a commune in Washington, D.C., and seven of us from the area were selected for the Fourth Venceremos Brigade after applying for the trip and being screened. We wanted to go to Cuba to cut sugar cane in support of Fidel Castro's Revolution. Two hundred of us were in this brigade, from all over the United States. We would spend seven weeks in a work camp and then tour the island for another two weeks. It was the ultimate in commitment to the lifestyle of being a radical. As far as the U.S. government was concerned, this trip was illegal, which only made it more enticing.

I had volunteer-worked my way up to this point in my radical career by being active in the civil rights movement, the women's movement, and the anti-war movement. I had even become an aboveground member of the Weather Underground through a boyfriend who was involved with them. It was the perfect time for me to get out of town since I had inadvertently taken part in an explosion in the U.S. Capitol building. I say "inadvertently" because my friend had surfaced to come visit me and had left a book on my shelf. When he picked it up later, he opened the front cover to show me: the book was hollow inside and it held blasting caps. No one had been hurt in the explosion, but I still felt guilty about my participation, and I felt guilty about feeling guilty, for it meant I was not a committed revolutionary and still had bourgeois tendencies.

My disillusionment with the Revolution began the moment I arrived in the work camp. The lack of individual rights was apparent. The one newspaper we saw, *Granma*, spelled "America" with a "k." The Cubans did not approve of the gay *brigadistas*, who were considered counter-revolutionary. This was the catchword of the moment, and to be branded such was the biggest insult imaginable and an invitation to being ostracized. It seemed to me that what was happening in Cuba was unrelated to my cultural values. Such thinking was, of course, counter-revolutionary.

There was a daily routine that provided structure. At sunrise, we had a shot of strong coffee, piled ourselves into claustrophobic

Soviet trucks, and sang revolutionary songs all the way to the fields. We worked until lunchtime, came back in the trucks (same singing routine, with a few shouted slogans thrown in), had a copious lunch, took a siesta, and went out again in the afternoon. Before each trip to the fields, we sharpened our machetes. At night, there were cultural activities—movies shown in the "Palm Theater," where we leaned against trunks of felled palm trees. Occasionally musicians came to perform for us. It was one big revolutionary party.

Social pressure worked subtly in the camp. We were "invited" to show up for work production meetings, where we were lectured on how to increase the amount of cane we cut. Occasionally, some important personage would come through the camp to give us a pep talk. We were expected to drop what we were doing, fall out in military fashion, line the path, and clap enthusiastically. It was like being in a cult.

Unfortunately, before coming to Cuba, I had become dependent on marijuana to elevate my mood. I had been in psychoanalysis for years, but the tendency to analyze and over-analyze had made me worse. So now, here I was, in a physically and emotionally trying situation, sleeping six to a tent, being covered in ash in the cane fields, often cutting myself with the blade of the machete, being harassed by the Cuban overseers who told us to cut faster and aim lower, and without my usual crutch (marijuana was not tolerated in Cuba).

There was also a lot of infighting among the different political factions. Doubt began to creep in, and I started questioning everything. If I had been wrong about the Cuban revolution, was I wrong about other beliefs? I came to the conclusion that I was wrong about everything; my life had been built on a lie. And then I became consumed by all-encompassing guilt for feeling that way. Everyone around me, except for a few of us doubters, seemed to be fully engaged in the revolutionary experience of cutting cane and mouthing the party line. So what was wrong with me? I took it all personally, lost my sense of perspective and, worst of all, my sense of humor.

The Cubans seemed fiercely patriotic and proud of their country, a great contrast to the constant criticism on the part of the North Americans against our own government and its policy toward Cuba. I started to feel weird about this, suspecting that the Cubans actually looked down on us for our lack of patriotism. They also were very anti-hippy and anti-drug, and they considered us spoiled and self-indulgent. They were determined to stamp these qualities out of us through hard work and indoctrination. I began to view my critical attitude toward Cuba as a symptom of overwhelming negativity. Was I just a rebel for the sake of rebellion? Was I doomed to see only the negative side of everything?

My self-confidence plummeted and I became more withdrawn, convinced that everyone suspected me of being a CIA agent. For one thing, I was being openly critical; for another, I was taking a lot of photos. The paranoia, both inside the camp and inside my own head, was not helped by the fact that one of the Cubans confided to me that before we had come, the Cuban government had taken them aside to warn them about us North Americans: we would try to seduce them sexually; we would try to poison their minds with our bourgeois, capitalist thinking; we were not really their friends. So it was all a sham—the forced companionship in the camp, the forced solidarity. My identity as a revolutionary was a sham, too, built on a false premise.

My world was falling apart. Going home was not an option, because joining the Brigade meant I was committed for the whole nine weeks and dependent on the Cubans for transport home. Clearly, I did not belong there, but where did I belong? It's ironic that I could have bragged about being more revolutionary than anyone because I was involved with the Weather Underground, but this was something that couldn't be revealed.

You realize you are in a prison of your own making. There is a wall separating you from others; how easily those fragile social connections you once took for granted are broken. You have forgotten how to engage in the proper behavior required for making contact. You feel detached from the human race, and this creates more self-blame.

This sense of detachment amidst people with whom I could not connect was the worst feeling of all. It was a signal to me that, emotionally, there was no turning back. I was doomed.

Somewhere down the spiral, after Blame, Guilt, and Detachment have arrived in full force, Anxiety suddenly appears. It's a rogue wave, slamming into your body, turning you upside down and saturating every pore. You are drowning, unable to surface for air. Once Anxiety seeps in, you realize it has been there all along, stalking you, hovering in the background like a rejected lover lurking outside your house, waiting for a moment when your guard is down and you have left a window cracked.

Fear is Anxiety's twin, for you now know there is no escape from your private descent into Hell. Sleep, when it comes, is full of nightmares. You awaken in the middle of the night, terrified, and filled with disgust at your terror. Morning arrives and you do not feel rested. Time becomes meaningless, for you are wrapped in the time zone of depression, your own private misery. The simplest act becomes a struggle: getting out of bed, brushing your teeth, combing your hair, dressing. Sheer maintenance wears you out. You are alone, falling faster into inner space.

As fear and despair took over, I experienced a loss of self, as if my core identity had been smashed and I had no way of reassembling it. I moved through the days like an automaton. So much of my energy was being taken up in this inner dialogue that little was left for interacting with my *compañeros* who, sensing my weirdness, began to distance themselves from me. This social isolation caused more anxiety. I was in a repetitive loop of self-criticism, self-loathing, guilt, despair, anxiety, loss of hope and, finally, thoughts of suicide.

The last two weeks of the trip were spent touring the island. This included a "forced march" in the Sierra Maestra. It was exhausting. By the time we returned home, in the hold of a ship, I was moving like a zombie, incapable of connecting, except with the other walking wounded. One of them was a drug addict who had spent the whole time in Cuba in a hospital, going through withdrawal. We spoke briefly, standing on deck, leaning against the rail. It was all I could do to keep from throwing myself overboard.

I vaguely remember the homecoming and being unable to articulate my experience or to connect with my friends. I vaguely remember buying sleeping pills and checking into a hotel. I vaguely remember writing a suicide note, explaining my "logical" reasons for doing this. I do remember the relief of gulping down those pills and lying down on the bed to sleep, forever. But it hurt, and I woke up: I was scared.

While unconscious, I had a vision of going down a tunnel, being led by a rabbit, and the thought had come to me that I was not ready to die. I did not want to follow that rabbit, and I forced myself to wake up. It was one of the hardest things I had ever done, pushing myself up off the bed and staggering into the hallway, where I incoherently flagged down a hotel guest and then passed out. When I awoke, I was on the locked ward of a hospital, having my stomach pumped. A good-looking young cop was standing over me, smiling, and I knew I was safe.

The first night in the hospital, I was rambling and carrying on, happy to be alive. They put me in solitary until I could calm down. The doctors laughed at me for trying to commit suicide with over-the-counter sleeping pills, and I felt like a failure again. This feeling came and went over the next few weeks. My analyst showed up (he must have felt like a failure himself). The approach in the hospital was group therapy and was much more directive than his Freudian method. I was surprised to see how many friends came to visit; some of them sought to "rescue" me in a guerrilla action from the evil clutches of conventional medicine, but I knew I needed to be there and refused to go with them.

The one failure in treatment was that I was not immediately put on antidepressants. The tranquilizers they gave me zonked me out but did nothing to quell my suicidal thought pattern. After three months, I entered a halfway house. This turned out to be a healing experience, and I gradually clawed my way back to mental health.

There were two crucial turning points. I learned that I could easily get a gun from one of the other residents, which would make committing suicide a definite possibility. I made a decision to stop thinking about suicide: I had regained my mind. Then, before moving into my own apartment, I had a brief affair with one of the staff, who made me feel like a desirable woman: I had regained my body.

I began to see a different psychiatrist, one with a new approach to the issue of depression. For him, it was simply a matter of proper brain chemistry, and he immediately put me on a tricyclic antidepressant. Amazingly, within two weeks, my energy and zest for life returned, and I became rational and more focused on my future. I was able to make social connections and appropriate decisions without second-guessing everything I did, a state of mind that had immobilized me since my breakdown.

The realization that my lifelong depression had a chemical and even a genetic component (my father had tried to commit suicide twice) relieved me of guilt and despair. I now had hope that I could recover.

And I did. I moved to the West Coast and went to law school for one year. I rented a beautiful apartment and got a job as a legal assistant at a law firm in San Francisco. With the money I saved, I bought property, becoming a real member of the establishment without any guilt. I became a massage therapist and took classes in painting. I maintained my interest in politics but worked within the framework of the Democratic Party, serving on the State Central Committee for two years. I met a man and fell in love. We traveled the world together, got married, and started what became a successful business.

Since my hospitalization more than three decades ago, I have had other bouts of depression, but I have learned to catch myself at the top of the spiral before I begin that terrifying descent. I heed those first warning signs—self-deprecating thoughts and debilitating anxiety—and, with the help of medication, I know I can stop the fall.

In 2003, I became interested in Cuba again and felt brave enough to go back for another look, legally this time. I no longer feel guilty about my negative perception of the Revolution. If someone called me a "counter-revolutionary" today, I would laugh and agree, taking it as a compliment.

I have now come out of the closet about my genetic tendency toward depression, although it still gives me a twinge of embarrassment to tell this story. I don't want depression to define me. I know how to conquer it and keep it under control. I know how to prevent that descent down the spiral.

A Kind of Quiet Most People Have Forgotten

PAM L. HOUSTON

It's July, 2014. I am guest teaching in the Chatham University Low
Residency MFA program in Pittsburgh, where I have been adopted
for these ten days by a couple of smart, talented, and beautiful young
women named Kyle and Maggie, and their handsome, entirely
self-possessed mutt, Apacha. It happens everywhere I go these days,
the coolest, hippest-dressed twenty-five-year-olds in any given program and their bandana-wearing dogs want to hang out with my
sturdy, laugh-lined, fleece and skort-clad, fifty-two-year-old self. It's
both surprising and flattering, and makes for a very satisfying do-over
from my teenaged years, during which the Kyle and Maggie equivalents would have rolled their eyes hard if I had taken one step in
their direction. Or perhaps I am wrong about that. Perhaps there were
no Kyle and Maggie equivalents in my teenhood, because along with
being the coolest girls in the MFA program, Kyle and Maggie are
almost preternaturally kind.

I can see by their eyes, though, that they each carry some large and not short-term sadness within them—which is the same thing people say about me when they look into my eyes for the first time, even on the rare days when I feel as though I don't have a care in the world. Maggie, I know, has recently lost her mother, who was very dear to her, and she is swimming in the deep waters of that grief. But Kyle's sadness, about which I have been told nothing, has a different flavor, one as familiar to me as my name, and I am nearly certain it has something to do with how she is letting herself be treated by a man.

The girls and I have taken Apacha for a walk through the huge, half-wild and glorious Frick Park on Pittsburgh's eastside, and now we are having a beer—well, they are having a beer—while we decide whether to stay where we are and eat vegetarian, or move on to BRGR for organic bison lettuce wraps. I am not drinking beer these days (or any other alcoholic beverage), nor am I drinking soda, coffee, or even green tea. I am not eating wheat, sugar, or anything packaged, processed, or inorganic, because when I went to the doctor for my yearly checkup a few months ago, I had the first high blood pressure reading of my life, along with a pre-cancer diagnosis in the form of HPV 16. The ecosystem that is me was quite clearly in trouble, and it was time, I decided, to clean up my act.

As the doctor was writing a prescription for the blood pressure meds, I asked her if I could have six months to right the ship. "No," she said, without looking up, so then I asked her if I could have three. "I'm writing the prescription," she said, "I won't be there to see whether you take the pills or not." Which I realized was true, and which I chose to interpret as permission.

Caffeine has always been my go-to antidepressant, and I've said for years that if I ever had to make the choice between giving up coffee or dying, I would choose death. But as it turned out, all death had to do to get me to quit caffeinated beverages cold turkey was to wave at me from the window of a bus at a distant intersection. To heal, I reasoned, my body needed sleep, and I had not slept properly in decades, if ever. Not if we define sleep as the state that, when you emerge from it, is like coming up from some deep oceany paradise of nothingness at the very bottom of the world.

Unsurprisingly, I spent my first ten non-caffeinated days wanting to kill myself.

And look just there, how I have used the phrase "wanting to kill myself" as a kind of mildly self-deprecating but good-humored figure of speech.

Surprising, one of my selves says to another. As I was likewise surprised when, a few weeks ago, I was standing behind a podium and in answer to a reader's too-personal question, I heard myself saying, "There was a period of my life when I would have considered killing myself, but that period is over now."

Is that so? That same self, the cynic, asked.

Yes, another answered (this one has a slightly imperious, almost British accent), *I feel quite confident that's where we are.*

Two mostly wonderful things about life after fifty: I'm never sure what I am going to say until I hear myself saying it, and it's hard to remember, with any real accuracy, feeling any way other than how I feel right now. But if a person's books are any reliable record of her life, and in my case they certainly ought to be, there were periods in both my thirties and forties where—and here I want to be careful with the wording—the possibility of suicide came up a lot.

In my thirties I wrote a book called *Waltzing the Cat,* and that book contains a story call "Cataract," about a river trip gone awry, and after the flip where both female characters nearly drown in one of the five largest runable falls in America, there is this moment of dialogue:

"Lucy," Thea said, "if you were to kill yourself ever, what would it be over?"

"A man," I said, though I didn't have a face for him. "It would only be over a man. And you?"

"I don't think so," she said. "Maybe something, not that."

"What then?" I said. But she didn't answer.

"If you are ever about to kill yourself over a man," she said, "get yourself to my house. Knock on my door."

"You do the same," I said. "For any reason."

"We'll talk about what it was like being under the water," she said, "what it was like when we popped out free."

The only decade of my life in which I don't remember having suicidal thoughts—until this one—was my twenties, possibly because I seemed to be trying so hard to kill myself in more socially acceptable ways. I rowed brutal Class V rapids during hundred-year floods in Utah, Colorado, Idaho, and Montana (I actually followed the high water north as the season progressed). I jumped off snow cornices into near-vertical "couloirs," with skis so long they look cartoonish by today's standards. During my years of guiding hunters, I kept watch all night over the carcasses of Dahl sheep, deep in the heart of the Alaska Range's grizzly bear country.

In those days, I seemed to gravitate toward natural disasters, riding out hurricane Gordon in the Atlantic ocean on a 52-foot sailboat built to cruise the Intercoastal Waterway (it was fat enough to hold a square dance in its main cabin), or trying to keep my skis on top of the leading edge of an avalanche in Colorado's backcountry. I slogged hip-deep through a mud slide in my long underwear in the Brooks Range, and more than once found myself flat on my back after being bucked off any number of green-broke horses.

I called the suicide hotline only once during that decade, after a horse shattered both bones in my forearm. A surgeon spent nearly nine hours taking eighteen pieces of pulverized bone out of my ulna and replacing it with cadaver bone from the bone bank, and then sent me home with two eight-inch scars and a bag full of Darvocet.

When the guy picked up the phone, I told him that I knew I ought to be happy. The last thing the surgeon had said to me before the anesthesia kicked in was that I should prepare myself to wake up from surgery with my arm amputated at the elbow, and yet here it still was, hurting like a son of a bitch, but more or less intact.

"Are you taking anything?" he asked, and when I told him about the Darvocet he said, "Well for Chrissake, stop! Haven't you ever heard of Advil?" Which turned out to be some of the best advice I've ever gotten in my life.

I spent a good portion of my forties writing a book called *Contents May Have Shifted*, and its working title, for all the years it lived in my laptop, was *Suicide Note, or 144 Reasons Not To Kill Yourself.*

Really? the cynic pipes up again. *Really? If you were ever actually suicidal, you must not have been very good at it.* And it's hard to argue with her now over our daily lunch of hibiscus tea and kale superfood salad. *It's bad business to deny your past*, the earnest self—the one who pays attention in therapy—tells her, and for now they (we) leave it at that.

Much was made of my working title in interviews I gave when *Contents* eventually came out, but I had never intended to call the published book *Suicide Note*. Too maudlin, too melodramatic, the contradiction within the longer version of the title dishonest, almost coy. The working title was simply a daily way to describe to myself what I was doing: prophylactically collecting and transliterating suicide prevention nuggets, gathering up all the things about this planet that made me want to stay on it, against some unknown future moment when I might feel it would be better not to. And, because I find myself here on the other side of fifty trying with all my might to stay alive, it seems reasonable to conclude that at least to some extent my strategy worked.

The waitress brings Kyle and Maggie their beers and me my Pellegrino with lime, and we are talking about favorite dogs or favorite bands, but Kyle is looking at me so intently with those sad, soulful eyes that the next thing I know I'm saying, "You know, there was a period of my life when I thought I might kill myself because a man I thought I loved didn't love me back. It embarrasses me a little to say so, but there it is."

Kyle's face is a mixture of stunned and relieved, which I take as a sign to continue. "I've always measured my sense of well-being on airplanes, when we hit turbulence. You know, how much—or how little—do I care if this plane goes down?" They nod. They both *do* know.

"I can remember actually willing the plane to tumble from the sky a few times, because some Joe I probably could not pick out of a lineup, were he here tonight, didn't call or went out with one of his four other girlfriends or lied about where he was last Saturday."

The girls are quiet—even Apacha has stopped licking his balls. It flashes through my mind that I might be grossing them out, like in the way you don't want your parents to mention the great sex they had over breakfast.

"You didn't ask me to dinner, I know, so I would sit here and rattle on with my old lady advice," I continue, "but I have been thinking a lot lately about how much power I used to give the men in my life to make me feel okay, or not okay. There are reasons for that—ugly childhood reasons—so I try to give myself a break. I'm not a regretter, exactly—I think all writers need something to push against, and maybe that was my thing to push against for a long time—and yet at fifty-two it seems absolutely mystifying to me that I would give men so much power. It's power I don't think most of them even really want."

Now Kyle is looking at me like I have crawled inside her brain. We are all silent for a while. "Maggie's got a good man," is what she finally manages to say.

I nod. I don't doubt it. Maggie's grief for her mom is palpable, piercing, but it is not full of the shadows and confusion that come when a little girl is treated badly in a hundred different ways by fathers or father figures, that insidious, everlasting training.

"I don't know anything about your past," I say to Kyle, "and I'm not trying to tell you how to live. Somebody could have said all this to me when I was your age—I'm sure someone did—and it would have probably just made me double down. I had to do it as long as I had to do it, chase those nasty cowboys." I smile and Kyle smiles, but her eyes never do. "I'm just saying, I guess, that there's another version, after this version, to look forward to. Because of wisdom or hormones or just enough years going by. If you live long enough you quit chasing things that hurt you; you eventually learn to hear the sound of your own voice."

Apacha groans, maybe signaling the end of the conversation, so I drain my Pellegrino and reach for the check, but Kyle stills my hand.

"What made it change," she asks, "for you?"

There are so many possible answers, including thirty-thousand dollars worth of therapy; several new age healing ceremonies—one involving a man who set his chest on fire and another involving a dust buster; five published books and a pre-cancer diagnosis, but I say the thing that feels first, truest, and most long-term: "I realized I could make my own life," I tell her. "I could have my own ranch. I finally realized that *I* could be the cowboy."

But now it is a grey, late-November morning, and I'm here, a cowboy on her very own ranch—120 acres of hard dirt and ponderosa, of sixty-mile-per-hour winds and blizzards that drop five feet of snow in 24 hours; of floods and drought; and last summer, the second largest fire in Colorado history; of blue columbine and quaking aspen and twelve-thousand-foot peaks all around; of unspeakable beauty and a kind of quiet, on a winter morning, that most people on the planet have forgotten exists. I am here, in the middle of all that, and I am pretty damn sad anyhow.

I have two very elderly horses that may not make the winter, and I can't decide if it is more humane to move them to a warmer place where everything would be unfamiliar, or try to heat the barn a few degrees with chicken lamps so they can live, or die, in the place they know. My ewes are in heat, and I can't seem to build a fence the ram can't tear down, and the wolfhound girl pup I got to cure my three-year-old hound's loneliness since his running partner died last May has so far only caused him to look at me with exasperation, incomprehension, and a kind of deep betrayal in his eyes. The days seem impossibly short already, and yet we'll lose daylight for another month before this planetary ship turns itself around.

Facebook has already made me cry four times this morning. First it was Ursula LeGuin reminding me that we don't write for profit, we write for freedom; next it was the Unist'ot'en Indiginous Camp Resistence trying to stop the Keystone Pipeline; and then it was the state of Nevada electing a man to their house of representative who said that "simple-minded darkies" show "lack of gratitude" to whites. Honestly, who wouldn't be sad waking up in this world? And then I clicked on The Prairie Fire Lady Choir singing a song my friend Annette wrote called "Not A Good Man"—a kind of Irving Berlin meets Laurie Anderson number, with all of them wearing lollipop-colored dresses and big hair and when *that* teared me up, I knew I might be in serious trouble.

Cry me a river, says the cynic. *How about we make a short list of all things that could be wrong and are not.* So I do. At this moment, none of my close friends are dying (except in as much as we are all dying). I have a job—I have several jobs—and at only one of them am I not respected. The man I love, who has been almost comatose with sadness for the better part of seven years, has decided, at last, to come back to life. I am not underwater on my mortgage. I have a barn full of hay and two cords of wood on the porch and a cabinet full of dark-chocolate-covered figs and almonds. My upstream neighbor has not gotten into bed with the frackers. My presence here means these 120 acres will not be subdivided, will not be paved over, will not be turned into dream homes for people who come here one week a year.

And still, this morning, that dark undertow, the feeling of looking up from the bottom of a dank, wet well . . .

Time to move. On this point, all selves are in agreement. *Put the smart wool on, lace your boots, don your barn coat. Cut the apples, cut the carrots, feed the equines from your hands. Cut the string that holds the bale of grass hay together, two flakes for the mini-donkeys, six for the horses, everything that is left for the sheep. Top off the horse water, top off the sheep water, double check the heaters in the troughs. Listen to the reassuring thump of cold boot soles on frozen ground, the comforting crunch of equine teeth grinding hay, the otherworldy woosh of wing beats overhead—the bald eagle who winters upriver, back after his one-year hiatus.*

The forecast is calling for wind and possibly snow tonight, but right now it is perfectly still and almost 20 degrees, too warm for my heavy barn coat. The creek at this time of year, with all the freezing and unfreezing, is an ice sculpture, the willows that line it pencil drawings, the mountaintop beyond it already feet deep in snow.

The puppy is charging and leaping to see above what's left of the tall grass, while William, the three-year-old, patrols the perimeter. From here I can see Middle Creek Road, Lime Creek Road, and the state highway across the river, and though this represents some fairly large percentage of all the roads in Mineral County, for the hour we'll be walking not one car will come by.

Out here, on this acreage, I've learned not only to hear my own voice, but to recognize what makes my heart leap up and then go toward it: the snowshoe hare—halfway through his biannual color change that William scares up along the back fence, his big white feet flashing as his still-tawny body gains distance. A coyote, sitting, dignified and still as a church 200 yards across the pasture watching us make our way to the wetland, and then the flash when William sees him, and he sees that William sees him, his total evaporation into thin air, like a ghost dog come from some other plane of being.

These are the things that have always healed me, it just took me half a lifetime to really trust them, to understand how infallible they are. Moving through space, preferably outdoor space, preferably outdoor space that maintains some semblance of nature—if not *this* nature, some other nature. When I'm happy, it's a carnival out here, and when I am sad it is almost too beautiful to bear—but not quite—it is definitely too beautiful to contemplate leaving. I climb the hill where the homesteader Robert Pinkley—the first man to build a cabin on this land—is buried, and I know well that when I claimed this 120 acres it also claimed me. We are each other's mutual saviors.

Toward the end of *Contents May Have Shifted*, I wrote the following lines: "I'm beginning to understand that when we want to kill ourselves, it is not because we are lonely, but because we are trying to break up with the world before the world breaks up with us." Which represents some progress, I realize, from what I wrote in *Waltzing the Cat*.

But the world, I have finally allowed myself to believe, is not out to hurt me, but to heal me, and I will hold on to it with both hands for as long as I am able. This is what I try to explain to Kyle and Maggie over a second round of beers and Pellegrino in Pittsburg.

We decide that bison burgers sound better than falafel, so Maggie drives me to BRGR while Kyle runs home to drop off Apacha. Maggie and I talk about the eleven-month trip she and her boyfriend took four months after her mother's death. "I was afraid I wouldn't survive her absence if I stayed still," she said, and I said, "Maybe you were collecting new things to love about the world."

We wait for Kyle for thirty minutes and then an hour. Finally she calls to say she is on her way, so we order for her, but by the time she actually gets there, her food is stone cold and she barely eats a bite.

She'll write me an email a few weeks later thanking me for the things I said to her, admitting that she had been driving around all that time we were waiting, sobbing, trying to pull herself together enough to come back out, but that I wasn't to worry too much about her because since that night she had been working on her writing and spending quality time with Maggie and Apacha and feeling a whole lot better. I wrote back and told her that though I thought of her often, that I hadn't, exactly, been worried. She sounded so solid, so grounded in her email, that I decided I didn't need to say the other thing I was pretty sure of: that she had cried that night, not so much for the disappointing past, as for the dawning possibility of an unspeakably beautiful future. I was pretty sure she already knew.

About the Contributors

Barbara Abercrombie has published novels, children's picture books, and books of nonfiction. Her essays have appeared in national publications and in many anthologies. Her most recent books are *Cherished: 21 Writers on Animals They've Loved & Lost; A Year of Writing Dangerously,* which was chosen by *Poets & Writers Magazine* as one of the best books for writers. (http://www.pw.org/best-books-for-writers); and her fifteenth book, *Kicking in the Wall,* published by New World Library. She received the Outstanding Instructor Award and the Distinguished Instructor Award at UCLA Extension, where she teaches creative writing. She also conducts private writing retreats and blogs at www.barbaraabercrombie.com and www.TheIntimidatedCook.com. She lives in Santa Monica and Lake Arrowhead, California.

Sherry Amatenstein, Licensed Clinical Social Worker, is the author of several books, including *The Complete Marriage Counselor: Relationship Saving Advice from America's Top 50+ Couples Therapists, Love Lessons from Bad Breakups,* and *Q&A Dating Book.* She runs relationship seminars around the country and works with patients in person and over the phone. She writes for many publications and websites and is frequently called upon to give love advice on national radio and TV programs including the *Today Show, Early Show, NPR, CBS News,* and *Huffington Post Live.* Her website is www.marriedfaq.com.

Regina Anavy was born in Minneapolis and received a BA in French Literature from the University of California, Berkeley, in 1965. She worked on voter registration with the Congress of Racial Equality, was involved in the womens' movement in Washington, D.C., and traveled to Cuba with the Fourth Venceremos Brigade in 1971. Anavy is the author and editor of *Larry's Letters,* a true story about a Jewish family in North Dakota (Hummingbird Press, 2005). Her memoir, *Out of Cuba: Memoir of a Journey,* was published by Cognitio Press in 2013. Her articles and essays have appeared in magazines, anthologies, and newspapers. Anavy is part of a worldwide network of volunteer translators for independent Cuban journalists who are censured in Cuba. She lives in San Francisco with her husband.

Chloe Caldwell is the author of the novella *Women* and the essay collection *Legs Get Led Astray* (Future Tense Books, 2012). Her work has appeared in *VICE, Salon.com, The Sun, Men's Health, Nylon,* and *The Rumpus.* Her essays have been anthologized in *Goodbye to All That: Writers on Loving and Leaving New York* (Seal Press) and *True Tales of Lust and Love* (Soft Skull). She lives in Hudson, New York. Learn more at www.chloecaldwell.com.

Jimmy Camp is a father, husband, son of a preacher, political consultant, musician, and tattooed white-trash punk. He lives in Southern California with his wife, author Samantha Dunn; their six-year-old son, Ben; and their two horses, two dogs, cat, pig, and Silverstreak trailer. Jimmy enjoys reading, gardening, hiking, camping, mountain biking, skateboarding, drinking, cussing, fighting, and other general forms of mayhem.

Zoe FitzGerald Carter is a graduate of Columbia Journalism School and has written for numerous publications, including the *New York Times,* the *San Francisco Chronicle, Vogue* and *Salon.* Her memoir, *Imperfect Endings* (Simon & Schuster, 2011) chronicles her mother's decision to end her life after living with Parkinson's for many years.

She lives in the Bay Area where she sings in a band, Do Wrong Right, and is a proud member of the San Francisco Writers Grotto. Details about her various classes and writing retreats can be found at: www. zoefitzgeraldcarter.com.

Debra LoGuerico DeAngelo is a columnist with McNaughton Newspapers, managing editor of the award-winning weekly newspaper *Winters Express*, and cofounder, coeditor, and CEO for iPinion Syndicate. She has received multiple first-place awards from the National Newspaper Association and California Newspaper Publishers Association for column writing and was the 2002 winner of the Front Porch Syndicate's national column-writing talent search. She has served as judge for the California Newspaper Publishers Association for twenty-two years and has written a weekly column for twenty-four years, covering topics ranging from humor to politics to parenting and, from time to time, cats. Debra's columns can be found at www.ipinionsyndicate. com. Read more at www.debradeangelo.com.

Marika Rosenthal Delan is a scientist/nurse by trade and an artist/ freedom fighter by birth who once choreographed her little brother and his friends in a rousing rendition of Divo's "Whip It," as performed by *Alvin and the Chipmunks*. After a severe back injury sidelined Marika from nursing, she has found her happy place in writing, music, and her family. She is coauthoring a book with her husband, Pastor Peter Delan, about the profound ways in which his near-death experience changed the course of their lives (visit www.tolunitedministries.org for the complete backstory). Her work has been featured on Jennifer Pastiloff's *The Manifest-Station, Elephant Journal*, and *The Huffington Post*. Visit her blog at www.bestillandstillmoving.com.

Hollye Dexter is author of the forthcoming memoir *Fire Season* (She Writes Press, 2015) and coeditor of the 2012 Seal Press anthology *Dancing at the Shame Prom*. Her essays and articles about women's issues, activism, and parenting have been published in anthologies as well as in Maria Shriver's *Architects of Change*, *Huffington Post*, *The Feminist Wire* and more. In 2003, she founded the award-winning non-profit *Art and Soul*, running arts workshops for teenagers in the foster care system. She currently teaches writing workshops and works as an activist for gun violence prevention in Los Angeles, where she lives with her husband and a houseful of kids and pets. Visit her at www .hollyedexter.blogspot.com.

Beverly Donofrio, recently dubbed a master memoirist by the *Daily Beast*, has published three memoirs: the New York Times bestseller, *Riding in Cars with Boys*, which was made into a popular movie; *Looking for Mary*, a Barnes and Noble Discover pick; and *Astonished*, called "astonishing" by more than one reviewer. Her latest children's book, *Where's Mommy*, was selected as *New York Times* Best Children's Book of 2014; she has written documentaries for NPR, and her essays have appeared in the *New York Times*, *Washington Post*, *Los Angeles Times*, *O, The Oprah Magazine*, *Marie Clair*, *More*, *Slate*, among others, as well as in numerous anthologies. She is an instructor at Wilkes University's low-residency MFA program and lives in Woodstock, New York, where she is working on an essay collection.

Beth Bornstein Dunnington is a writer, editor, singer/actor, and stage director who lives on the Big Island of Hawaii. She leads bimonthly women's writing workshops, as well as the Big Island Writers' Workshop. She wrote and performed the stage play *Que Sueñes Con Las Angelitas*, and cowrote the documentary film *The Road To Q'ero: A Journey Home*. Her essays have appeared in a number of anthologies, and she was a scriptwriter and story editor for animated TV series, including *Tiny Tunes Adventures*, *Batman*, *GI Joe*, *Transformers*, *My Little Pony*, *Doug*, *Thundercats*, and more. Beth is married to developer Steve Dunnington and has two kids, Marena and Sean. Read more at her blog: http://wakingupinhawaii.com.

Matt Ebert lives and works on a dairy farm in Sheshequin, Pennsylvania. He spent his life pursuing a variety of odd jobs in movies, technology, labor, agriculture, and now as a writer. The author is an activist for progressive politics, and a staunch advocate for healthcare reform, the environment, and workers' rights. In 2014, he began publishing a blog in *The Huffington Post*. He is currently at work on his first novel.

Betsy Graziani Fasbinder's debut novel, *Fire & Water*, was published by She Writes Press in 2013 with the audiobook released in 2014. Her works have been honored with the Floyd Salas Award for Fiction, a silver medal in the Wishing Shelf Book Awards, a Jack London Award, and two East of Eden Awards. "Search for the Silver Cup" is a memoir piece she wrote as part of a healing journey following the loss of her brother. Betsy is a psychotherapist, practicing for more than twenty-five years, and lives in Marin County, California, with her husband in their newly empty nest. Learn more at www.betsygrazianifasbinder.com.

Pam L. Houston is the author of two collections of linked short stories, *Cowboys Are My Weakness* and *Waltzing the Cat*; the novel, *Sight Hound*; a collection of essays, *A Little More About Me*; and her most recent novel, *Contents May Have Shifted*, all published by W.W. Norton. Her stories have been selected for *Best American Short Stories*, *The O. Henry Awards*, *The 2013 Pushcart Prize*, and *Best American Short Stories of the Century*. She is Professor of English at UC Davis, directs the literary nonprofit Writing by Writers, teaches in the low-residency MFA program at the Institute of American Indian and at writer's conferences around the world. She lives on a ranch in Colorado near the headwaters of the Rio Grande. Visit her at https://pamhouston.wordpress.com or on Facebook and Twitter.

Mark S. King has written about his experiences living with HIV since he tested positive the week the HIV test became publicly available in 1985. His book, *A Place Like This*, is a personal chronicle of Hollywood, the phone sex trade, and the dawn of AIDS in Los Angeles during the 1980s. Mark attributes his thirty-year survival to AIDS activism, patient empowerment, the love of a good man, and double-chocolate brownies made from scratch. His writings and videos can be found on his award-winning blog www.MyFabulousDisease.com.

David Lacy began writing for a daily city newspaper when he was fifteen, covering county politics, features, and occasionally sports. In 2003, his weekly column, "Growing Younger," won First Place in the California Newspaper Publishers Association's Better Newspapers Contest. He has a BA in English from UC Davis and an MA in English from UC Irvine. He has written for multiple magazines and newspapers. He is a full-time writing specialist and former lecturer at UC Irvine and part-time Professor at Orange Coast College. He has also taught at CSU Long Beach. David is the cofounder of iPinionSyndicate.com, an online column and blogging site. The Northern California native now resides in Orange County, California, with his fiancée and two dogs.

Caroline Leavitt is the *New York Times* bestselling author of *Is This Tomorrow* and *Pictures of You*, and eight other novels. *Pictures of You* was on the Best Books of the Year from the *San Francisco Chronicle, Bookmarks Magazine, The Providence Journal* and *Kirkus Reviews*. Caroline teaches writing online at Stanford and UCLA Extension Writers Program and also works with private clients. A book critic for *People*, the *Boston Globe*, and the *San Francisco Chronicle*, she has also published essays and stories in the *New York Times, Salon, More, Redbook*, and various anthologies. She lives with her husband, the writer and editor Jeff Tamarkin, near New York City and has a college-age son. Visit her at www.carolineleavitt.com, on Twitter @leavittnovelist, and Facebook https://www.facebook.com/carolineleavitt.

Patti Linsky was a highly regarded Cantor at Temple Ahavat Shalom for over twenty-four years when a life-threatening condition forced her to retire. She embarked on a spiritual quest that led her to write a funny, poignant one-woman musical memoir, *Altar EGO*, which debuted in 2013. In addition to her show, Patti remains active in the Jewish community as a freelance Cantor officiating for Lifecycle events, performing in concerts, recording in the studio, and as visiting Artist-in-Residence throughout the country. Patti and her husband have two children and live in Los Angeles. Learn more at http://www.pattilinsky.com.

Karen Lynch was a Homicide Investigator for San Francisco Police Department, and prior to being promoted, she worked as a street patrol officer for nine years. After twenty-nine years of police work and a bout with breast cancer, she retired to become a full-time writer. Her 2014 memoir, *Good Cop, Bad Daughter: Memoirs of an Unlikely Police Officer*, tells the story of how being raised by a bipolar mother and a tribe of hippies provided her the perfect training to become a cop. She is a native San Franciscan, and proud UC Berkeley Cal Bear. She has been married to Greg for twenty-five years, with whom she has three children.

Lira Maywood holds a BA in Humanities and Creative Writing from The New School in New York City and has studied fiction and creative nonfiction writing at Columbia College of Chicago and the UCLA Extension Writer's Program. Following her husband's suicide in 2010, Lira started a blog (https://hourbeforedawn.wordpress.com) that chronicled her grief and gradual healing process. Her commitment to writing on the blog for a full year was also a promise to herself and her loved ones to keep going, no matter how dark her road to healing became. Her current blog, about caregiving for her mother with dementia, can be found at https://momentsandstories.wordpress.com. Lira lives in Los Angeles and is working on a full-length memoir.

C.O. Moed grew up on the Lower East Side of New York City when it was still a tough neighborhood. A recipient of the Elizabeth George grant for fiction, her short stories and dramatic works have been published in several anthologies and literary reviews. She chronicles brief moments and old memories that still survive in a disappearing city in the multimedia project, "IT WAS HER NEW YORK" at https://myprivateconey.blogspot.com. The rest of the time she works a day job and lives in New York City with her partner, fellow writer Ted Krever, and their two cats.

Mark Morgan is an American film and television producer. His credits include such commercial successes as *The Wedding Planner,* the *Cody Banks* franchise, *The Riches,* the *Percy Jackson* franchise, and the *Twilight Saga* franchise. He currently heads Mount Diablo Entertainment.

Linda Joy Myers is president of the National Association of Memoir Writers and has been a therapist for thirty-five years. She's the award-winning author of *Don't Call Me Mother—A Daughter's Journey from Abandonment to Forgiveness, The Power of Memoir—How to Write Your Healing Story, The Journey of Memoir* and *Becoming Whole—Writing Your Healing Story. Don't Call Me Mother* and *Becoming Whole* were finalists in the *Foreword Magazine's* Book of the Year Award. Linda coteaches the program Write Your Memoir in Six Months, and offers editing and coaching for writers. Visit www.namw.org and http://memoriesandmemoirs.com for more information.

Christine Kehl O'Hagan is the author of *Benediction at the Savoia,* a novel, and the memoir *The Book of Kehls.* Both books received starred reviews in *Kirkus Reviews,* the latter a Kirkus Best Book of 2005 selection. Her essays have appeared in thirteen anthologies, the *New York Times, Newsday,* and several Long Island publications. She is a recipient of the Jerry Lewis Writing Award and a former writing instructor at Hofstra University. Christine lives on Long Island with her husband, Patrick, and is working on a second memoir.

Jennifer Pastiloff is a writer, yoga teacher, and creator of the popular website The Manifest-Station. Jennifer and her Manifest-Station workshops and retreats have been featured on *Good Morning America* and CBS News, and in *New York* magazine, Salon, The Rumpus, Oprah. com, and more. She studied poetry and writing at NYU and Bucknell University and is currently finishing her first book, *Girl Power: You Are Enough*. She lives with her husband in Los Angeles (when she's not on an airplane), but you can find her online at jenniferpastiloff.com and on Twitter and Instagram as @jenpastiloff.

Angela M. Giles Patel's work has appeared in *The Healing Muse, The Nervous Breakdown* and *The Manifest-Station*. She tweets as @domesticmuse, and when inspired, updates her blog at www.the nervousbreakdown.com. She lives in Massachusetts where she conquers the world, one day at a time.

Ruth Pennebaker's most recent novel was *Women on the Verge of a Nervous Breakthrough*, the story of three generations of women living under one roof. The author of six other books, Ruth was a columnist for the *Dallas Morning News*, and her work has appeared in the *New York Times, Texas Monthly*, and other national publications. She is currently working on *Pucker Up! The Subversive Woman's Guide to Aging with Wit, Wine, Drama, Humor, Perspective, and the Occasional Good Cry* with artist Marian Henley. She lives in Austin with her mad-scientist husband and blogs at www.geezersisters.com.

Alexa Rosalsky is a sophomore at the College of William and Mary. She loves fencing, college, skiing, writing, reading, her family, her friends, linguistics, and making the world better (not necessarily in that order). She spent the summer after her freshman year working at an orphanage in Nepal and is the middle child between two brothers.

Elizabeth Rosner is a bestselling novelist, poet, and essayist living in Berkeley, California. Her first novel, *The Speed of Light*, was translated into nine languages and won several literary prizes. Her second novel, *Blue Nude*, was a *San Francisco Chronicle* Best Book of the Year. Her

2014 novel, *Electric City*, was among NPR's Best Books of the Year and was released alongside her poetry collection, *Gravity*. Hers essays have appeared in the *New York Times Magazine, Elle*, the *Forward, Hadassah Magazine*, and several anthologies; her poems have been published by *Poetry Magazine, Southern Poetry Review*, and many others. She teaches writing workshops and lectures on contemporary literature. Her book reviews appear frequently in the *San Francisco Chronicle* and the *Los Angeles Review of Books*. Visit her at www.elizabethrosner.com.

Kathyn Rountree is a former radio and TV personality. Currently she has her own voiceover recording business and is the voice for companies all over the country. She is an advertising sales executive for Performance Santa Fe and is in the process of finishing her first screenplay. Katie is married and the mother of two children and lives in Santa Fe, New Mexico.

Kitty Sheehan is a former teacher, corporate trainer, consignment store owner, and graphic designer. Now a writer, editor, and photographer, she is the founder and director of the annual Dartbrook Writers Retreat in Keene, New York. She is also a freelance copywriter, social media editor, and consultant for several brands. Her resume makes her own head hurt. Kitty is a past contributor to *Hudson Valley Magazine* and, like almost everyone else she knows, is also working on a book. When she's not writing, she makes jewelry and collages. Visit her at www.kittysheehan.com and on Twitter at @KittyASheehan.

Jenna Stone is a Fulbright Scholar and a former high school teacher. She is a published author/digital artist, a cohost of the radio show "You've Got Moxie," a columnist for iPinion, and a Creative Regressionist for CreateShops. She currently hangs her hat on a tall Saguaro in Arizona. Visit her at www.linkedin.com/in/jstonesquared.

judywhite is the award-winning author and photographer of several nonfiction books, including the encyclopedia, *Taylor's Guide to Orchids*

(Houghton Mifflin). Principal photographer at GardenPhotos.com, she has thousands of photo credits in major magazines, books, and the advertising world. A former research neurobiologist, judywhite began her writing career as a humor columnist for *Seventeen Magazine.* Her first screenplay, *Lies I Told My Little Sister,* dealing with the aftermath of the death of her older sister, has been made into an award-winning drama-comedy feature film, to be released in 2015. Visit the website at www.liesitoldmylittlesister.com

Samantha White's writing career began when she wrote, directed, and starred in her sixth-grade class play, "A Christmas in France." She had never visited France nor met anyone who had but felt confident in her project because she knew the word "crèche." Samantha studied creative writing with Joseph Heller and Kurt Vonnegut and developed writer's block when they both offered to introduce her to their agents. She participated in the Emerging Playwrights series at Theater Rhinoceros in San Francisco. Her work has been produced in New York, London, San Francisco, and if you count the French play, North Carolina. She is currently working on a book trilogy for tweens.

About the Editor

Amy Ferris is an author, screenwriter, editor, and playwright. She has contributed to numerous magazines and literary anthologies, and her memoir, *Marrying George Clooney: Confessions from a Midlife Crisis* (Seal Press, 2009), was adapted into an Off-Broadway play in 2012. Ferris co-edited (with Hollye Dexter) *Dancing at the Shame Prom* (Seal Pess, 2012), and authored the young adult novel *A Greater Goode* (Houghton Mifflin, 2000). Ferris has written for film and television, a she was nominated for best screenplay for *Funny Valentines*. She serves on the advisory board of the Women's Media Center and is an instructor for the San Miguel Writers' Conference. She lives in northeast Pennsylvania with her husband, Ken, and two cats who think they're human.